Lecture Notes in Economics and Mathematical Systems

Antoine Billot

Economic Theory of Fuzzy Equilibria

An Axiomatic Analysis

Springer-Verlag
Berlin Heidelberg New York
London Paris Tokyo
Hong Kong Barcelona
Budapest

Author

Dr. Antoine Billot
Department of Economics
University of Paris 2 (Panthéon-Assas)
92, rue d'Assas
F-75006 Paris

ISBN 3-540-54982-X Springer-Verlag Berlin Heidelberg New York
ISBN 0-387-54982-X Springer-Verlag New York Berlin Heidelberg

Typesetting: Camera ready by author
Printing and binding: Druckhaus Beltz, Hemsbach/Bergstr.
42/3140-543210 - Printed on acid-free paper

In memoriam of Guillaume Artur du Plessis

Acknowledgements

My thanks go to Maurice Desplas, Didier Dubois, Victor Ginsburgh, Bertrand Munier, Pierre Salmon, Bernard Walliser, Hans-Jürgen Zimmermann and Daniel Vitry, who read large parts of the manuscript based on my Ph.D. dissertation ; the book owes much to their detailed suggestions. Of course, all errors remain my responsability.

I should also like to thank Marc Chenais and Cyrille Piatecki for their helpful comments and David Sarfas for his translation.

Finally, my greatest debt is to Claude Ponsard. His comments have been more than perceptive : he saved me from several errors and made numerous suggestions which have resulted in a considerably wider perspective for this book. He was my Ph.D. Director and I hope to have been one of his friends.

The writing and translation of this book were supported by the Centre d'Economie Financière et Bancaire of the University of Paris 2, Panthéon-Assas. I should like to thank their Directors, Michèle de Mourgues and Claude Vedel.

Preface

Fuzzy set theory, which started not much more than 20 years ago as a generalization of classical set theory, has in the meantime evolved into an area which scientifically, as well as from the point of view of applications, is recognized as a very valuable contribution to the existing knowledge. To an increasing degree, however, fuzzy set theory is also used in a descriptive, factual sense or as a decision making technology. Most of these *applications* of fuzzy set theory are in the areas of fuzzy control, multi-criteria analysis, descriptive decision theory and expert systems design. In economics, the application of fuzzy set theory is still very rare. Apart from Professor Ponsard and his group, who have obviously recognized the potential of fuzzy set theory in economics much better than others, only very few economists are using this new tool in order to model economic systems in a more realistic way than often possible by traditional approaches, and to gain more insight into structural interdependences of economic systems. I consider it, therefore, particularly valuable that Dr. Billot, in his book, makes a remarkable contribution in this direction.

There seems to be one major difference between Dr. Billot's contribution and the other publications in which fuzzy set theory is applied to either game theory, group decision making or economic theory : Some authors use fuzzy set theory in order to gain a mathematically more attractive or efficient model for their problems of concern, others use a specific problem area just in order to demonstrate the capabilities of fuzzy set theory without a real justification of whether this "fuzzification" of a traditional theory makes sense or is justified by better results. For Dr. Billot, not surprisingly similar to Professor Ponsard, the economic thinking seems to be the predominant factor and fuzzy set theory is only a tool to improve an economic model or theory where it seems possible or appropriate. Hence, his book should not primarily be considered as a contribution in fuzzy set theory, but as one in economic theory, which merges microeconomic considerations with macroeconomic observations.

On an axiomatic basis, the author analyses first how the assumption of specific fuzzy preferences bear on equilibria of classical and newly defined economic systems. He proceeds in three steps : In the first chapter of his book, he presents specific kinds of fuzzy individual preferences and in a second chapter, he investigates their repercussions on aggregation procedures in the sense of group decision making or welfare economics, in the third chapter he focuses his attention on fuzzy cooperative and non-cooperative games. In both fourth and fifth chapters, he applies the results of the first three chapters to the analysis of equilibria in a specific market model.

In introducing his view of fuzzy preferences, Dr. Billot does not follow the so-called "Anglo-saxon, cardinalist school", but he proceeds along the lines of the European or French school in concentrating on orders and allowing for different degrees of preferences. He also distinguishes between relative, absolute, local and global preferences and postulates the "dominated irrationality principle". He can thus prove that given a certain preference structure $(X, \mathcal{R}(.,.))$, there exists a fuzzy utility function if X is a totally preordered, countable set. To arrive at that result he introduces a number of notions and definitions which partly deviate from those used in classical fuzzy set theory. This concerns particularly the notions of reflexivity and transitivity and also that of a fuzzy preorder which for Dr. Billot is a fuzzy relation which is reflexive (f.s.) And f-transitive. New is also the introduction of a "fuzzy incoherent preference" which is a binary fuzzy relation which is reflexive (f.s.) but not transitive. For the following parts of his book, the author bases to a large extent of his proof of the existence of a continuous utility function, given that there exists a fuzzy preorder and continuous fuzzy preferences as well as a connected set of decision alternatives (it is also shown in the first part that Boolean preorders are a special case of above).

The second chapter focuses on the aggregation of fuzzy preferences and on the social choice, i.e. the usual problem of the theory of group decision making. Dr. Billot first describes traditional theory (evaluation cycles of "Condorcet") and Arrow's impossibility theorem. In the framework of Arrow's axiomatic system, he now defines requirements for a group decision function which is supposed to be analogue to an individual preference function. His axioms are essentially that the group preference constitutes a fuzzy preorder, that the group preferences are a function of the individual preferences, the axiom of unanimity, the independence of alternatives and the request that the group decision function be not dictatorial. Dr. Billot reformulates the requirements for a social welfare function in his axioms P1 through P6, introduces a "planner" as an artifact, focuses on specific lexicographic aggregation rules and eventually shows in his theorems 4 and 5, respectively, that - given fuzzy preference relation for the agents - a translation from the Arrovian dictator into a more democratical structure is possible. I find the new structures introduced by Dr. Billot, even though they are sometimes surprising, intuitively appealing and productive.

Two further major topics are of concern to Dr. Billot : Equilibrium points of fuzzy games and fuzzy economic equilibria. In the third chapter of the book, he first focuses on non-cooperative games and then he analyses cooperative games. He presents some generalizations to the theorem of Kakutani and an application to Nash equilibria. Then, the agents of the game are equipped with non-dichotomous behaviours which eventually yield ordinal strategic utility functions. It should be noted that the term *f*-convex defined and used by the author does not refer to the membership function, as in fuzzy set theory, but to the support of a fuzzy set. Of particular importance is the introduction by the author of the notion of a *peripheral core* which is defined to be a specific fuzzy set. He can then show that this core under certain circumstances is non-empty. In effect, the author transforms the situations without equilibria by introducing fuzzy behaviours of the agents and by augmenting the number of equilibrium solutions.

The author then proceeds to investigate the compatibility of this fuzzy behaviour in an economy with production. He focuses his attention on the factor labour and eliminates for the sake of transparency other possible activities in an economy. Essentially, he tries to show that the introduction of fuzzy preferences does not impeach the existence of a general equilibrium. He also tries to show that this behavioural fuzziness can generate some non-standard equilibria for the Walrasian approach. After the examination of different approaches existing already in the literature, he presents a model of this simplified economy which he calls a GLE (for Good-Labour-Economy). He then presents two results concerning the existence of equilibria, one concerning an GLE in the sense of Ponsard in which the goals of the agents and their constraints are fuzzy and the other concerning an GLE in which only preferences are fuzzy in the sense of the first chapter of this book. The principal result of this chapter is the verification of the consistency of fuzzy choice behaviour and the existence of a general equilibrium.

In the last chapter, he focuses on dis-equilibria in the labour market including different kinds of unemployment. The demonstration of the possible existence of an unvolontary unemployment which should be compatible with a Walrasian general equilibrium depends on the notion of free disposal and on that fuzzy preference relations. The author shows that there exists some Walrasian general equilibria with disequilibria of tasks by using the usual definition of a free disposal equilibrium. In characterizing the unemployed, the author focuses on those agents whose preference relations are typically that of unvolontary Walrasian unemployed who persist in offering labour even if the equilibrium wage is and stays zero. Those unemployed are locally coherent and globally indifferent between a zero-offer and a non-zero-offer of tasks, but the absolute preferences of the non-zero offer is bigger than the absolute preference for the zero-offer. By contrast to the traditional microeconomic theory in which behaviour of the agents is more or less unified for the analysis, the author studies diverse agents and examines the pertinence of the usual equilibria when he introduces a new behavioural mode within the theoretical models of traditional economic theory. He defines, for the economy under consideration, an equilibrium for unemployment and shows that these equilibria exist under certain conditions.

Altogether, this book presents a very intriguing analysis of classical problems with new tools which lead to interesting results. The author can be congratulated on his results and it can be hoped that many economic theorists start from Dr. Billot's work and advance economic theory along the lines indicated.

Aachen, January 1991 *H.-J. Zimmermann*

Contents

General Introduction

With regards to dictionaries, five possible definitions may be alternatively used to define the adjective *precise*, each one referring to exactitude. For the word *imprecision*, there is generally a brief definition : "*which lacks precision*". However, the english language is rich with many expressions that can help us to understand imprecision. "Vague", "ambiguous", "general", or "fuzzy" are indistinctively used adjectives expressing the imprecise character of a phenomena or an idea.

If we can consider that the imprecision of laboratory apparatus in physics does not change the characteristics of the observed phenomena, could we say that economics and especially microeconomics study a world where ambiguity and shade are absent ?

Determining the path of an electron as a function of the environment leads to *unifying* the behaviour of electrons ; in other words, electron *a* is not allowed to be different from electron *b* if placed in similar conditions. Who can say that agents behave as electrons do ?

Nevertheless, the classic theory of preference implicitly assumes the Walrasian *mechanist* inspiration. By defining one and only one rule of behaviour, one describes the agents as they behave in a systematic manner, just as a computer always replies the same way to an unchanged stimulus. If physics study physical objects, economics study economical objects (goods) and economical *subjects* (agents).

Of course, usual microeconomics succeed in solving problems that derive from agents whose preferences are intransitive or partially complete. But it never aggregates coherent and incoherent agents, short-sighted ones (indifferent by alternative clusters) and others whose acuity is more or less efficient, in order to study their consistency (by using equilibrium analysis for example). It always unifies behaviours. Hence, one deduces a particular type of rationality that forbids differences. The economic subject is then deprived of a simple liberty : the agent cannot have another behaviour than his neighbour's one ; conceptually, he *is* his neighbour.

We can now consider that the agent's *liberty* described by the usual theory consists in only allowing the preferences to change from an individual to another even though their *choice behaviour* is the same. A question arises straight away : what remains of the theory if some agents come into the analysis, who do not correspond to the chosen standard of behaviour ?

Defining a new standard of behaviour which could be enough weak to include many types of coherences and many types of preferences (from the usual reflexive and transitive relation, to the non-reflexive and non-transitive fuzzy relation) is unfortunately insufficient in the sense that a *microeconomic* improvement of the description of individual choice behaviour does not give us any information on what the explicit goal of this approach is. This goal is, actually, the economic equilibrium. Studying the consistency of individual decisions leads to the second main concept in microeconomics : the equilibrium. Here again, the question is to know what remains of the conditions for the equilibrium existence if all agents do not conform to a single standard of preference.

Our work tries to solve the two following problems : can we define a system of preferences that allows the introduction of many behaviours ? Under what conditions economic equilibria with such behaviours is consistent ? Our approach consists in theoretically defending the *fuzzy* preference behaviour and showing that it corresponds to a new standard of behaviour (in the sense that it can describe very different agents).

The *fuzzy* behaviour of preference tries to introduce individuals whose preferences are not necessarily clear or coherent. It opposes Boolean behaviour of preference (i.e. usual micro-economic theory) which only allows three decisions at the end of a comparison between x and y : the preference for x, the preference for y and the indifference between x and y. The object that is turned down into choice has no more quality for the agent before he compares it again to a third one : the preference is cut short. The agent completely prefers the chosen object to the other. The agent who has imprecise preferences is much more shaded. He evaluates the qualities of x relatively to the ones of y, then the ones of y relatively to x. He evaluates the qualities of each object before *locally* deciding to choose the object whose qualities are the greatest. Therefore, we introduce the possibility for local choices (i.e. the preferences) to be *updated* at a *global* level (i.e. the utility function), if the agent is not coherent. In others words, the fuzzy agent prefers *evaluating* the qualities of each object relatively to the others than directly choosing. On the contrary of a Boolean agent (sometimes called a *crisp* agent), the fuzzy agent (also called the *soft* agent) cannot decide anything with his only preferences. Those ones contribute in evaluating his opinion but he has to interpret them in order to be able to translate his preferences into a utility function and finally to decide. If we want to sum up both attitudes in a precise way, we can say that Boolean agents are self-confident when fuzzy agents are indecisive and doubt on their own preferences (we later prove they can contradict them at a global level).

However, in spite of their introduction into microeconomics, these fuzzy agents must not imply a new and *single* standard of behaviour. They must necessarily cohabit with agents whose behaviour is usual, within standard theory. The question is to allow the theory to describe some different behaviours and not *to reduce* them to a new single formulation. The tool that allows to improve the usual model of preference must have the ability of describing diversity. It is the main quality of the fuzzy subsets theory to lead to an infinity of interpretations because of an infinity of possible solutions.

The notion of *fuzzy subset* appeared in a 1965 paper, by an American mathematician from the University of Berkeley, California, Lofti. A. Zadeh. This notion tries to show that an object corresponds *more or less* to the particular category we want to assimilate it to ; that was how the idea of defining the membership of an element to a set not on the Aristotelician pair $\{0, 1\}$ any more but on the continuous interval $[0, 1]$ was born. In Boolean mathematics, the set of *tall men* needs a binary criterion to be defined (more than one meter and 60 centimeters, for example). If someone measures 1m50, he does not belong to the set at all (the value of the membership degree is 0). If he measures 1m61 or 2m15, he belongs to it in the same way ; that is, completely (the value of the membership degree is 1). Hence, the notion of fuzzy subset intuitively deals with the idea according to which a man who measures 2m15 being taller than a man measuring 1m61, belongs more to the set of *tall men* than the man measuring 1m61. Therefore, the binary criterion is not justified any more. The midget belongs to the set at level 0,1, the average man at level 0,5, and the giant at level 1. The fuzzy subset of *tall men* therefore describes that men are *more or less tall* and not that mankind is binary divided in two complement sets, tall and small men.

The idea of describing all shades of reality (cf Billot [1987b], chapter 1) was for long the obsession of some logicians. Lukasiewicz [1922], for example, by proposing an infinite system of logical values, develops the basis of an analysis about the *"more or less"*.

Some economists also inquired into fuzziness ; Arrow ([1951], [1963] p.71) expressed the desire of a utility indicator defined on the interval $[0, 1]$. This indicator precisely looks like a membership function as had underlined Dubois ([1983] p.270). With the notion of *potential surprise*, Shackle [1961], [1971] defined a behavioural standard of decision that is directly related to a fuzzy membership function (Dubois [1983]).

As soon as the studied world is not totally *precise*, either observed objects and/or subjects are imprecise in their behaviour or that the language used in describing such behaviours is imprecise (the Wittgenstein's *puzzles* [1921], [1961]), the resort to fuzzy sets theory is one of the possibilities to the researcher in order to integrate imprecision. A way of summing up both conceptions consists in saying that Boolean mathematics are mathematics of *all or nothing* while fuzzy mathematics are mathematics of *more or less*. It is not the economist who makes the world imprecise ; economic agents are men, and it can be better to introduce their doubts and shades, their hesitations and especially their differences. Montaigne wrote : "*Wealth must be diverse to be fecund*" ; all reducing (even scientific) is an impoverishment if not logically necessary. Our purpose is to defend imprecise preferences because they increase diversity of behaviours that improve micro-economic tradition to which they are nevertheless clearly linked.

CHAPTER 1

Individual Fuzzy Relation of Preference

The main purpose of the theory of fuzzy preference is to introduce some new behaviours. The existing literature is generally divided in two schools, according to the position the authors adopt relatively to the axiom of Independence of Irrelevant Alternatives (I.I.A.)[1]. Actually, most of the works using fuzzy preferences are based on additive measures of satisfaction (Orlovsky [1978], [1980], Kaufmann [1973], Zadeh [1971b], Nahmias [1980], Dubois & Prade [1979], Bazu [1984] and Butnariu [1980;1985;1987]).

Works with such preferences, that forbid intra/inter personal comparisons, do not usually satisfy the I.I.A. (Ponsard [1980;1981;1982a; 1982b;1984;1986], Chakraboty & Sakar [1987], Montero & Tejada [1986], Chakraboty & Das [1985]). Because of the particular form of fuzzy transitivity that is used, it implies an obvious dependence of choices. Besides, there are only few papers with purely ordinal preferences satisfying the I.I.A. (Luo [1986], Billot [1986;1987a]).

This chapter is devoted to the presentation of these new fuzzy behaviours.

In section one, we present the new system of preferences. In section two, we prove that a distinction between intrinsic preference and relative one can provide the basis of an axiomatic solution for the indecision paradox. Then, in section three, we prove the existence of a utility

---

1 We call I.I.A. the axiom according to which a third object never interferes with a comparison between two other objects.

function translating fuzzy preferences on a countable referential set and finally, in section four, we try to generalize such a result to the case of a convex referential.

SECTION ONE : THE FUZZY BINARY RELATION OF PREFERENCE

A IVth century B.C. philosopher, Eubulides, has defined the following paradox : a pile of sand is a set of sand grains. There is not a precise number N from which the sand grains form a pile. In other words, let us imagine an agent placed in front of a sand pile who would take away a grain of sand, then another and so forth until the pile disappears : it would be impossible for him to know exactly when the sand pile disappears, i.e. what particular grain corresponds to it.

This paradox was the origin of some logical criticisms elaborated by Pierce, Alston, Russel and Black[2] who developed logical systems based on three values of truth, up to Lukasiewicz [1922] who proposed the first approach in terms of infinite logic based on a continuum of values of truth. In fact, as a pile of sand, a bald or a small person are not precise notions ; there is no number of hairs N that lets a man be declared bald if he just has $(N-1)$ hairs. There exists a lot of concepts, mostly coming from natural language, in philosophy, linguistics or economics, that lead to criticize the Aristotelician logic using two values of truth. One of the possible ways to introduce fuzziness is to model the *"vague"* or the *"bad-defined"* (the word belongs to Russel) with the help of a new set theory.

In economics, and especially in preference theory, we are not trying to "treat" of the conceptual fuzziness (a treatment of the semantic imprecision deals with another analysis ; see Lefaivre [1974] and Zadeh [1971a]). In other words, the preference is not really *"bad-defined"* ; nevertheless, the usual preferences system implies a reducing of behaviour because based upon a binary (or Boolean) process : it just allows three kinds of final attitude, to prefer, not to prefer, to be indifferent.

Moreover, if we consider the intrinsic agents' ability to discriminate between two terms not to be perfect (they may be "short-sighted"), the usual preferences model is unfit to interpret this incapability since usual preferences are transitive and complete.

By the way, the proposition "I prefer a Ferrari to a bicycle" is identically "written" as the proposition "I prefer a Ferrari to a Porsche". But, it is not exaggerated to consider the agent's choice process to make a difference between the terms of both propositions.

---

2 Noted by **Haak** [1974].

I.1. Binary relation and fuzzy binary relation

I.1.1. Usual set

Let us consider the set X of men living on earth. We call X the referential set. If we want to give a definition of set A, the usual subset of X including *men living on earth who are "Doctors in Economics"*, we resort to the equality between the proposition "x is an element of A" and the proposition "x is an element of X and satisfies the property p" (p corresponds to *"being a doctor in Economics"*). So, we have :

$$A = \{x \in X, p(x)\}.$$

The set of x belonging to A is a usual subset of X because the property p is totally binary ; either one is doctor in Economics or not at all ! In other words, it is impossible to be a *"bit doctor"* or *"nearly completely doctor"*. The property p can only take the values 0 or 1 depending on the degree of the considered man living on earth.

I.1.2. Fuzzy set

Let us still consider the set X of men living on earth. We try to define the subset $\mathcal{B}$ of men living on earth who satisfied the property *"to be bald"* (by taking Black's example). It is possible to consider that a man is *"nearly bald"* or *"slightly bald"* and then the membership to the set $\mathcal{B}$ cannot be considered in a binary way, which means that the property *"to be bald"* does not take its values on $\{0,1\}$ but on the interval $[0,1]$, called the Zadeh set or sometimes the Lukasiewicz set. Therefore, a man living on earth who looses much of his hair belongs to $\mathcal{B}$ at 0,7 when another man living on earth, having much hair belongs to $\mathcal{B}$ at 0,01 (even though he looses a few hairs). In order to define the fuzzy subset $\mathcal{B}$, we have :

$$\mathcal{B} = \{x \in X;\ \mathscr{b},\ \mathscr{b}(x) \in [0,1]\}$$

where $\mathscr{b}(.)$, is the membership function that translates the satisfaction level of the property *"to be bald"*.

By putting together these two definitions and subsets A and $\mathcal{B}$ of X, we see that the only difference consists in the membership set that we write $\underline{M}$:

$$A = \{x \in X;\ p(x) \in \underline{M} = \{0,1\}\}. \qquad (1)$$

$$\mathcal{B} = \{x \in X;\ \mathscr{b},\ \mathscr{b}(x) \in \underline{M} = [0,1]\}. \qquad (2)$$

However, the membership set $\underline{M}$ is not always restricted to the Zadeh set. We will see, in Chapter two, how it can be productive to define $\underline{M}$ on the real set R (see for example Chang [1968], Zadeh [1965], Orlovsky [1978] or Mjelde [1986]).

I.1.3. The Boolean binary relation

Let us keep the referential set X of men living on earth. Let us admit the relation *"to be the legal father of"*. We generate a graph of the relation $R(.,.)$ *"to be the legal father of"* between elements of X. The relation $R(.,.)$ is Boolean in an obvious way ; it is not possible to be *"nearly the legal father of"* or *"a bit the legal father of"*. Hence, the levels of realization of the relation can only be 0 or 1, which corresponds to the usual Boolean $\underline{M}$. Therefore, the graph G of the relation $R(.,.)$ is written as follows :

$$G = \{(x,y) \in X^2; R(x,y) \in \underline{M} = \{0,1\}\}. \tag{3}$$

I.1.4. The fuzzy binary relation

Let us still consider our referential set X of men living on earth, and now let us try to put them in relation by using the property *"being the neighbour of"*. The notion of proximity is not binary ; there is no fixed measure that defines proximity. This notion is exactly the same as the one about being "small" or "bald". That is why the levels of realization of the relation between two elements of X cannot be reduced to 0 and 1. It is possible of being *"a close neighbour of"* whereas others are *"far away neighbours"*. The graph $\mathcal{G}$ of the relation $R(.,.)$ *"being the neighbour of"* is written as follows :

$$\mathcal{G} = \{(x,y) \in X^2; \mathcal{R}(x,y) \in \underline{M} = [0,1]\}. \tag{4}$$

We note that it is generally necessary to open the lower bound of $\underline{M}$ to keep the elements of X that are *"really"* in relation (see Prevôt [1977]).

I.2. The fuzzy relation of preference and its properties

I.2.1. The fuzzy preference

Preferences when defined with psychological foundations (Barthelemy & Mullet [1986], Moulin [1982;1983], Mullet [1986]) show an implicit process of ordering that is not modelled. Apart from resorting to multicriterion analysis (Moscarola & Roy [1976], Roy [1985], Morviller & Lepage [1974], Farreny & Prade [1981]) or *Lancasterian* approach of the economy, the usual process of preferences leads to a result that cannot describe the details of choice.

Actually, we want "*to come out the black box of preferences*".

We are not contented any more with the Boolean result. In that case, the agent must conceal his hesitations, his eventual irrationality and his difficulties to discriminate. According to the graph of a fuzzy relation, we note two levels of relation to exist. It is not necessary - but not excluded - to equalize them. If the fuzzy relation is a relation of preference, the agent gives two degrees ; the highest is called "*high preference degree*" and the lowest "*low preference degree*". In evaluating the relative qualities of x with respect to y, he defines $g(x,y)$. Then, he does the same for y with respect to x and defines $g(y,x)$. The model "*locally*" concludes by comparing both degrees.

Let us consider an agent calling on a wallpapers salesman. This salesman can choose between two possible attitudes. The first is called *usual* : the agent is showed in a room where all wallpapers are and the salesman let him choose. He has previously told him :"Classify them and we shall see what you can buy with your budget". The salesman will only know the final preorder. He will always ignore what has happened in the client's mind ; the room, where is the agent, corresponds to the *black box* of the model.

The second attitude - called *fuzzy* - consists for the salesman in escorting his client into the wallpapers room and in acknowledging the client's hesitations as facts, his difficulties to discriminate and his incoherences too. Then, we can see the salesman trying to solve inconsistencies, hesitations or incoherences. The room, where the salesman and the agent are, is the *clear box* of the model.

In the first case, the client leaves the room with his preorder already defined in a secret manner ; if some wallpapers have similar textures or colours or on the contrary, are so different that it is not possible to compare them, the client is compelled to be indifferent because unable to discriminate.

In the second case, the salesman attends the definition of the preorder : the client takes two batches of wallpaper. He examines the *intrinsic qualities* of each one in order to define the level of fuzzy reflexivity. Then, he examines the *relative qualities* of batch x with respect to y, and finally, the ones of batch y with respect to x in order to define his two *degrees of preference* $g(x,y)$ and $g(y,x)$. If $g(x,y)$ is greater than $g(y,x)$, the salesman concludes his client to *locally* prefer x. If $g(x,y)$ and $g(y,x)$ are equal, he knows the client to be *locally* indifferent between both. If both batches are not comparable, the salesman knows that it corresponds to an *equality* of both preference degrees at zero-level. The relation "*greater or equal*", which is by definition complete, is the relation that links the preference degrees. The fuzzy attitude case (which refers to a membership set $\underline{M}$ whose cardinal is strictly greater than 2) leads to four cases :

a- The batch x is *locally preferred* to y : $g(x,y) > g(y,x)$.

b- The batch y is *locally preferred* to x : $g(x,y) < g(y,x)$.

c- x is *locally but actively indifferent* to y : $g(x,y) = g(y,x)$ with $g(.,.) \in]0,1]$.

d- x is *locally incomparable* to y : $g(x,y) = g(y,x) = 0$.

Let us come back to a usual situation and consider the four following situations (the membership set is $\{0,1\}$) :

a- $g(x,y) > g(y,x)$ i.e. $g(x,y) = 1$ and $g(y,x) = 0$.

b- $g(x,y) < g(y,x)$ i.e. $g(x,y) = 0$ and $g(y,x) = 1$.

c- $g(x,y) = g(y,x)$ i.e. $g(x,y) = g(y,x) = 1$.

d- $g(x,y) = g(y,x)$ i.e. $g(x,y) = g(y,x) = 0$.

The fourth situation - d - is excluded thanks to the axiom of completeness but it implicitly exists when $\underline{M} = \{0,1\}$. With fuzzy preferences, completeness of the individual relation of preference is acquired with the relation *"greater or equal"*.

Nevertheless, let us suppose a local indifference with level α between two batches of wallpaper x and y[3]. An axiom is not necessary to exclude incomparabilities. Actually, if α is different from 0, it means on one hand, that the relative qualities of both batches are equal and on the other, that the agent is able to discriminate. If α is equal to 0, it means that comparing has no meaning or that both batches are without interest.

However, a relation of fuzzy preference can be reflexive and/or transitive.

I.2.2. Fuzzy reflexivity and fuzzy transitivity

I.2.2.1. Fuzzy reflexivity

It is possible to consider two specific schools according to different treatments of fuzziness. This distinction, between French and Anglo-saxon[4] approaches, deals with the measure of fuzzy preferences, sometimes ordinal and sometimes cardinal. Beyond this criterion, the French school defines fuzzy reflexivity in a very special way. In the first articles (Zadeh [1971b], Bellman & Zadeh [1970], Shimura [1973], Tamura, Huguchi & Tanaka [1971] up to Kaufmann's [1973] book), reflexivity has a clearly binary inspiration. The definition is called Anglo-saxon[5] :

Definition 1 : Let X be a non-fuzzy referential set and $\underline{M}$, the Zadeh membership set, [0,1]. $\forall x \in X$, the fuzzy relation $\mathcal{R}(.,.)$ is reflexive (A.s.) $\Leftrightarrow \mathcal{R}(x,x) = 1$.

Let us now explain this definition in an economic way. $\mathcal{R}(x,x)$ is the preference level of x with respect to x ; when comparing a batch x with respect with itself, we just evaluate the qualities of x : i.e. the *intrinsic* qualities (Billot [1987b]). Hence, it is not necessary to compare two different elements in order to define their intrinsic qualities.

Moreover, this definition of reflexivity remains binary. Indeed, if $\mathcal{R}(x,x) \neq 1$ for one element of X at least, the relation $\mathcal{R}(.,.)$ is not reflexive.

---

3 i.e. $g(x,y) = g(y,x) = \alpha \in \underline{M} = [0,1]$

4 Actually, it means the *"rest of the world"*.

5 (A.s.) for Anglo-saxon school. (F.s.) for French school.

These two arguments are the reasons why the French school does not use any more this kind of reflexivity which forbids the interpretation in terms of intrinsic qualities. The definition of fuzzy reflexivity we propose is written as follows :

Definition 2 : Let X be a non-fuzzy referential set and $\underline{M}$, the membership set, [0,1]. $\forall x \in X$, the fuzzy relation $\mathcal{R}(.,.)$ is reflexive (F.s.) $\Leftrightarrow \mathcal{R}(x,x) \in [0,1]$.

If an object is intrinsically satisfying, the indifference between the object and itself corresponds to the highest level of satisfaction : $\mathcal{R}(x,x) = 1$. If, on the contrary, another object is without any interest, then the indifference between this object and itself corresponds to the lowest level of satisfaction : $\mathcal{R}(x,x) = 0$. In other words, if one of the elements is in a non-reflexivity situation, it does not condemn the relation to be non-reflexive.

Definition 3 : A fuzzy relation $\mathcal{R}(.,.)$ is totally reflexive if : $\forall x \in X$, $\mathcal{R}(x,x) = 1$.

Definition 4 : A fuzzy relation $\mathcal{R}(.,.)$ is totally nonreflexive if : $\forall x \in X$, $\mathcal{R}(x,x) = 0$.

Any intermediate situation between these two Boolean definitions derives from the fuzzy reflexivity that describes the shades of reflexivity.

I.2.2.2. Fuzzy transitivity

In order to deduce a preorder (case of a coherent behaviour), we need a definition of fuzzy transitivity. We are going to present the different formulations that exist, without forgetting the "*credo*". The "*credo*", here, consists in imposing the different formulations to describe fuzzy transitivities and usual one when the membership set is restrained to {0,1}. Any form of transitivity that is presented satisfies the *credo*. But, we finally reject them in order to propose a last one that is used when the economic agents are coherent in their choices. This formulation is justified *a contrario*, according to criticisms that are elaborated against the other types of transitivity.

A. Max-Min transitivity

This definition is the most commonly used. It was introduced by Zadeh [1971b], and agreed by Orlovsky [1978;1980] (we shall present his work). From Hashimoto [1983] to Bezdek & Harris [1978], everybody (Dubois & Prade [1980], Ponsard [1980,1981,1982, 1984,1986]) utilizes it. Moreover, it is the only type of fuzzy transitivity proposed by Prevôt [1977] and Roubens & Vincke [1986]. Nevertheless, we are going to see how much its implications can be criticized in an economic way because of the I.I.A. violation. The definition of Max-Min transitivity is :

Definition 5 : Let X be a non-fuzzy referential set. $\forall(x,y,z) \in X^3$, a fuzzy relation $\mathcal{R}(.,.)$ is Max-Min transitive $\Leftrightarrow \mathcal{R}(x,y) \geq \text{Max}_y[\text{Min}\{\mathcal{R}(x,y), \mathcal{R}(y,z)\}]$.

Let us read Kaufmann's defence : "*We know that the transitivity is defined by :* $\forall(x,y,z) \in X^3$; $\{(x,y) \in X^2, (y,z) \in X^2\} \Rightarrow \{(x,z) \in X^2\}$.

This relation explains that there exists at least one element "y" such that : $(x,y) \in X^2$ *and* $(y,z) \in X^2$ *; if* $\mathcal{R}(x,y) = 1$ *and* $\mathcal{R}(y,z) = 1$, *then* $\mathcal{R}(x,z) = 1$ *and* $(x,z) \in X^2$.

Operator "Min" corresponds to the logic "and" and operator "Max" to the result that can be obtained with the implication "$\Rightarrow$*"*"[6].

Let us notice this defence of Max-Min transitivity to consist in insisting on what we already called the "*credo*" : since the usual transitivity holds when the membership becomes binary, therefore the Max-Min transitivity is justified. We can also note that Kaufmann's defence is based on a perfect (apparent) relation between operators that *generalize* (Max and Min) and logic operators (*"and"* and "$\Rightarrow$"). It still remains valid for any membership set $\underline{M}$. If the first argument (credo) is strong, the second is weaker. In fuzzy sets algebra, the operator that translates intersection, i.e. the logic *"and"*, is the operator "Min" (Zadeh [1965]). On the contrary, the result of the logical implication *"*$\Rightarrow$*"* does not correspond to the operator that translates the union of fuzzy subsets which is operator "Max". Hence, the last part of this defence is not intuitively convincing, by the confusion introduced between *"or"* (i.e. *"union"*) and the logical implication *"*$\Rightarrow$*"*.

There exists a better defence that is more coherent from a theoretical point of view. This defence was elaborated by Orlovsky [1978] and repeated by Montero & Tejada [1986]. It is based on the fuzzy set of *nondominated alternatives*. Orlovsky introduces a fuzzy relation of strict preference as follows : $\mathcal{R}^S(x,y) = \text{Max}\{\mathcal{R}(x,y) - \mathcal{R}(y,x), 0\}$.

The membership function of the fuzzy set of *nondominated alternatives* is defined as follows : $\mathcal{Nd}(x) = \inf_{x \in X}[1 - \mathcal{R}^S(y,x)]$, expression that corresponds to :

$$\mathcal{Nd}(x) = 1 - \sup_{x \in X}[\mathcal{R}^S(y,x)],$$

where X is the referential set and $\underline{M} = [0,1]$.

$\mathcal{Nd}(x)$ is the degree on and after which x is never dominated (*preferred*) by another element belonging to X. Straight away, Orlovsky transforms the problem of choice rationality into a maximization program of $\mathcal{Nd}(.)$. Next, he proves that if X is a finite referential set, $\mathcal{R}(.,.)$ a reflexive (A.s.) and Max-Min transitive fuzzy relation, then the set of *"non fuzzy and nondominated solutions"*, noted $X_{\mathcal{R}}^{\text{UND}}$ is nonempty :

$$X_{\mathcal{R}}^{\text{UND}} = \{x \in X; \mathcal{Nd}(x) = 1\} \neq \emptyset.$$

6 Kaufmann [1973], Tome 1, p.80.

He concludes that it is necessary to use Max-Min transitivity when working with relations of fuzzy preference such that the set of *nondominated solutions* is nonempty. Nevertheless, we cannot accept this defence because of two reasons.

1- Let us note that the most important argument to justify the Max-Min transitivity deals with a particular fuzzy relation of preference that implies a particular membership function for the fuzzy set of *nondominated solutions*. Next, when looking the two definitions, $\mathcal{R}^S(x,y) = \text{Max}\{\mathcal{R}(x,y) - \mathcal{R}(y,x), 0\}$ as well as $\mathcal{N}d(x) = 1 - \sup_{x \in X}[\mathcal{R}^S(y,x)]$, it is obvious that both are based on an additive measure and thus, the I.I.A. is violated.

2- Apart from the advantage of such an approach in terms of *nondominated* alternatives, it is amazing to defend a type of transitivity that remains ordinal, by means of cardinalism.

This defence is based on cardinalism of preferences. But, Bazu [1984] develops a criticism against the Max-Min transitivity that leads to prefer some weighed transitivities ever since one accepts cardinal relations of preference.

"*Let us suppose that* $X = \{x,y,z\}$ *and* $\mathcal{R}(x,y) = \mathcal{R}(y,z) = 0{,}5$. *Then the smallest level for* $\mathcal{R}(x,z)$ *is* $0{,}5$. *Let us now alternatively consider* $\mathcal{R}(x,y) = 1$ *and* $\mathcal{R}(y,z) = 0{,}5$ *; even in this case, the smallest level for* $\mathcal{R}(x,z)$ *is* $0{,}5$. *In the second case, we shall think that* $\mathcal{R}(x,z)$ *is greater than* $\mathcal{R}(x,z)$ *of the first case.*"

Bazu's argument is very strong even though related to a particular weakness of the Max-Min transitivity. But, it is still true that for any (ordinal or cardinal) utilization of the Max-Min transitivity, the I.I.A. is finally violated. This is why we reject it.

Actually, if the referential set has a cardinal greater than 3, the Max-Min transitivity implies the alternatives not to be considered in an independent way. All along this book, we shall prefer another transitivity based on ordinal fuzzy relations that satisfy the I.I.A.

B. Max-* transitivity

Zadeh [1971], like Bezdek & Harris [1978], presents some other kinds of transitivity, associated to other fuzzy compositions than the Max-Min one, as Med, Proj...(see Dubois [1983], Chap.2, p.111).

Let us suppose any binary relation[7], defined on [0,1], that we call *"connection operator"* ; we say a fuzzy relation $\mathcal{R}(.,.)$ to be Max-* transitive iff :

$$\forall (x,y,z) \in X^3,\ \mathcal{R}(x,z) \geq \text{Max}_y[\mathcal{R}(x,y) * \mathcal{R}(y,z)].$$

---

7 If *=Min, we find again def.5.

C. *Weighed* transivity

Bazu [1984] proposes a type of transitivity that solves the problem which appeared in his example. A fuzzy relation $\mathcal{R}(.,.)$ is *w*-transitive iff :

$$\forall(x,y,z)\in X^3;$$

$$\mathcal{R}(x,z)\geq\alpha\,\mathrm{Max}\{\mathcal{R}(x,y),\mathcal{R}(y,z)\}+\beta\,\mathrm{Min}\{\mathcal{R}(x,y),\mathcal{R}(y,z)\}$$

with $(\alpha+\beta=1)$ and $(\alpha>0,\beta>0)$.

It is obvious that we find again cardinalism and thus violation of the I.I.A.

D. f-transitivity

We reject any transitivity that does not respect the I.I.A. i.e., based on an additive measure implying cardinalism. We consider the theoretical necessity of the I.I.A. to be sufficient since cardinalism implies its violation. This necessity leads us to define a transitivity that respects the *"credo"* and satisfies the I.I.A.

Definition 6 : A fuzzy relation $\mathcal{R}(.,.)$ is f-transitive iff :

$$\forall(x,y,z)\in X^3;$$

$$[\mathcal{R}(x,y)\geq\mathcal{R}(y,x)\text{ and }\mathcal{R}(y,z)\geq\mathcal{R}(z,y)]\Rightarrow[\mathcal{R}(x,z)\geq\mathcal{R}(z,x)].$$

Each time the agents are supposed to be *"coherent"*, we use preorders of fuzzy preference, i.e. reflexive (F.s.) and f-transitive relations, except when we explicitly refer to Ponsard's works. f-transitivity has not appeared in literature before Luo [1986] and Billot [1986;1987b] ; a fuzzy preorder is a reflexive (F.s.) and f-transitive relation. When the agents are *"coherent"*, their preferences correspond to a fuzzy preorder. The *"incoherent"* behaviour can be modelled with the help of a simple fuzzy relation of preference.

I.2.3. "Incoherent" fuzzy preferences and dominated irrationality

We consider some agents, with a poor ability to discriminate, to be *"incoherent"*. We call *incoherent fuzzy preferences* a binary fuzzy relation that is only reflexive (F.s.). Preferences are not transitive (none of the different types of transitivity is satisfied). The agent can just *locally* choose, i.e. between two objects. Without any condition of coherence, the I.I.A. implies an *irrational* definition of preference degrees. For example, an *"incoherent"* agent presents the following preferences : $\forall(x,y,z)\in X^3$, $\mathcal{R}(x,y)=0{,}5$, $\mathcal{R}(y,x)=0{,}2$, $\mathcal{R}(y,z)=0{,}6$ and $\mathcal{R}(z,y)=0{,}4$; but when the agent *locally* compares x and z, $\mathcal{R}(x,z)=0{,}5$ while $\mathcal{R}(z,x)=0{,}6$.

Such a behaviour would be impossible to model in a relevant way if the relation of preference were Boolean. On the contrary, we can discriminate between *local* and *global* preferences (the *global* preference can only be a preorder) when preference are fuzzy. This distinction allows agents whose local behaviour is incoherent to generate some theoretically strange or paradoxical situations.

Nevertheless, it is necessary to link *local* and *global* preferences. In microeconomics, the fuzzy preorder must be represented by a utility function in order to be maximized on the agent's budget. This transition from *local* to *global* preference consists in *dominating the agent's irrationality*. The principle of *"dominated irrationality"* corresponds to the *first projection of the fuzzy relation* $\mathcal{R}(.,.)$. The *locally* incoherent agent decides to assign the maximum degree of $\mathcal{R}(x,.)$ to each x. This maximum degree corresponds to the membership level of x to the fuzzy preordered subset $\mathcal{X}$, $\mathcal{X} \subset X$:

Definition 7 : $\forall x \in X$, let $\mathcal{R}(.,.)$ be a reflexive (F.s.)[8] fuzzy relation. The *principle of dominated irrationality* consists in defining a fuzzy subset $\mathcal{X}$ such that :

$$\chi(x) = Proj[\mathcal{R}(x,y)] = \text{Max}_{y \in X}[\mathcal{R}(x,y)].$$

Finally, this *principle* will be very useful in the last chapter of this book. Nevertheless, the proof of the existence for a continuous utility function representing a fuzzy preorder is the main point of both following sections of this chapter.

SECTION TWO : THE PARADOX OF INDIFFERENCE

The paradox of Buridan's donkey deals with indecision in indifference context[9]. It means that the usual preference theory does not *explain* decisions deriving from choice but only choice. Buridan's donkey is indifferent between a peck of bran and a pick of oats. Its fate will be tragic because it cannot decide which peck is going to feed it. Here, we find the idea, already expressed by Vuillemin [1986], according to which preference theory is not a theory of action because sometimes unable to imply effective decisions without any exogeneous algorithm as uncertainty (heads or tails). Preference theory is a *reflexive* theory that does not ever come out of agents : *"it is only a meaning of choice."*[10]

---

8 $\chi(.)$ is the membership function of fuzzy subset $\mathcal{X}$, defined on the Zadeh set [0,1].

9 This is the reason why we sometimes talk about the *indifference paradox.*

10 Vuillemin [1986], p.381.

II.1. Reflexivity and indifference

The means presented by Schmidt [1984] in order to solve this paradox are based on the introduction of a *sensibility* of preferences relatively to three possible intrinsic characters : *good, bad* and *neutral.* This corresponds to three possible values for $\mathcal{R}(x,x)$; the membership set $\underline{M}$ differs from the Boolean set {0,1} according to a third value corresponding to *"neutrality"*[11]. If mixing the fuzzy reflexivity (F.s.) with a continuous membership set $\underline{M}$, it is possible to consider an axiomatic solution for the paradox of Buridan's donkey that always yields an *action*, even based on a choice indifference.

II.2. The axiomatic solution

II.2.1. The absence of ideal object (A1)

There is no *intrinsically* perfect object. In other words, the qualities of some objects can be infinitely great without always defining the ideal object, i.e. the one having all possible intrinsic qualities[12]. Let X be the referential set and $\mathcal{R}(.,.)$ a fuzzy relation of preference defined on $\underline{M} = [0,1] : \forall x \in X, \mathcal{R}(x,x) \in]0,1[$.

II.2.2. If relative preferences are equal, satisfactions are equal (A2)

If two objects have relative qualities of same importance, they both generate the same satisfaction for the agent : if I am indifferent between an apple and a pear, the satisfaction I get from their consumption is identical :

$$\forall (x,y) \in X^2, \mathcal{R}(x,y) = \mathcal{R}(y,x) \neq 0 \Rightarrow u(x) = u(y)$$

where $u(x)$ is the agent's satisfaction when consuminge x[13].

II.2.3. Identity (A3)

If two objects have the same intrinsic qualities and the same relative ones (if comparable), then they must be the same object :

---

11 We can recognize here the principle of Kunztmann's Φ-Boolean calculus devoted to a three values system, 0, 1 and Φ, where Φ is a *undetermined* value.

12 We assume any x to be always comparable to itself, i.e. : $\forall x \in X, \mathcal{R}(x,x) \neq 0$.

13 (A2) is strong : it forbids local incoherences and yields any relation of preference to be a *fuzzy preorder*. That is the reason why it disappears in the rest of this book and especially in Section four of this Chapter. Moreover, it implies an immediate equivalence between *local* and *global* preferences.

$$\forall (x,y) \in X^2, [\mathcal{R}(x,y) = \mathcal{R}(y,x) \text{ and } \mathcal{R}(x,x) = \mathcal{R}(y,y) \neq 0] \Rightarrow [x = y].$$

II.2.4. Max-satisfaction (A4)

The agents assign to any x, as *"evaluated satisfaction"*, denoted $u(x)$, the maximum level of relative or intrinsic qualities. If x is indifferent to y with level α, and indifferent to another z with level β, the agent associates to x the maximum of levels α, β and $\mathcal{R}(x,x)$.

$$\forall x \in X, \ u(x) = \text{Max}\{\mathcal{R}(x,y);\ \mathcal{R}(x,y) = \mathcal{R}(y,x)\}.$$

We have to point out here (A4), that is the basis of an utility function in the case of a countable referential set, to proceed from Ponsard [1980;1982;1986].

II.2.5. Comparability and intrinsic qualities (A5)

Intrinsic qualities are always lower or equal to relative ones when x and y are precisely comparable, i.e. when $\mathcal{R}(x,y)$ and $\mathcal{R}(y,x)$ are equal but different from 0. If not, two incomparable elements still have intrinsic qualities. In this case, intrinsic qualities are greater than relative ones which are null. Let us consider a bicycle and a motorcycle. The qualities of one compared to the other (if it is the agent's conviction) are greater than intrinsic qualities of each one, (both cycles are trivially *comparable*) since it is natural to consider the level of satisfaction, while comparing, to be influenced by the intrinsic qualities of both cycles.

Therefore, the intrinsic qualities of a Ferrari are so great that they influence the comparison level between the Ferrari and the bicycle or the motorcycle. Moreover, the poor intrinsic qualities of the bicycle influence the preference degree $\mathcal{R}$(bicycle, Ferrari), dragging it to the lower bound of $\underline{M}$.

$$\forall (x,y) \in X^2, 0 \le \mathcal{R}(x,x) \le \mathcal{R}(x,y) \text{ and } 0 \le \mathcal{R}(y,y) \le \mathcal{R}(y,x)$$

$$\text{or } 0 = \mathcal{R}(x,y) \le \mathcal{R}(x,x) \text{ and } 0 = \mathcal{R}(y,x) \le \mathcal{R}(y,y).$$

II.3. Solution

The method that we propose is based on the information proceeding from the preference levels that correspond to fuzzy reflexivity. We have to divide the solution in two parts : a first one dealing with the *"active"* indifference (when objects are comparable) and a second analyzing the *"passive"* indifference (when objects are not comparable).

II.3.1. Case of active indifference

Let us consider Buridan's donkey in front of its two pecks. We note x the oat peck and y the bran one.

We know Buridan's donkey to be indifferent between the two pecks, i.e. the relative qualities of oat and bran are equal. The fuzzy relation of preference of Buridan's donkey's, $\mathcal{R}(.,.)$, is such that $\mathcal{R}(x,y)=\mathcal{R}(y,x)$. The donkey is also assumed to know the tastes of both pecks. It can assign levels of intrinsic qualities by defining fuzzy reflexivity levels, $\mathcal{R}(x,x)$ and $\mathcal{R}(y,y)$. (A2) ensures the donkey to have the same satisfaction in eating one or the other. Therefore, we can write : $u(x)=u(y)$. (A4) implies :

$$u(x)=\text{Max}\{\mathcal{R}(x,x),\ \mathcal{R}(x,y)\}=u(y)=\text{Max}\{\mathcal{R}(y,y),\ \mathcal{R}(y,x)\}.$$

(A5) yields $\mathcal{R}(x,x)\leq\mathcal{R}(x,y)$ and $\mathcal{R}(y,y)\leq\mathcal{R}(y,x)$.

Let us assume the donkey to consider that both pecks, the bran peck as the oat one, have intrinsic qualities strictly lower than relative ones. Under this assumption, the satisfaction deriving from oat as the one deriving from bran are equal and ensures the indifference between both pecks. Nevertheless, are the intrinsic qualities of both pecks equal in terms of level ? (A3) implies the contrary since, by definition, oat is not bran. Therefore, as soon as $\mathcal{R}(x,x)\neq\mathcal{R}(y,y)$, i.e. when the intrinsic qualities are different, it is always possible to *actively* choose which of both pecks has the greatest intrinsic qualities. Henceforth, Buridan's donkey chooses the peck that has the greatest intrinsic qualities. Formally [14]:

$$\mathcal{R}(x,y)=\mathcal{R}(y,x)\neq 0$$

$$\Leftrightarrow \quad \text{(A2)} \quad u(x)=u(y)$$

$$\Leftrightarrow \quad \text{(A4)} \quad \text{Max}\{\mathcal{R}(x,x),\ \mathcal{R}(x,y)\}=\text{Max}\{\mathcal{R}(y,y),\ \mathcal{R}(y,x)\}$$

$$\Leftrightarrow \quad \text{(A5)} \quad \mathcal{R}(x,x)\leq\mathcal{R}(x,y) \text{ and } \mathcal{R}(y,y)\leq\mathcal{R}(y,x)$$

$$\Leftrightarrow \quad \text{(A4)} \quad u(x)=\mathcal{R}(x,y)=\mathcal{R}(y,x)=u(y)$$

$$\Leftrightarrow \begin{cases} \alpha- & \mathcal{R}(x,x)=\mathcal{R}(x,y)=\mathcal{R}(y,x)=\mathcal{R}(y,y) \quad \Leftrightarrow \quad \text{(A3)} \quad x=y \\ \beta- & \mathcal{R}(x,x)<\mathcal{R}(y,y) \quad \Leftrightarrow \quad \text{choice of y} \\ \gamma- & \mathcal{R}(x,x)>\mathcal{R}(y,y) \quad \Leftrightarrow \quad \text{choice of x.} \end{cases}$$

---

14 The case $\alpha-$ has no interest for Buridan's donkey since by definition, oats are not bran.

II.3.2. Case of passive indifference

When objects are not comparable, the paradox disappears. Actually, in this case, (A5) implies the intrinsic qualities of each object to be necessarily greater than the relative ones. Then, (A4) yields the satisfaction deriving from both objects to be equal to the valuation of these intrinsic qualities. Hence, the paradox comes down to the case where the intrinsic qualities of both objects are identical, which means according to (A3) that both objects are the same. Finally, it excludes - because (A1) - the initial incomparability. Formally :

$$\mathcal{R}(x,y)=\mathcal{R}(y,x)=0$$

$$\Leftrightarrow \quad \text{(A5)} \quad \mathcal{R}(x,y)\leq \mathcal{R}(x,x) \text{ and } \mathcal{R}(y,x)\leq \mathcal{R}(y,y)$$

$$\Leftrightarrow \quad \text{(A4)} \quad u(x)=\mathcal{R}(x,x)=\mathcal{R}(y,y)=u(y)$$

$$\Leftrightarrow \quad \text{(A3)} \quad x=y$$

$$\Leftrightarrow \quad \text{(A1)} \quad \mathcal{R}(x,y)=\mathcal{R}(y,x)=\mathcal{R}(x,x)=\mathcal{R}(y,y)\neq 0 \quad \Rightarrow \quad \text{contradiction.}$$

SECTION THREE : FUZZY UTILITY FUNCTION ON A COUNTABLE SET

In 1881, Edgeworth introduced the basic idea according to which a mathematical function can represent the agent's preferences.

Nevertheless, there are three good reasons that allow to resort to a utility function, even knowing the agent's preorder of preference, (which is sufficient for an important part of microeconomics). First, there are fundamental and *classic* results that we cannot exhibit with a preferences system, even though transitive, reflexive and complete. Next, mathematical difficulties are less important. Finally, the supplementary hypotheses that must define the preorder of preference in order to obtain a continuous utility function are not stronger than the basic ones (except the preferences continuity).

We must distinguish two very different versions of what is called a *fuzzy utility function.* In this section, the referential set of objects is *countable*. The transition operator is *Max* and the agents are all *coherent*, their fuzzy relations of preference are reflexive (F.s.) and Max-Min transitive.

Before presenting *Ponsard*'s fuzzy utility function, it is necessary to define some properties related to the considered system of fuzzy preferences.

III.1. Subrelations of similitude

A fuzzy relation of indifference, denoted $\mathcal{I}(.,.)$ yields indifference classes that form among them similitude subrelations - SSR - (not necessarily disjoint). A SSR is a reflexive fuzzy relation (F.s.), Max-Min transitive and symmetric[15] denoted $s\mathcal{I}(.,.)$. The fuzzy class is noted $\mathcal{C}(.)$.

Definition 8 : We call *fuzzy quotient-set*, the following set : $X/s\mathcal{I}(.,.) = \{\mathcal{C}(x), \forall x \in X\}$.

There exists a bijection from $X/s\mathcal{I}(.,.)$ to $X/\sim$ ($\sim$ denoting usual indifference). The relation between the different similitude classes is necessarily antisymmetric (Negoita & Ralescu [1978], Ponsard [1986]). It is obvious that there exists a fuzzy order between the similitude classes. Hence, it is easy to describe this process by considering the similitude classes as *fixed* on an indifference level (belonging to $\underline{M}$).

$$\text{If } (x,y) \in \mathcal{C}(x)^2 \text{ and } \mathcal{I}(y,z) = \mathcal{I}(z,y) \quad \Rightarrow \quad \mathcal{I}(x,z) = \mathcal{I}(z,x).$$

For a relation of preference[16] $\mathcal{R}(.,.)$, reflexive (F.s.) and Max-Min transitive, we have :

$$\text{If } (x,y) \in \mathcal{C}(x)^2 \text{ and } \mathcal{R}(y,z) > \mathcal{R}(z,y) \quad \Rightarrow \quad \mathcal{R}(x,z) > \mathcal{R}(z,x).$$

III.2. The transition operator

Let us consider the membership set $\underline{M}$ to be the Zadeh set [0,1]. We assume :

If $\mathcal{I}(x,y) = \mathcal{I}(y,x) = \mu_x \in [0,1] \Rightarrow \chi(x) = \text{Max}\,\mu_x$ (where $\chi(.)$ is the membership function of $\mathcal{X}$, fuzzy subset of X preordered by $\mathcal{R}(.,.)$) :

$$\mathcal{X} = \{x \in X,\ \chi(x) = \text{Max}\,\mu_x \in [0,1]\}. \qquad (P1)$$

This postulate means any fuzzy relation of preference to lead to a fuzzy subset proceeding from the transition operator, Max. The utility function corresponds to the membership function $\chi(.)$, which implies that the continuity of a fuzzy utility function depends on the continuity of the membership function of $\mathcal{X}$. Actually, by taking the maximum levels of indifference, we ensure incomparable objects not to be out of utility[17].

---

15 $\mathcal{I}(.,.)$ is a *symmetric* fuzzy relation $\Leftrightarrow \forall (x,y) \in X^2,\ \mathcal{I}(x,y) = \mathcal{I}(y,x)$.

16 A fuzzy relation of preference that is a fuzzy preorder, i.e. a reflexive (F.s.) and Max-Min transitive relation, is based on a relation of indifference, reflexive (F.s.), Max-Min transitive and symmetric (which is noted here, $\mathcal{I}(.,.)$) and a relation of strict preference which is reflexive (F.s.), Max-Min transitive and antisymmetric.

17 In Ponsard's works, the conceiving of transition from the relation towards the function has evolved. In one of his last papers devoted to the subject (Ponsard [1986]), Ponsard suggests the degree of reflexivity to derive from the maximum of the indifference degrees. However, the analysis in terms of intrinsic and relatives qualities is inconsistent with this last conceiving ; moreover, this approach is unfit to integrate those objects which are only comparable with themselves.

It is also obvious that the ideal object, i.e. the one whose level of reflexivity is equal to 1, always leads to the maximum of satisfaction ; it confirms the economic interpretation of fuzzy reflexivity (F.s.).

III.3. Utility and fuzzy reflexivity

The *transition* postulate assigns a level of satisfaction to the maximum of the indifference levels. Using Ponsard's analysis, the concept of "intrinsic qualities" gets its full meaning by *equalizing* the maximum of degrees of relative preference to the degree of intrinsic one. This degree is evaluated thanks to the fuzzy reflexivity (F.s.). The model seems correct but the particular problem of the objects that are just comparable with themselves is not solved : hence, there are cases where this transition procedure is irrevelant.

In the first annex of Billot [1987b], we proved the *necessary* equality of the level of fuzzy reflexivity and the membership level to the subset $\mathcal{X}$ when the *transition* operator is Max. This observation implies the elementary remark according to which this equality ruins the relevance of a preference theory that dispenses with comparisons between the objects. In order to improve this approach, one proposed the level of intrinsic preference to be theoretically justified as soon as all the comparisons between all the objects are be done. Actually, the level of intrinsic preference would be equal to the maximum level of relative preferences. In other words, we should first compare the objects, next, we should assign the maximum level of relative preferences to the one of intrinsic preference. Nevertheless, this leads to the fact that a fully *incomparable* object has an intrinsic level of preference equal to zero.

III.4. Totally ordered fuzzy topological space

For the structure $(X, \mathcal{R}(.,.), \mathcal{T})$ to become a totally ordered fuzzy topological space (where X is the set of objects, $\mathcal{R}(.,.)$ the fuzzy preorder of preference, $\mathcal{T}$ a fuzzy topology), the preferences must be continuous, the set $\mathcal{X}$ closed and X connected.

III.4.1. Fuzzy topology

We call *fuzzy topology* defined on a referential set X, a family $\mathcal{T}$ of fuzzy parts O_i, ($i \in I$ where I is an index set), called *"open sets"* and verifying three axioms :

Axiom 1 : X and $\emptyset$ are open : $X \in \mathcal{T}$; $\emptyset \in \mathcal{T}$.

Axiom 2 : $\forall i \in I$, $O_i \in \mathcal{T}$: $\cup_{i \in I} O_i \in \mathcal{T}$.

Axiom 3 : $\forall i \in I$, $O_i \in \mathcal{T}$: $\cap_{i \in I_n} O_i \in \mathcal{T}$.

(I_n is a *finite* subset of I)

III.4.2. Assumption of preferences continuity

Let us consider $\mathcal{A}(x)$ as the satisfaction degree consistent with the postulate [P1] and $(\mathcal{A}(y))_n$, $n \in N$, as a finite sequence of satisfaction degrees for the objects that tends to $\mathcal{A}(z)$, where z is an element of the referential X. If n tends to infinity, thus, for any n, $(\mathcal{A}(y))_n$ is *at most as great as* or *at least as great as* $\mathcal{A}(x)$. This means that $\mathcal{A}(z)$ is *at most as great as* or *at least as great as* $\mathcal{A}(x)$: i.e. z is *at most indifferent* or *at least indifferent to* x. Mathematically :

$$X^+ = \{y \in X;\ \mathcal{R}(x,y) \geq \mathcal{R}(y,x)\} \text{ and}$$

$$X^- = \{y \in X;\ \mathcal{R}(x,y) \leq \mathcal{R}(y,x)\} \text{ are closed sets in } X.$$

This fuzzy topology which is relevant to a fuzzy preorder defines a totally preordered space of fuzzy preferences on a countable set.

Studying the compatibility between the preferences structure and the totally preordered topological space is easy in the case of a countable set. The existing literature is essentially based on Usawa's theorem [1960].

III.5. A fuzzy utility function

The function that links an element from the interval [0,1] to the level of fuzzy preferences is based on the quotient-set $X/s\mathcal{l}(.,.)$. Because of the isomorphism between the quotient-set $X/s\mathcal{l}(.,.)$ and the usual set $X/\sim$, we have :

$$f: X/\sim\ \rightarrow [0,1]$$

$$\mathcal{C}(x) \rightarrow f[\mathcal{C}(x)] = \mathcal{I}(x,y) = \mu_x.$$

This function is increasing : $\forall (x,y) \in \mathcal{C}(x)^2, \forall (z,t) \in \mathcal{C}(z)^2$ and $\mathcal{I}(x,y) = \mu_x$ and $\mathcal{I}(z,t) = \mu_z$ for $\mu_x > \mu_z$; $f[\mathcal{C}(x)] > f[\mathcal{C}(z)]$.

The increase of f means that indifference can correspond to different degrees of satisfaction. "To be indifferent between a Ferrari and a Porsche" does not mean the same thing as "to be indifferent between a bicycle and a motorcycle". Let us consider the first projection[18] : *Proj*

$$Proj : X \rightarrow X/\sim$$

$$x \rightarrow Proj[\mathcal{C}(x)] = \text{Max}[\mathcal{C}(x)].$$

---

18 This projection is mathematically identical to the one we use when *"dominating irrationality"* of the agents. But here, it is applied to the quotient-set $X/\sim$ and not to the fuzzy subset X.

The associated utility function is therefore : $f \circ Proj = u$.

$$
\begin{array}{llllll}
u: & X & \rightarrow & X/\sim & \rightarrow & [0,1] \\
 & x & \rightarrow & Proj[\mathcal{C}(x)] & \rightarrow & f(Proj[\mathcal{C}(x)]) = f(\mathrm{Max}[\mathcal{C}(x)]) \\
 & & & & & = \mathrm{Max}\, I(x,y) \\
 & & & & & = \chi(x) \\
 & & & & & = u(x).
\end{array}
$$

We can define *Ponsard's* fuzzy utility function thanks to the basic principle : "equal relative qualities yield equal satisfaction" :

$$\forall (x,y) \in X^2, \text{ if } \mathcal{R}(x,y) = \mathcal{R}(y,x) \Rightarrow u(x) = u(y).$$

This definition that defines identity between *local* preference and *global* one also implies two *incomparable* objects to yield the same level of satisfaction ; that is a deceiving result. If there exists a fully *incomparable* object, i.e. :

$$\exists x \in X; \forall y \in X, \mathcal{R}(x,y) = \mathcal{R}(y,x) = 0,$$

it implies : $\forall y \in X,\ u(x) = u(y)$.

But this generalized indifference is going to spread at zero-level since by definition :

$$\chi(x) = \mathrm{Max}\, I(x,y) \text{ and so } \chi(x) = 0 = u(x).$$

To prevent this case, we just have to assume a fully *incomparable* object not to exist in X.

For the structure $(X, \mathcal{R}(.,.))$, the utility function is an homomorphism of $(X, \mathcal{R}(.,.))$ on $([0,1], \geq)$.

THEOREM 1 (Ponsard [1986]) : *Let a preferences structure* $(X, \mathcal{R}(.,.))$. *There exists a fuzzy utility* $u(.)$ *if* X, *the set of objects, is a countable set totally preordered by* $\mathcal{R}(.,.)$.

Proof : $\mathcal{R}(.,.)$ is a total preorder, the set $X/s\ell(.,.)$ is an isomorphism of $X/\sim$ (defined thanks to the similitude classes $\mathcal{C}(.)$), $X/\sim$ is totally ordered by [P1] and X is a *countable* set. Hence, it implies the quotient-structure $X/\sim$ to be *countable*. Moreover, any chain $(A, \geq)$ is homomorph to the real chain $(R, \geq)$, therefore to $([0,1], \geq)$. Thus, the homomorphism f exists, from $(X, \mathcal{R}(.,.))$ to $([0,1], \geq)$. The application $f \circ Proj$ is also an homomorphism from $(X, \mathcal{R}(.,.))$ to $([0,1], \geq)$; we have : $f \circ Proj = u$.

□

SECTION FOUR : FUZZY UTILITY FUNCTION ON A CONVEX SET

First, we define the fuzzy utility function on a countable subset ; next, we cover the whole convex set by widening this utility. This is why the existence of a fuzzy utility on a countable referential is a necessary step.

We need to present some properties related to fuzziness of the used sets and relations, and also some assumptions.

IV.1. Assumptions on X

We do the same as Debreu [1959] did about the consumption set :

A1 : X, the set of objects is closed.

A2 : X is a convex set (therefore connected).

IV.2. Assumption and definition on the associated fuzzy set $\mathcal{X}$

Definition 9 : A fuzzy subset $\mathcal{X}$ is f-connected[19] $\Leftrightarrow \forall(\mathcal{X}_1, \mathcal{X}_2)$, two nonempty, disjoint[20] and closed fuzzy subsets included in $\mathcal{X}$, $\exists x \in \mathcal{X}$, so that : $\chi(x) \neq \text{Max}[\chi_1(x), \chi_2(x)]$.

A3 : $\mathcal{X}$ is a f-connected fuzzy subset of X.

IV.3. Analysis of assumptions

α- A1 means any object x^t of a converging sequence ($t = 1,2,..$ *ad infinitum*) to define an object that belongs to X ; therefore the object x', limit of x^t also belongs to X.

β- A2 means that if any two objects belong to X, then any convex combination of these two objects also belongs to X.

γ- A3 requires from the fuzzy subset $\mathcal{X}$ to be f-connected.

IV.4. Continuity of fuzzy preferences

We consider agents who have fuzzy relations of preference $\mathcal{P}_i(.,.)$; they are going *to order* the elements of X thanks to the information deriving from their preferences but also to the first

---

19 A fuzzy subset $\mathcal{A}$ is included in a fuzzy subset $\mathcal{B} \Leftrightarrow \forall x \in X$, (X referential set) : $a(x) \leq b(x)$.

20 Two fuzzy subsets $\mathcal{A}$ and $\mathcal{B}$ are disjoint $\Leftrightarrow \forall x \in X$, $\text{Min}[a(x), b(x)] = 0$.

Operator of union corresponds to Max : $\forall x \in X$, $[a \cup b](x) = \text{Max}[a(x), b(x)]$.

projection of their relations, without which there is no possible *ordering*. So, the agents are either *coherent* or *incoherent*, but in the last case, they dominate their irrationality[21].

Proj is reflexive (F.s.) : $\forall x \in X, Proj(x) = \text{Max}_y[\mathcal{R}(x,y)] \Rightarrow Proj(x) \in]0,1]$.

Proj is f-transitive : $\forall (x,y,z) \in X^3$, if $Proj(x) > Proj(y)$ and $Proj(y) > Proj(z)$

$\Rightarrow Proj(x) > Proj(z)$.

These two *properties* are obvious and come from the usual properties of the relation "≥". In order to ensure the existence of a fuzzy utility function, we just need to preorder[22] X. The *Proj* operator determines the membership function to the fuzzy subset $\mathcal{X}$:

$$\mathcal{X} = \{x \in X, \chi(x) = Proj(x) \in]0,1]\}$$

IV.5. Assumption of continuity for fuzzy preferences

The two following fuzzy subsets[23] :

$$\mathcal{X}^+ = \{y \in X, \chi(x) \geq \chi(y) \text{ with } \chi^+(y) = \chi(y)\}$$

$$\mathcal{X}^- = \{y \in X, \chi(x) \leq \chi(y) \text{ with } \chi^-(y) = \chi(y)\}$$

are fuzzy closed subsets.

Let us note these two fuzzy subsets to differ in their topological nature from the ones which are exhibited by Ponsard. The two fuzzy subsets $\mathcal{X}^+$ and $\mathcal{X}^-$ are fuzzy closed, i.e. their complement sets in X are open :

$$\mathcal{COMP}_X(\mathcal{X}^+) = \left\{ y \in X, comp_{\mathcal{X}^+}(y) = 1 - \chi^+(y) \right\} \text{ and}$$

$$\mathcal{COMP}_X(\mathcal{X}^-) = \left\{ y \in X, comp_{\mathcal{X}^-}(y) = 1 - \chi^-(y) \right\}.$$

The particular definition of fuzzy complement sets - which implies a nonempty intersection between a fuzzy subset and its complement - modifies the proof of existence of a utility function when compared to Debreu's one [1959]. The assumption of the fuzzy preferences closure is based on a notion of closed fuzzy set which is associated to an open nondisjoint complement.

This assumption of continuity for fuzzy preferences means more explicitly :

---

21 If agents are coherent, $\mathcal{R}(.,.)$ is a reflexive (F.s.) and Max-Min transitive fuzzy relation (the first projection keeps the constituted preorder, Prevôt [1977]), or else $\mathcal{R}(.,.)$ is only reflexive (F.s.). We assume the objects to be always comparable to themselves : $\forall x \in X, \mathcal{R}(x,x) \in]0,1]$.

22 Here, we make a distinction between local and global preferences. The principle "equal relative qualities imply equal satisfactions" is not necessarily satisfied.

23 It is possible to deduce the continuity of any function by the topological nature, *closed* here, of both sets covering the referential for any element belonging to the referential. But we cannot deduce that $\chi(.)$ is continuous because $\mathcal{X}^+$ and $\mathcal{X}^-$ are *fuzzy* closed. Actually, the support of $\mathcal{X}$ would be a usual closed. For that, the membership function would be already continuous.

if $x \in \mathcal{X}^+$, $\chi^+(x) = \chi(x)$ and $\chi^-(x) = 0$

if $x \in \mathcal{X}^-$, $\chi^-(x) = \chi(x)$ and $\chi^+(x) = 0$.

IV.6. Preliminary results

LEMMA 1 : *Let $\mathcal{X}$ be a fuzzy subset of R^m. There exists a fuzzy subset $\mathcal{D}$ included in $\mathcal{X}$ such that : (1) the closure of $\mathcal{D}$, noted $\overline{\mathcal{D}}$, is equal to $\mathcal{X}$, (2) the exclusive support, noted supp $\mathcal{D}$, is countable (strong α-cut[24] of level 0).*

Proof: $\mathcal{X}$ is a fuzzy subset of X which is a subset of R^m, for any m. Hence, $\mathcal{X}$ is a fuzzy subset of R^m. Because of the decomposition theorem (Kaufmann [1977], Dubois [1983]), we know that : $\mathcal{X} = \text{Max}_\alpha[\alpha \cdot X_\alpha]$ where X_α is an α-cut and $\alpha \in]0,1]$.

As any α-cut, X_α is a subset of R^m, which means that X_α also contains a usual countable subset that we note D_α. D_α is such that $\forall \alpha \in]0,1], \overline{D}_\alpha = X_\alpha$ where $\overline{D}_\alpha$ is the closure of D_α (Dixmier [1981]). We can assign to any α a couple (X_α, D_α) that satisfies the following property : $\cup_\alpha D_\alpha = D$ and $\overline{D} = X$ because $\cup_\alpha \overline{D}_\alpha = \overline{D} = X$.

This result proceeds from the property according to which the closure of a union of usual closed sets is equal to the union of closures of usual closed sets.

Let us consider the decomposition theorem ; we have :

$$\alpha \cdot \overline{D}_\alpha = \alpha \cdot X_\alpha, \ \forall \alpha \in]0,1], \text{ because } \overline{D}_\alpha = X_\alpha.$$

It implies :

$$\text{Max}_\alpha[\alpha \cdot \overline{D}_\alpha] = \text{Max}_\alpha[\alpha \cdot X_\alpha] \Rightarrow \overline{\mathcal{D}} = \overline{\mathcal{X}}$$

As the strong support of $\mathcal{D}$, noted *supp* $\mathcal{D}$ is equal to $\cup_\alpha D_\alpha$, this implies, since the union of countable sets is a countable set : $D = \textit{supp}\ \mathcal{D}$ is a countable set.

□

LEMMA 2 : $\forall (x,y) \in X^2$, *if* $0 < d(x) \leq d(y)$, *then* $0 < \chi(x) \leq \chi(y)$.

Proof: The closure[25] of $\mathcal{D}$, $\overline{\mathcal{D}}$ is such that if $d(x) > 0$, therefore $d(x) = \overline{d}(x)$ for any x element of $\mathcal{D}$. So, if we have $d(x) \leq d(y)$, this means $\overline{d}(x) \leq \overline{d}(y)$. Since we know that $\overline{\mathcal{D}} = \mathcal{X}$, we can conclude : $0 < \chi(x) \leq \chi(y)$.

□

---

24 An α-cut is a tool that yields the usual set which corresponds to the fuzzy one.
A strong α-cut : $X_\alpha = \{x \in \mathcal{X}; \chi(x) > \alpha\}$. If $\chi(x) > \alpha \Rightarrow x \in X_\alpha$. Otherwise, $x \notin X_\alpha$.
A weak α-cut : $X_\alpha = \{x \in \mathcal{X}; \chi(x) \geq \alpha\}$. If $\chi(x) \geq \alpha \Rightarrow x \in X_\alpha$. Otherwise, $x \notin X_\alpha$.

25 If $d(.)$ is the membership function of the fuzzy subset $\mathcal{D}$, $\overline{d}(.)$ is the membership function of $\overline{\mathcal{D}}$, closure of $\mathcal{D}$.

Proving the existence of a continuous fuzzy utility function representing a fuzzy relation of preference consists in the identification of this function from the membership function $\chi(.)$. Henceforth, we assume the referential X to be a subset of R^m (which is explicit in lemma 1), without specifying its dimension.

The trivial case where any object of X leads to the same satisfaction (i.e., $\mathcal{R}(.,.) =$ constant) is settled by using a real constant continuous function on X. From now on, we exclude this case of generalized indifference (which means that all needs have the same intensity). Our argument is based on the existence of a fuzzy subset $\mathcal{D}$ included in the associated fuzzy set $\mathcal{X}$, having a strong countable support and being *totally dense* , i.e. for any object of X, therefore of $\mathcal{X}$, there exists another object belonging to $\mathcal{D}$ that is very nearby. We first define the utility on *supp* $\mathcal{D}$, thanks to $d(.)$. Then we extend this utility up to X thanks to $\chi(.)$.

LEMMA 3 : *Let* $(x,y) \in X^2$ *and* $\mathcal{X}$ *be a* f*-connected subset of* X*, with* $\chi(x) < \chi(y)$*. Then,* $\exists z$*,* $z \in$ *supp* $\mathcal{D}$*,* $\mathcal{D}$ *being a fuzzy subset having a strong countable support included in* $\mathcal{X}$*, such that :* $\chi(x) < \chi(z) < \chi(y)$.

Proof : Let us consider the two following fuzzy subsets :

$$\mathcal{X}' = \{x' \in \mathcal{X};\ \chi(x') \leq \chi(x)\} \text{ and}$$

$$\mathcal{X}'' = \{x'' \in \mathcal{X};\ \chi(x'') \geq \chi(x)\}.$$

$\mathcal{X}'$ and $\mathcal{X}''$ are two disjoint fuzzy subsets since $\chi(x) < \chi(y)$; they are nonempty and closed because of the assumption of continuity for fuzzy preferences. We know that $\mathcal{X}$ is a f-connected fuzzy subset. This means that there exists an object belonging to $\mathcal{X}$, noted a, such that $\chi(a) \neq \text{Max}[\chi'(a), \chi''(a)]$. Let us present the logic denial of the proposition to prove and let us conclude in its mathematical irrelevance. This negation can be written as follows : there is no $z \in \mathcal{D}$ such that $\chi(x) < \chi(z) < \chi(y)$. This means that if such a z exists, defined by $\chi(z) \in]\chi(x), \chi(y)[$, then it does not belong to $\mathcal{D}$, i.e. : $d(z) = 0$.

It means : $d(z) \neq 0 \Leftrightarrow \chi(x) \geq \chi(z)$ or $\chi(y) \leq \chi(z)$.

To sum up : $d(z) \neq 0 \Leftrightarrow z \in \mathcal{X}' \cup \mathcal{X}''$.

Moreover, we know that $\mathcal{D} \subseteq \mathcal{X}$, i.e. : $d(z) \leq \chi(z), \forall z \in \mathcal{D}$. But :

$$\text{if } d(z) \neq 0 \Rightarrow d(z) \leq \text{Max}[\chi'(z), \chi''(z)], \tag{1}$$

since $d(z) \leq \chi(z)$. With the assumption of continuity for fuzzy preferences :

$$\chi(z) = \chi'(z) \text{ if } z \in \mathcal{X}' \text{ or } \chi(z) = \chi''(z) \text{ if } z \in \mathcal{X}''.$$

But we know that $\overline{\mathcal{D}} = \mathcal{X}$, i.e. :

$$\overline{d}(z) = \chi(z), \forall z \in \mathcal{D}. \tag{2}$$

Let us now combine (1) and (2) : $d(z) \leq \chi(z) = \overline{d}(z)$.

Since $\mathcal{X}'$ and $\mathcal{X}''$ are closed then, if $\mathcal{D} \subseteq \mathcal{X}' \cup \mathcal{X}''$, it implies $\overline{\mathcal{D}} \subseteq \mathcal{X}' \cup \mathcal{X}''$, because a union of closed sets is also a closed set. Hence, we have :

$$\bar{d}(z) = \chi(z) \leq \text{Max}[\chi'(z), \chi''(z)].$$

By definition of continuity for fuzzy preferences, it is relevant if :

$$\chi(z) = \text{Max}[\chi'(z), \chi''(z)].$$

This means that $d(z) \neq 0 \Leftrightarrow z \in \mathcal{X}' \cup \mathcal{X}'' \Leftrightarrow \mathcal{X} = \mathcal{X}' \cup \mathcal{X}''$. But $\mathcal{X}$ is supposed to be f-connected, i.e. : $\mathcal{X} \neq \mathcal{X}' \cup \mathcal{X}''$. Then, the proposition $[d(z) \neq 0 \Leftrightarrow z \in \mathcal{X}' \cup \mathcal{X}'']$ is wrong. We can deduce : $\exists z \in \mathcal{D};\ \chi(z) \in]\chi(x), \chi(y)[$.

□

Now the density of $\mathcal{X}$ is ensured. Since the strong support of $\mathcal{D}$, which corresponds to D, is a usual countable set and the membership set on which is defined the fuzzy reflexivity (F.s.) is limited to $]0,1]$, we can apply to $\mathcal{D}$ the existence result of a fuzzy utility function on a countable set.

LEMMA 4 : *Let $\mathcal{D}$ be a fuzzy subset having a strong countable support. Then, there exists a continuous utility function on supp $\mathcal{D}$.*

Proof : this one is identical to Ponsard [1986] where the set of objects is limited to the countable case, theorem 1.

□

This utility function is obtained on a countable set from the existence of a structure of topological space which is totally preordered. This utility function is now going to be extended from the strong support of $\mathcal{D}$ to X which represents the strong support of $\mathcal{X}$. We note $v(.)$ this continuous utility function defined over D, with :

$$\forall x \in supp\,\mathcal{D} = D,\ v(x) = d(x).$$

First, it is necessary to verify the following property :

LEMMA 5 : *Let $v(.)$ be the utility function defined on the strong support of $\mathcal{D}$, $supp\,\mathcal{D} = D$, and :* $\mathcal{D}' = \{x' \in \mathcal{D};\ d(x') \leq d(x)\}$, $\mathcal{D}'' = \{x'' \in \mathcal{D};\ d(x'') \geq d(x)\}$. *Then :* $\text{Sup}\, v[\mathcal{D}'] = \text{Inf}\, v[\mathcal{D}'']$.

Proof : It is clear that the strong supports of $\mathcal{D}'$ and $\mathcal{D}''$ have a nonempty intersection containing x : $supp\,\mathcal{D}' \cap supp\,\mathcal{D}'' = [x]$ (where $[x]$ represents the indifference class of x). We know that $v(x') = d(x')$. Hence :

$$\text{Sup}\, v[\mathcal{D}'] = v([x]) = \text{Sup}\, d'(x') = d'(x) = d(x).$$

Identically :

$$\text{Inf}\, v[\mathcal{D}''] = \text{Inf}\, d''(x'') = d(x).$$

□

IV.7. Extension of $\nu(.)$ on X and existence of a continuous utility function $u(.)$

We call $u(.)$ the common value of both fuzzy subsets $\mathcal{D}'$ and $\mathcal{D}''$.

$$\nu(x) = d(x) = u(x).$$

Lemma 2 shows the preorder to remain while extending it on X. We can write :

$$u(x) = \kappa(x).$$

THEOREM 2 : *Let $X \subseteq R^m$ be a connected referential set of objects, preordered by the first projection of a fuzzy relation of preference $\mathcal{R}(.,.)$. Under the assumption of continuity for fuzzy preferences, there exists a continuous fuzzy utility function on supp X.*

Proof : We are now going to show that for any α belonging to the open set $]0,1[$, the inverse image of the closed interval $[\alpha,1]$ by $u(.)$ is a closed *fuzzy* subset belonging to X. We could exactly do the same proof in the case of the other closed interval $[0,\alpha]$.

Let us consider $\eta \in]0,1[$ and both fuzzy sets :

$$X_\eta = \{x \in X;\ u(x) \le \eta\} \text{ and } X^\eta = \{x \in X;\ u(x) \ge \eta\}.$$

Consider the following identity :

$$[\alpha, 1] = \bigcap_{\substack{\alpha \ge \beta \\ \beta \in N}} [\beta, 1],$$

where $N = \{\beta \in [0,1];\ \exists x \in \mathcal{D},\ d(x) = \beta\}$.

Now, let us take the inverse images :

$$u^{-1}([\alpha, 1]) = \bigcap_{\substack{\alpha \ge \beta \\ \beta \in N}} u^{-1}([\beta, 1]).$$

This can also be written with X^η and X_η :

$$X^\alpha = \bigcap_{\substack{\alpha \ge \beta \\ \beta \in N}} X^\beta.$$

Consider $a \in X$ such that $\kappa(a) = \beta$, i.e. :

$$X^\beta = \{x \in X;\ u(x) \ge \beta\}.$$

The subset X^β also corresponds to :

$$X^\beta = \{x \in X;\ \kappa(x) \ge \kappa(a)\}.$$

X^β is a closed fuzzy subset by continuity of preferences. Moreover, the intersection of closed sets is a closed set ; since $\beta \in N$ and N is a countable set because defined on $\mathcal{D}$, X^α is a closed set. That expresses the fact that the inverse image of the interval $[\alpha,1]$ is a closed fuzzy subset and thus, that the fuzzy utility function $u(.)$ is continuous.

□

Final remarks

The introduction of fuzziness inside the preference theory has not changed coherence and relevance of the choice analysis. The goal of this chapter was to explain the changes that we have done when "fuzzyfying", and to prove their perfect adequacy to the acquired rules. If there may be a gain of understanding, there is no loss of generality, since the usual model - restricted to Boolean preorders - is a case corresponding to the particular membership set $\{0,1\}$.

CHAPTER 2

Aggregation of Fuzzy Preferences

There are many ways of approaching the transition from individual to collective. We can either study the conditions under which the vote is an efficient procedure of collective decision - consistent with the principle "*a man, a vote*" -, (Moulin [1985], Saari [1986], Hosomatu [1978], Satterthwaite [1975]), or inflect the field of individual preferences in order to develop a collective preference (Kim & Roush [1981], Dutta [1977], Mas-Colell & Sonnenschein [1972]) ; it is also possible to analyze collective preference by the means of the conflict between individual interests (Salles & Wendel [1977]). We therefore model them thanks to the game theory or by using typological methods (Lemaire [1981]) or even by giving to the space of preferences some metric structures which yield functions of social choice (Heuchenne [1970], Luce [1956], Barthelemy & Monjardet [1979]).

We do not search for producing specific conditions of aggregation but rather to analyze the modifications of the problem of aggregation when the agents' preferences are fuzzy (in an *ordinal* way à la Ponsard [1981;1986;1988], Billot [1986;1987] and *non cardinal* à la Orlovsky [1978;1980], Chakraboty & Sarkar [1987], Chakraboty & Das [1985], Roubens & Vincke [1985], Shimura [1973], Ovchinnikov [1981;1988], Zadeh [1971]). We try also to emphasize the main role of the particular agents, called *leximin* and *leximax*, in the fuzzy process of aggregation.

We sum up the general subject of this kind of works as follows: how can we fight against the logical inconsistency between *social choice* and *individual interest* or *selfish motive*, so called by Schmidt [1985][1] ? There are many ways of expressing this question, from the most famous - Arrow's theorem of impossibility - to the most technical - the topological equivalence elaborated by Chichilinsky [1982] between the Arrowian dictator and Pareto optimality. However, if we try to trace back to the origins of the paradox between individual and collective, we find, on one hand, the Marquis de Condorcet's memoir in 1785, "Essai sur l'Application de l'Analyse à la Probabilité des Décisions Rendues à la Pluralité des Voix", and on the other, the Jean-Charles de Borda's one in 1781, "Mémoires de l'Académie Royale des Sciences".

Black [1958], in his book "The Theory of Committee and Elections", explains the starting point of this analysis to be based on the fact that a group of votes, he calls it *plurality of votes* for several candidates, can easily lead to a final (collective) incoherent decision. By extending the vote to the preference, we certainly come to a more modern and more mathematical expression of a binary relation. Economists and logicians tried to overstep this paradox, once admitted Arrow 's theorem of impossibility (as a generalization of Condorcet's cyclicities).

In order to do it, they first tried to weaken the conditions related to the aggregation functions (among others, independence of alternatives, transitivity of preferences, unanimity). A first step consisted in weakening the requirement of transitivity for the collective preference (Blair, Bordes, Kelly & Suzumura [1976], Deb & Blau [1977], Sen [1969], [1977]). Since results were not very significant, they turned to the side of preferences field - in order to restrict them - (Black [1948], Dutta [1977], Grandmont [1978], Kalai & Ritz [1980], Schofield [1977]).

Our approach is not independent from Arrow's theorem of impossibility. We try to link this theorem and May [1952]. This last shows the required conditions to find a collective solution proceeding from the majority rule when applied to the individual preorders of preference.

On one hand, we are going to link fuzzy preferences to the traditional field of the theory of collective choice (see Barret, Pattanaik & Salles [1985], Pattanaik & Salles [1983]). On the other hand, we assume the utility to typically remain ordinal. This takes us apart from the works of Roubens & Vincke [1985], Cholewa [1985] and Switalski [1988]. Finally, we point out a mathematical but meaningful relation between two very different theorems, May's one and Arrow's one.

SECTION ONE : ARROVIAN DICTATOR AND FUZZY PREFERENCES

The basic purpose of this chapter is to bring out the relation between the planner's requirement and the difficulty of transition from individual to collective as well as the theoretic relation

1 in Schmidt [1985] *op.cit* p.103.

between this requirement and the extremist agents. It is advisable to give an economic meaning to this requirement : we see that it corresponds to the necessity of *implication* for each agent in the group. This one proceeds from the choice. If I prefer object A to object B, then I belong to the group of "the agents preferring A to B". But, the more A is preferred to B, the more I belong to this group. The planner who solves and decides, just takes into consideration the preference of the agent who seems to be implicated : this is called the planner's *requirement*. This approach depends on the nature of preorders of preference.

I.1. Imprecise behaviour and fuzzy individual preferences

We suppose economic agents to be coherent : their fuzzy relations of preference are f-transitive and reflexive (F.s).

I.1.1. Reflexive fuzzy relation of preference (F.s.)

Let X be a referential set of objects. The agent i's fuzzy relation of preference (the usual set of agents is denoted S) is noted $\mathcal{P}_i(.,.)$ and defined from X^2 to $\underline{M} = [0,1]$. We say $\mathcal{P}_i(.,.)$ to be a reflexive (F.s.) relation of fuzzy preference, iff, for any object x of X, the valuation of its intrinsic qualities is included in [0,1] : $\forall(x,x) \in X^2$, $\mathcal{P}_i(x,x) \in [0,1]$.

I.1.2. Fuzzy f-transitive relation of preference

We say the fuzzy relation of preference $\mathcal{P}_i(.,.)$ to be f-transitive iff :

$$\forall(x,y,z) \in X^3, \text{ if } \mathcal{P}_i(x,y) \geq \mathcal{P}_i(y,x) \text{ and } \mathcal{P}_i(y,z) \geq \mathcal{P}_i(z,y)$$

$$\text{then } \mathcal{P}_i(x,z) \geq \mathcal{P}_i(z,x).$$

We can notice that it is sometimes possible to define a metric procedure of aggregation without assuming a measure of intensity of preference (see Guilbaud [1952], Moon [1968], Kendall [1962], Barthelemy [1979], Abdi, Barthelemy & Luong [1980], Clause [1982]).

I.1.3. "Condorcet"'s cyclicities

Condorcet's cyclicities actually bring out a paradox resulting from the application of the majority rule to preorders of individual preference in order to extract a collective relation. A supplementary condition is to be precised. Preorders have to be complete but from now on (Billot [1987]), we know this condition not to be necessary any more when preorders are fuzzy in the meaning of Ponsard and Billot, as the relation "*greater or equal*" directly makes the preference complete.

I.1.3.1. From preferences to utility

We have stated in the first chapter the existence of a continuous utility function translating a fuzzy preorder. This existence is proved on the basis of both assumptions of continuity for fuzzy preferences and connectedness of the referential set. We therefore assume those two hypotheses and we note $u_i(.)$ the agent i's utility function, defined from X to [0,1] - sometimes called *global preference* -, deriving from his fuzzy preorder of preference $\mathcal{P}_i(.,.)$ - sometimes called *local preference.*

I.1.3.2. The paradox

Let us consider society S of three agents. Let us decide to generate arbitrarily the fuzzy collective preorder $\mathcal{P}_S(.,.)$ (i.e. the fuzzy collective utility function $u_S(.)$) by applying the majority rule. In other words, if two agents out of three consider x to have greater relative qualities than y, then society considers x to have greater relative qualities than y.

We assume the principle according to which the aggregate preference does not cancel local preference. In others words : $\forall i \in S$, $\forall (x,y) \in X^2$, if $\mathcal{P}_i(x,y) \geq \mathcal{P}_i(y,x) \Leftrightarrow u_i(x) \geq u_i(y)$.

In that way : $\forall (x,y) \in X^2$, if $\mathcal{P}_S(x,y) \geq \mathcal{P}_S(y,x) \Leftrightarrow u_S(x) \geq u_S(y)$.

Let us consider three objects (x,y,z) belonging to the referential X. The three agents (i,j,k) are asked to express their opinion, i.e. to order the three objects (x,y,z) which are presented.

1- Agent i arranges the objects as follows :

$$u_i(x) > u_i(y) > u_i(z).$$

2- Agent j arranges the objects as follows :

$$u_j(y) > u_j(z) > u_j(x).$$

3- Agent k arranges the objects as follows :

$$u_k(z) > u_k(x) > u_k(y).$$

Let us now apply the majority rule. Agents i and k feel more satisfied with x than with y. Hence, society thus concludes by stronger utility for x than for y, i.e. :

$$u_S(x) > u_S(y).$$

In the same way, agents i and j prefer y to z, so :

$$u_S(y) > u_S(z).$$

Finally, agents j and k assign a stronger utility to z than to x, In other words :

$$u_S(z) > u_S(x).$$

We are now able to yield the social ordering and we point out the cyclicity by combining it with the f-transitivity.

We know that : $u_S(x) > u_S(y)$, $u_S(y) > u_S(z)$ and $u_S(z) > u_S(x)$. So we can write :

$$u_S(x) > u_S(y) > u_S(z) > u_S(x).$$

Applying the f-transitivity to the preorder (which corresponds to usual transitivity for utility functions), we obtain : $u_S(x) > u_S(x)$, which is absurd ; the associated social preorder is : $\mathcal{P}_S(x,y) > \mathcal{P}_S(y,x)$, $\mathcal{P}_S(y,z) > \mathcal{P}_S(z,y)$ and $\mathcal{P}_S(z,x) > \mathcal{P}_S(x,z)$ which becomes by f-transitivity : $\mathcal{P}_S(x,x) > \mathcal{P}_S(x,x)$.

This cyclicity, analyzed by the Marquis de Condorcet, in his memoir - from which the phrase "Condorcet's cyclicity" - brings out an occurrence of irrelevance of the procedure, which is enough to declare the majority rule unable to model social preferences.

Arrow generalizes the impossibility of aggregation by stating definitely the subjacent axioms.

Remarks :

α- First, it is obvious that a usual utilization of fuzzy preorders of preferences does not change the fundamental opposition between collective preorder and individual ones. Arrow's theorem when applied to fuzzy relations of preference confirms this analysis.

β- Second, we can state that if all the agents have the same ordering, society has it too (which is called unanimity). Thus, the relation of social preference is f-transitive and also ordinal. The majority rule studied by Condorcet is based on the whole set of individual preorders. These statements are the basis of the four axioms defined by Arrow.

I.2. Fuzzy preferences and collective decision : Arrow's axioms

We paradoxically ought to corroborate the general problematic of aggregation before conferring it a different meaning if the agent's preferences are fuzzy. Arrow's theorem depends on a group of axioms that we are now going to develop.

I.2.1. Individual preferences

Individual preferences are modelled thanks to a reflexive (F.s.) and f-transitive relation, noted $\mathcal{P}_i(.,.)$, (for any agent i from S).

I.2.2. The collective preference is a fuzzy preorder [A1]

The relation of social preference $\mathcal{P}_S(.,.)$ is reflexive (F.s.) and f-transitive. Under the same assumptions of continuity for the collective preference and connectedness of X, it leads to a continuous social utility function, noted $u_S(.)$. Our problem is then to find a rule noted *CCR* (Collective Choice Rule) which allows to build a social preorder $\mathcal{P}_S(.,.)$ from individual preorders $\mathcal{P}_i(.,.)$, $\forall i \in S$.

I.2.3. The collective choice rule [A2]

The collective Choice Rule, *CCR*, is defined as follows : $\mathcal{P}_S(.,.) = CCR_{i \in S}\{\mathcal{P}_i(.,.)\}$.

It produces the criterion which allows to *socially* compare the elements of the referential set X.

I.2.4. Unanimity axiom [A3]

It means that if all the agents of society S agree to prefer x to y, then society prefers x to y :

$$\text{if } \forall i \in S, \forall (x,y) \in X^2, \mathcal{P}_i(x,y) \geq \mathcal{P}_i(y,x) \text{ then } \mathcal{P}_S(x,y) \geq \mathcal{P}_S(y,x).$$

I.2.5. Independence of Irrelevant Alternatives [A4]

To compare an object x with an object y, the collectivity forgets about the other objects belonging to the referential set X. The only thing which founds the social preference is "*who prefers x*" and "*who prefers y*". This axiom, however strongly contested, implies some logical rationality : when the question is to compare a car with a bicycle, to choose between them, the agent's decision is not affected at all by the fact that the referential set may count a boat and a plane, or only a plane. Formally : let $\{\mathcal{P}_i(.,.)\}$ and $\{\mathcal{H}_i(.,.)\}$ be two families of fuzzy individual preorders ($i \in S$) :

$$\mathcal{P}_S(.,.) = CCR_{i \in S}\{\mathcal{P}_i(.,.)\} \text{ and } \mathcal{H}_S(.,.) = CCR_{i \in S}\{\mathcal{H}_i(.,.)\}.$$

Let (x,y) be a couple of objects belonging to X :

$$\text{if } \forall i \in S, \forall (x,y) \in X^2, \mathcal{P}_i(x,y) \geq \mathcal{P}_i(y,x) \Leftrightarrow \mathcal{H}_i(x,y) \geq \mathcal{H}_i(y,x)$$

$$\text{then } \mathcal{P}_S(x,y) \geq \mathcal{P}_S(y,x) \Leftrightarrow \mathcal{H}_S(x,y) \geq \mathcal{H}_S(y,x).$$

It should be observed from the definition of *CCR*, that if individual preorders are cardinal then, the social preorder deduced from them, is also cardinal.

I.2.6. The different kinds of CCR

The definition of a rule for collective choice is hardly restrictive. We know the majority rule to yield Condorcet's cyclicities. There are many *CCR*, satisfying very diverse specificities. Let us note Sen's one [1969] issued from a quasitransitive preference and Mas-Colell & Sonnenschein's one [1972], using *binary dictator* and *monotonicity* notions. Schwartz's one [1972], [1980], the most famous, is based on the GOCHA (General Optimum CHoice Axioms) principle and upon both assumptions of *reducibility* and *narrowness* applied to the group of dominated solutions.

The four criterions from which we can judge a *CCR* are the following :

1- A *democracy* criterion based on the power division between the agents.

2- A *sovereignty of the agents group* criterion, expressed by the unanimity axiom.

3- A *choice discriminance* criterion, related to the completeness of preorders.

4- A *choice coherence* criterion, related to the transitivity of preorders.

Generally, it is possible to find Collective Choice Rules satisfying three of these criterions but impossible to find one which simultaneously satisfies the four criterions. For example, in Arrow's dictator theorem, when defining the *CCR* as follows :

$$\mathcal{P}_S(.,.) = CCR_{i \in S}\{\mathcal{P}_i(.,.)\} = \mathcal{P}_i(.,.),\ i \in S,$$

it involves *coherence, discriminance* and *sovereignty* but obviously contradicts the *democracy* criterion.

I.2.7. The dictatorial CCR

This rule consists in designating an agent i to choose for the whole society. In other words, the social preorder is identical with agent i's one. The axioms of independence and unanimity are trivially satisfied. This rule can be summed up by the famous words "*what is good for General Motors is good for America*".

I.2.7.1. Arrow's theorem : first version

Let us assume a new axiom : The *CCR* is not dictatorial [A5].

THEOREM 1 : *[A1], [A2], [A3], [A4] and [A5] are inconsistent.*

This formulation corresponds to the *pessimistic* approach of the impossibility theorem.

I.2.7.2. Arrow's theorem : second version

THEOREM 1bis : *Let CCR be a non dictatorial rule satisfying [A3]. Then CCR does not satisfy [A4].*

This version is more *optimistic* as it directly points out the *logical place* of impossibility.

I.2.8. P-decisive coalitions (power-decisive)

Definition 1 : A P-decisive coalition C is any usual subset of S which can enforce society to prefer x against y (x and y belonging to X).

C is P-decisive for x against $y \Leftrightarrow$

$\forall i \in C \subset S, \mathcal{P}_i(x,y) \geq \mathcal{P}_i(y,x)$ and

$\forall j \notin C, \mathcal{P}_j(y,x) \geq \mathcal{P}_j(x,y)$ then $\mathcal{P}_S(x,y) \geq \mathcal{P}_S(y,x)$.

I.3. Proof of the dictator theorem with fuzzy preferences

I.3.1. First intermediate result

LEMMA 1 : *There exists two objects (x,y) belonging to X^2 and a coalition C such that $Card C = 1$ and C P-decisive for x against y.*

Proof : Let P be the usual set of P-decisive coalitions for a given couple of objects.

$$P = \{C \subseteq S \,/\, \exists (x,y) \in X^2 : C \text{ is p-decisive for } x \text{ against } y\}.$$

Axiom [A3] means that P is nonempty because S is obviously not P-decisive : $S \in P$.

Let C be one of the coalitions of P with the smallest cardinal.

$$\forall A \in P, Card A \geq Card C \text{ i.e. } |A| \geq |C|.$$

The empty set, $\emptyset$, does not belong to P, because S belongs to P. If $|C| = 1$, we have the result. So, let us suppose $|C| > 1$ which also means $|C| \geq 2$.

Let us note (x,y) the two objects of X^2 for which C is P-decisive for x against y.

If $|C| \geq 2$, we can split up C into a single element d and the rest of the coalition, i.e. the subset B.

$$C = \{d\} \cup B \text{ with } B \subset C \text{ and } d \notin B.$$

Let us now take a third element z, different from x and y, belonging to X. We suppose d to prefer x against y and y against z.

$\mathcal{P}_d(x,y) \geq \mathcal{P}_d(y,x)$ and $\mathcal{P}_d(y,z) \geq \mathcal{P}_d(z,y)$.

$\forall j \in B$: $\mathcal{P}_j(z,x) \geq \mathcal{P}_j(x,z)$ and $\mathcal{P}_j(x,y) \geq \mathcal{P}_j(y,x)$.

$\forall i \in S-C$: $\mathcal{P}_i(y,z) \geq \mathcal{P}_i(z,y)$ and $\mathcal{P}_i(z,x) \geq \mathcal{P}_i(x,z)$.

We know C not to belong to P and to be P-decisive for x against y. Hence, society decides what C decides for (x,y) : $\mathcal{P}_S(x,y) \geq \mathcal{P}_S(y,x)$.

It is also obvious that we cannot finally have :

$$\mathcal{P}_S(z,y) \geq \mathcal{P}_S(y,z) \quad (1)$$

because, if it were, it means B to be P-decisive for z against y. Now, if B is P-decisive, it belongs to P. But, if $B \in P$ and, in the same time, has a smaller cardinal than C, it contradicts, $\forall A \in P$, $|A| \leq |C|$. In other words, if $|B| < |C|$, which is true, $B \notin P$. Therefore :

$$\mathcal{P}_S(z,y) < \mathcal{P}_S(y,z). \quad (2)$$

Axiom [A1] enforces $\mathcal{P}_S(.,.)$ to be a fuzzy f-transitive relation of preference, and with (1) and (2), we obtain $\mathcal{P}_S(x,z) \geq \mathcal{P}_S(z,x)$, which corresponds to d's preferences. Then, it means that $\{d\}$ is P-decisive for x against z, i.e. $\{d\} \in P$. But $\{d\}$ is a single element and $|C| \geq 2$. Therefore, the coalition C of P, such that $\forall A \in P, |A| < |C|$, is one of the coalitions such that $|C| = 1$.

□

I.3.2. Second intermediate result

LEMMA 2 : *The coalition C with a single element, is P-decisive.*

Proof : Lemma 1 reveals the existence of the element d who is P-decisive for x against z. Let us envisage y belonging to X. This object, y, is different from x and z. We suppose $d \in C$ to have the following preferences : $\mathcal{P}_d(x,z) \geq \mathcal{P}_d(z,x)$ and $\mathcal{P}_d(z,y) \geq \mathcal{P}_d(y,z)$, and the other agents, $\forall i \in S-\{d\}$: $\mathcal{P}_i(z,y) \geq \mathcal{P}_i(y,z)$ and $\mathcal{P}_i(y,x) \geq \mathcal{P}_i(x,y)$.

Let us show what is the implied social preference, $\mathcal{P}_S(.,.)$: $\mathcal{P}_S(x,z) \geq \mathcal{P}_S(z,x)$, because $\{d\}$ is P-decisive for x against z.

Axiom [A3] of unanimity means : $\mathcal{P}_S(z,y) \geq \mathcal{P}_S(y,z)$.

Because of f-transitivity, Axiom [A1] means : $\mathcal{P}_S(x,y) \geq \mathcal{P}_S(y,x)$.

Axiom [A4] of independence allows us to make z disappeared from the relation. Then, we deduce : $\mathcal{P}_d(x,y) \geq \mathcal{P}_d(y,x)$ and $\forall i \in S-\{d\}$, $\mathcal{P}_i(x,y) \leq \mathcal{P}_i(y,x)$.

It implies $\{d\}$ to be P-decisive for x against y. Taking a fourth object t would lead to the same result. Therefore, we have obtained that $\{d\}$ is P-decisive for any t, x or y belonging to X.

□

I.3.3. Dictator theorem with fuzzy preferences

THEOREM of "Fuzzy" dictator : *The single element d of C is a dictator (i.e.* $\mathcal{P}_d(.,.) = \mathcal{P}_S(.,.)$ *).*

Proof : We know $C = \{d\}$ to be P-decisive. We have just to prove that d's preferences are exactly the same as society's ones and thus that the collective choice rule is really the dictatorial CCR. Let us consider three objects of X, x, y and z and the d's preferences as follows : $\mathcal{P}_d(x,z) \geq \mathcal{P}_d(z,x)$ and $\mathcal{P}_d(z,y) \leq \mathcal{P}_d(y,z)$.

The other agents defining the rest of society, are such as $\forall i \in S - \{d\}$:

$$\mathcal{P}_i(z,x) \geq \mathcal{P}_i(x,z) \text{ and } \mathcal{P}_i(z,y) \geq \mathcal{P}_i(y,z).$$

The element d of C enforces his choice because C is P-decisive, then :

$$\mathcal{P}_S(x,z) \geq \mathcal{P}_S(z,x).$$

Axiom [A3] leads to : $\mathcal{P}_S(z,y) \geq \mathcal{P}_S(y,z)$.

The relation of preference is f-transitive with [A1] ; we can conclude :

$$\mathcal{P}_S(x,y) \geq \mathcal{P}_S(y,x).$$

Finally, we obtain the following proposition :

$$\mathcal{P}_d(x,y) \geq \mathcal{P}_d(y,x) \Rightarrow \mathcal{P}_S(x,y) \geq \mathcal{P}_S(y,x).$$

Because x and y are any elements of X, it is possible to invert the position of x and the one of y, inside the proposition :

$$\mathcal{P}_d(y,x) \geq \mathcal{P}_d(x,y) \Rightarrow \mathcal{P}_S(y,x) \geq \mathcal{P}_S(x,y).$$

The relation $\geq$ is complete upon R and thus upon [0,1]. Therefore, we can conclude :

$$\forall (x,y) \in X^2, \mathcal{P}_d(x,y) \geq \mathcal{P}_d(y,x) \Leftrightarrow \mathcal{P}_S(x,y) \geq \mathcal{P}_S(y,x).$$

□

SECTION TWO : FUZZY COALITIONS AND DEMOCRACY

In terms of power, the most important theoretical opposition can be summarized by two very famous theorems, Arrow's and May's. The first one determines the minimal group of axioms under which the only feasible collective choice rule corresponds to the identity between the collective relation of preference and any individual preorder. The second one determines the minimal group of axioms under which the majority rule (*quantitative* comparison of individual choices) is a feasible collective choice rule. The object of this section is to link them in a single approach which would have the ability to describe them as extreme cases. We make the connection using the aggregation lexicographic rule of individual choices and then, we specify the two fuzzy coalitions with the help of which the majority rule takes all its meaning. We have to introduce some notions as *justice*, *equity* (à la Rawls) and *utilitarism*. About this tradition, see d'Aspremont & Gevers [1977], Hammond [1976], Deschamps & Gevers [1978], Bordes [1980]), Bentham (Halevy [1903]), Sen & Williams [1982], Rawls [1971], Sen [1974] or Strasnick [1976].

II.1. Axioms of May's theorem

II.1.1. The choice of axioms

There are many presentations of these axioms. We only retain Deschamps & Gevers [1978] one. Even though the conditions produced by May [1952], deal with three basic binary axioms, *independence*, *anonymity* and *duality* and a fourth of *monotonicity* (Bordes [1980]), we prefer introducing the two conditions of *minimal equity* and *extensive neutrality* in order to define the lexicographic rule which has an obvious economic meaning.

II.1.2. The new axiomatic

II.1.2.1. Referential and society

We assume the referential set to include more than three objects and society more than three agents :$|X| \geq 3$ and $|S| \geq 3$. It means that $|X|$ is the cardinal of the set X. We considered X to be expressed as follows : $X = \{x, y, z, \ldots\}$, and $S = \{1,2,3,\ldots,i,\ldots,n\}$ (i.e. $|S| = n$).

II.1.2.2. Set of fuzzy preorders

We note $\mathcal{P}(X)$ the set of fuzzy preorders defined on X. Furthermore, for any preorder $\mathcal{P}(.,.)$ of $\mathcal{P}(X)$, $\forall (x,y) \in X^2$, $\mathcal{P}(x,y) \geq \mathcal{P}(y,x)$ means that x is at least indifferent to y. (Indifference corresponding to the equality of the two preferences degrees.)

II.1.2.3. From individual to society

Our problem here is to develop a satisfying process of transition from fuzzy individual preferences to a fuzzy collective one. First of all, let us recall that under the assumptions of connectedness of X and continuity for preorders, we can associate a fuzzy function $u_i(.)$, from X to $\underline{M}$, where $\underline{M}$ is a membership set, to each individual preorder $\mathcal{P}_i(.,.) \in \mathcal{P}(X)$. Next, we call $\mathcal{U}(X)$, the set of utility functions that translate a preorder of $\mathcal{P}(X)$.

The existence of a planner is justified by his ability to judge and compare relative preferences of the agent i and those of another agent j. The following proposition, $[\forall x \in X, \exists i \in S\,;\ u_i(x) > u_i(y)]$, means that the planner enquires into the information according to which agent i considers the object x to have relative qualities greater than y ones. If there is another agent, $j \in S$, such that $u_i(x) > u_j(x)$, this corresponds to the fact that the planner considers the object x to be more preferred by i than j, without j being constrained to prefer x to y.

II.1.2.4. Social welfare functions *SWF*

This notion, introduced by Sen [1970], corresponds to the process which allows to *functionally*[2] aggregate individual preferences into a collective one. It is an application from the Cartesian product of the n individual sets of preorders of preference to the set of preorders $\mathcal{P}(X)$.

f is a function of social welfare or *SWF* if : $f : \prod_{i \in S} \mathcal{P}(X) \rightarrow \mathcal{P}(X)$.

II.1.2.5. Formal writing of a *SWF*

We have just seen a *SWF* to be any application from the Cartesian product $\prod_{i \in S} \mathcal{P}(X)$ to $\mathcal{P}(X)$. Another way of specifying a *SWF*, noted W, is the following :

$$\forall u(.) \in \mathcal{U}(X), \exists \mathcal{P}(.,.) \in \mathcal{P}(X) \,/\, \mathcal{P}(.,.) = W[u(.)].$$

II.1.3. Binary independence of alternatives [P1]

Let a pair of fuzzy utility functions $(u_1(.), u_2(.))$ belonging to $\mathcal{U}(X)$, and a subset Y of the referential set X, to be such that[3] $|\, Y \,|= 2$; the fuzzy preorder $\mathcal{P}_1(.,.)$ corresponds to the fuzzy preorder $\mathcal{P}_2(.,.)$ on Y if : $\forall (x,y) \in Y,\ u_1(x) \geq u_1(y) \Leftrightarrow u_2(x) \geq u_2(y)$.

II.1.4. Strong-Pareto principle [P2]

Let any pair (x,y) belonging to X, and $u(.)$ a utility function belonging to $\mathcal{U}(X)$.

If $\forall i \in S - \{j\}$, $\mathcal{P}_i(x,y) \geq \mathcal{P}_i(y,x)$, there is an agent j, $j \in S$, so that : $\mathcal{P}_j(x,y) > \mathcal{P}_j(y,x)$, then $\mathcal{P}_S(x,y) > \mathcal{P}_S(y,x)$, i.e. : if $u_i(x) \geq u_i(y)$ and $u_j(x) > u_j(y)$, then $u_S(x) > u_S(y)$.

---

2 That is the difference between a *CCR* and a *SWF*.

3 This condition, $|\, Y \,|= 2$, *explains* the term *binary*.

II.1.5. Extensive neutrality [P3]

Let any pair $(w,z) \in X^2$, and a fuzzy utility function $u^1(.) \in \mathcal{U}(X)$ or $\mathcal{P}^1(.,.) \in \mathcal{P}(X)$.

$$\mathcal{P}_S^1(w,z) \geq \mathcal{P}_S^1(z,w) \text{ (resp. } \mathcal{P}_S^1(w,z) > \mathcal{P}_S^1(z,w))$$

iff, $\exists(x,y) \in X^2, \exists u^0(.) \in \mathcal{U}(X)$ or $\mathcal{P}^0(.,.) \in \mathcal{P}(X)$, so that $\forall i \in S$:

$$u_i^0(x) = u_i^1(w),\ u_i^0(y) = u_i^1(z) \text{ and } \mathcal{P}_S^0(x,y) \geq \mathcal{P}_S^0(y,x) \text{ (resp. } \mathcal{P}_S^0(x,y) > \mathcal{P}_S^0(y,x)).$$

Some authors (Fishburn [1973]) suggest an interpretation of *neutrality* in terms of duality : this condition requires the agents to have preferences which could be reversed. Choices are therefore inversed in order to ensure the objects that were rejected before the inversion to be chosen after.

II.1.6. Intermediate result

The first interesting result we can produce corresponds to the following property : if the *SWF* *W* satisfies the binary independence and strong-Pareto principle, then *W* satisfies the extensive neutrality. The proof is based on a generalization of d'Aspremont & Gevers [1977].

LEMMA 3 : *If the SWF W satisfies [P1], [P2], then it satisfies [P3].*

Proof: Generally, we have to consider three cases corresponding to the fact that the intersection between the two pairs (x,y) and (w,z) can be empty, single or including two elements. Let us consider the last case and assume that for any agent $i, i \in S$:

$$u_i^1(x) = u_i^0(y) = a_i \text{ and } u_i^1(y) = u_i^0(x) = b_i.$$

We know the cardinal of the referential set X to be greater than 2, $|X| > 2$. Therefore, we can consider a third element of X, that we note v, with v different from x and y, and three fuzzy utility functions belonging to $\mathcal{U}(X)$, $u^2(.)$, $u^3(.)$ and $u^4(.)$ and which would describe the following scheme[4] :

4 In that scheme, the emptiness of $u^0(.)$ and $u^1(.)$ means : $\forall u^0(.), \forall u^1(.)$.

	$u^0(.)$	$u^1(.)$	$u^2(.)$	$u^3(.)$	$u^4(.)$
x	b	a	a	b	b
y	a	b	b	b	a
v	*	*	a	a	a

According to [P1], we can write :

$$\mathcal{P}_S^1(x,y) \geq \mathcal{P}_S^1(y,x) \quad \text{if} \quad \mathcal{P}_S^2(x,y) \geq \mathcal{P}_S^2(y,x)$$
$$\mathcal{P}_S^2(v,y) \geq \mathcal{P}_S^2(y,v) \quad \text{if} \quad \mathcal{P}_S^3(v,y) \geq \mathcal{P}_S^3(y,v)$$
$$\mathcal{P}_S^3(v,x) \geq \mathcal{P}_S^3(x,v) \quad \text{if} \quad \mathcal{P}_S^4(v,x) \geq \mathcal{P}_S^4(x,v)$$
$$\mathcal{P}_S^4(y,x) \geq \mathcal{P}_S^4(x,y) \quad \text{if} \quad \mathcal{P}_S^0(y,x) \geq \mathcal{P}_S^0(x,y).$$

Identically [P2] allows to write :

$$\mathcal{P}_S^2(x,y) \geq \mathcal{P}_S^2(y,x) \quad \text{if} \quad \mathcal{P}_S^2(v,y) \geq \mathcal{P}_S^2(y,v)$$
$$\mathcal{P}_S^3(v,y) \geq \mathcal{P}_S^3(y,v) \quad \text{if} \quad \mathcal{P}_S^3(v,x) \geq \mathcal{P}_S^3(x,v)$$
$$\mathcal{P}_S^4(v,x) \geq \mathcal{P}_S^4(x,v) \quad \text{if} \quad \mathcal{P}_S^4(y,x) \geq \mathcal{P}_S^4(x,y).$$

Combining these different results, we can conclude as follows :

$$\mathcal{P}_S^1(x,y) \geq \mathcal{P}_S^1(y,x) \Leftrightarrow_{(P1)} \mathcal{P}_S^2(x,y) \geq \mathcal{P}_S^2(y,x) \Leftrightarrow_{(P2)} \mathcal{P}_S^2(v,y) \geq \mathcal{P}_S^2(y,v) \Leftrightarrow_{(P1)}$$
$$\mathcal{P}_S^3(v,y) \geq \mathcal{P}_S^3(y,v) \Leftrightarrow_{(P2)} \mathcal{P}_S^3(v,x) \geq \mathcal{P}_S^3(x,v) \Leftrightarrow_{(P1)} \mathcal{P}_S^4(v,x) \geq \mathcal{P}_S^4(x,v) \Leftrightarrow_{(P2)}$$
$$\mathcal{P}_S^4(y,x) \geq \mathcal{P}_S^4(x,y) \Leftrightarrow_{(P1)} \mathcal{P}_S^0(y,x) \geq \mathcal{P}_S^0(x,y).$$

It yields by removing intermediate steps :

$$\mathcal{P}_S^1(x,y) \geq \mathcal{P}_S^1(y,x) \Leftrightarrow \mathcal{P}_S^0(y,x) \geq \mathcal{P}_S^0(x,y).$$

□

It is obvious that strict collective preference (strict inequality) would be obtained according to the same process.

If (x,y) and (w,z) have less than two elements in common, i.e. 1 or 0, the proof would be similar, however shorter, and would allow to obtain the same result.

II.1.7. Anonimity axiom [P4]

Let $\sigma(.)$ be a *permutation* defined on S : let us consider two fuzzy utility functions, $u^1(.)$ and $u^2(.)$, belonging to $\mathcal{U}(X)$; we can say that $\mathcal{P}^1(.,.)$ and $\mathcal{P}^2(.,.)$, the two associated fuzzy preorders belonging to $\mathcal{P}(X)$, are identical if for any agent i, $i \in S$, and whatever an object x, $x \in X$: $u_i^1(x) = u_{\sigma(i)}^2(x)$.

This condition of *anonymity*, means that the *SWF W* does not *need* to know *who* prefers *what*. If some agents exchange their preferences, the aggregate result will not be modified.

II.1.8. Equity axiom [P5]

Let any fuzzy utility function $u(.)$ belonging to $\mathcal{U}(X)$, any pair (x,y) belonging to X^2 and any pair (i,j) of S^2 :

$$\forall g \in S-\{i,j\},\ u_g(x)=u_g(y) \text{ and } u_i(y)<u_i(x)<u_j(x)<u_j(y)$$

then $u_S(x) > u_S(y)$.

This axiom means that even though every agent except $\{i,j\}$ is indifferent between two objects (x,y), if both agents $\{i,j\}$ are in conflict and if j strictly prefers both objects, then society will reproduce the preferences of the *less satisfied agent*.

II.1.9. From the lexicographic preorder to the leximin rule

The *leximin* principle or *CCR* leximin, is a refinement of *utilitarianism*. The transition from the lexicographic rule to the leximin rule is founded upon the only supplementary requirement of anonymity [P4]. The associated social choice function, the corresponding welfare function *SWF W*, sometimes considered as equalitarian, maximizes the welfare of the less satisfied agent; it is based on interpersonal comparisons of utility but not on intrapersonal ones. It can weakly represent an anonymous social lexicographic preorder but not completely, as proved by Chichilinsky [1982].

We only present two results ; a leximin theorem (resp. leximax) and May's one. We distinguish them thanks to [P5], and try to find the relation with Arrow's theorem.

II.1.9.1. Lexicographic preorder

Let $u(.)$ a fuzzy utility function belonging to $\mathcal{U}(X)$; we define a function $i_x(.)$ (notations Deschamps & Gevers [1978]), from the ranks set, $N=\{1,2,3,\dots,n\}$ to S. This function satisfies the following condition : $\forall h,k \in N, \forall x \in X,\ u_{i_x(h)}(x) < u_{i_x(k)}(x) \Leftrightarrow h<k$.

In other words, if agent i's satisfaction is *lower* than agent j's one for a same object x, the rank assigned to agent i is lower to that assigned to agent[5] j : i.e. the bigger the satisfaction is, the higher the rank is.

II.1.9.2. Leximin principle (resp. leximax)

We can define the leximin principle as follows : for any pair of objects (x, y) belonging to X^2, the social relation of preference $\mathcal{P}_S(.,.)$ is such that : $\forall u(.) \in \mathcal{U}(X)$, if $\exists m \in N$ (m is a rank) such that $\forall k \in N$ with $k < m$, we have :

$$u_{i_x(k)}(x) = u_{i_y(k)}(y) \text{ and } u_{i_x(m)}(x) > u_{i_y(m)}(y),$$

$$\text{then } u_S(x) > u_S(y) \text{ or } \mathcal{P}_S(x,y) > \mathcal{P}_S(y,x).$$

(In reversing the inequalities, we obtain a characterization of the *leximax* principle.)

In other terms, society makes the choice of the first less satisfied agent when he is not indifferent. The social preference is an indifference only if all agents are indifferent.

II.1.10. Axioms for the Leximin Principle

We present without proving them two generalizations with fuzzy preorders of lemmas by Hammond [1976] and Strasnick [1976] (see the proof for partial results in Annex 1, 2 and 3).

LEMMA 4 (Hammond) : $\forall (x, y) \in X^2$, $\forall u(.) \in \mathcal{U}(X)$, *if SWFW satisfies [P1], [P2] and [P4], then if :* $u_S(x) = u_S(y)$, $\exists \sigma(.)$, *a permutation over* S, *such that :* $\forall i \in S$, $u_i(x) = u_{\sigma(i)}(y)$.

LEMMA 5 (Strasnick) : $\forall (x, y) \in X^2$, $\forall u(.) \in \mathcal{U}(X)$, $\forall C \subseteq S$, C *a coalition such that :* $C = \{j \in S, u_j(x) < u_j(y)\}$. *If SWFW satisfies [P1], [P2] and [P5] and if there exists an agent* $i, i \in S$, *such that :* (1) $u_i(x) > u_i(y)$ (2) $\forall j \in C, u_j(x) > u_i(y)$ *then :* $u_S(x) > u_S(y)$.

THEOREM 2 : *SWF W-leximin is the only SWF satisfying axioms of binary independence [P1], strong-Pareto principle [P2], anonymity [P4] and minimal equity [P5].*

Proof . First step :

---

5 i.e. : $i_z(h) = i$ and $i_x(k) = j$.

Let us suppose that $\mathcal{P}_S(x,y)=\mathcal{P}_S(y,x)$ (i.e. $u_S(x)=u_S(y)$, which is identical for X connected and $\mathcal{P}_S(.,.)$ continuous). If indifference between two objects x and y is social, it means that all agents are indifferent, i.e. : $\forall i \in S$, $u_i(x)=u_i(y)$.

In terms of ranks, we have : $\forall k \in N$, $u_{i_x(k)}(x)=u_{i_y(k)}(y)$.

Let us take now, the following permutation $\sigma(.)$: $\forall i \in S$, $u_{i_x(k)}(x)=u_{\sigma(i_y(k))}(y)$, which also means : $u_i(x)=u_{\sigma(i)}(y)$, and when applying lemma 1, we know that it corresponds to a social indifference. In cases where the agents are unanimously indifferent, we produce the *SWF* which satisfies axioms [P1], [P2] and [P4] thanks to a permutation $\sigma(.)$.

Second step :

We now have to prove the necessity of axiom [P5] by using lemma 2. Let us suppose : $\mathcal{P}_S(x,y)>\mathcal{P}_S(y,x)$ where $\mathcal{P}_S(.,.)$ is the social preorder proceeding from the social welfare function W : $\mathcal{P}_S(.,.)=W^L[u(.)]$ (W^L the leximin principle). One supposes that there is a rank m, such that $m \in N$, with :

α- $\forall k \in N, k<m$: $u_{i_x(k)}(x)=u_{i_y(k)}(y)$ and

β- $u_{i_x(m)}(x)>u_{i_y(m)}(y)$.

Let us consider the rest of the referential set X without the pair (x,y). Let us take an object z in $X-\{x,y\}$ and a fuzzy utility function $u^0(.)$ satisfying the axiom of binary independence [P1] such that $u^0_{i_y(k)}(y)=u_{i_z(k)}(z)$ and this, $\forall k \in N$, which corresponds to a generalized indifference for y and z. As in the first step, we can conclude thanks to a permutation $\sigma(.)$ of S and thanks to the axiom [P2], that it follows : $u^0_S(y)=u^0_S(z)$, i.e. $\mathcal{P}^0_S(y,z)=\mathcal{P}^0_S(z,y)$.

Third step :

We now have to show that $\mathcal{P}^0_S(x,z)>\mathcal{P}^0_S(z,x)$, in order to make the relation with the result of the second step. Therefore, we use lemma 3. Let an agent i belonging to society such that :

α- $\mathcal{P}^0_i(x,z)>\mathcal{P}^0_i(z,x)$ and

β- $\forall j \in S-\{i\}$, $\mathcal{P}^0_j(z,x)>\mathcal{P}^0_j(x,z)$ with $\mathcal{P}^0_i(x,z)>\mathcal{P}^0_i(z,x)$.

[P1] and [$u_{i_x(m)}(x)>u_{i_y(m)}(y)$,] means : $u^0_{i_x(m)}(x)>u^0_{i_y(m)}(y)$.

We know also : $u^0_{i_y(m)}(y)=u^0_{i_z(m)}(z)$. Hence, we obtain : $u^0_{i_x(m)}(x)>u^0_{i_z(m)}(z)$, which can be written like this : $\mathcal{P}^0_i(x,z)>\mathcal{P}^0_i(z,x)$, which corresponds to the characteristic (1) of lemma 5.

Let us suppose now : $\mathcal{P}^0_j(z,x)>\mathcal{P}^0_j(x,z)$.

This means, in terms of rank :

$$u^0_{j_z(k)}(z)>u^0_{j_x(k)}(x). \tag{1}$$

But we also know that $u^0(.)$ is defined such that : $\forall i \in S$, (i.e. $\forall k \in N$) :

$u^0_{i_y(k)}(y) = u^0_{i_z(k)}(z)$.

We can deduce, $\forall k \in N : u^0_{j_y(k)}(y) = u^0_{j_z(k)}(z)$ with (1) $\Rightarrow u^0_{j_y(k)}(y) > u^0_{j_x(k)}(x)$, that is : $\forall j \in S$, $\mathcal{P}^0_j(y,x) > \mathcal{P}^0_j(x,y)$.

[P1] allows to write : $\forall j \in S, \mathcal{P}_j(y,x) > \mathcal{P}_j(x,y)$, which corresponds to the second condition of Strasnick's lemma.

But, the condition defining the individual preferences for the pair (x,y) in the second step, allows to restrain this inequality to ranks k which are lower than rank m. For $k > m$ and thanks to W^L, we have :

$$u^0_{i_x(k)}(x) \geq u^0_{i_x(m)}(x). \tag{2}$$

Now, we can identify the two conditions of lemma 5 :

1- There is an agent $i, i \in S$, such that $u^0_i(x) > u^0_i(z)$.

2- There is a coalition C which corresponds to agents j represented by ranks k that are superior to rank m. This coalition can be defined as follows : $C = \left\{ j \in S,\ u^0_{i_z(k)}(z) > u^0_{i_x(k)}(x) \right\}$. When combining this definition with the result of equation (2), it means $u^0_j(x) > u^0_i(x)$, because the rank m corresponds to agent i.

As we know : $u^0_{i_x(k)}(x) \geq u^0_{i_x(m)}(x) > u^0_{i_z(m)}(z)$, and thus : $u^0_{i_x(k)}(x) > u^0_{i_z(m)}(z)$, i.e. $u^0_j(x) > u^0_i(z)$.

From this result, we can conclude, applying lemma 5 :

$u^0_S(x) > u^0_S(z)$, i.e. $\mathcal{P}^0_S(x,z) > \mathcal{P}^0_S(z,x)$.

Combining this result with the one we obtained at the end of the second step, i.e. $\mathcal{P}^0_S(z,y) = \mathcal{P}^0_S(y,z)$ we obtain : $\mathcal{P}^0_S(x,y) > \mathcal{P}^0_S(y,x) \Leftrightarrow_{(P1)} \mathcal{P}_S(x,y) > \mathcal{P}_S(y,x)$, which corresponds to the result we tried to obtain at the beginning of the second step and which ends the proof.

□

This theorem means that when modifying some of Arrow's axioms and specifying the FBS, we come to a rule of aggregation - called *leximin* - which allows a first step towards the majority rule. Actually, the anonymity axiom is a strong version of the axiom of non-dictatorship [A5]. The independence remains (even though binary), the axiom of strong-Pareto principle is a weak formulation of Arrow's unanimity and the axiom of minimal equity introduces some interpersonal comparisons of utility which were basically forbidden by Arrow.

Let us introduce a new axiom.

II.1.11. Monotonicity [P6]

$\forall u(.) \in \mathcal{U}(X)$, $\forall i \in S$, $\forall (x,y,z) \in X^3$, iff $\mathcal{P}_S(x,y) \geq \mathcal{P}_S(y,x)$ and $\forall j \in S-\{i\}$, $u_j(z) = u_j(x)$, when $u_i(x) = u_i(y) < u_i(z)$, then $\mathcal{P}_S(z,y) > \mathcal{P}_S(y,z)$.

It is obvious for a *SWF* to be satisfying, that it generally has to be "*discriminant*", namely it does not systematically leads to indifference situations. However, it is not necessary to totally suppress the possibilities of indifference. In other words, this condition of *monotonicity* consists in getting *instable* all the indifference situations.

Finally, [P6] means that if all the agents except one are indifferent between x and z while society nonstrictly prefers x to y then it strictly prefers z to y while the *single* agent prefers z to y and is indifferent between x and y.

At first sight, the power of i may appear in relation with Arrow's dictator. However, this power is only *efficient* when a situation of social indifference appears. A binary dictator cannot even be concerned as, independently from the other agents' fuzzy preferences, there is no *systematic* power and no given couple of objects (x,y), such that i constitutes, *always and everywhere*, a p-decisive coalition or a determinant set, according to Arrow's own words. Perhaps, we could say, it is a *fortuitous dictator.*

II.1.12. Social-welfare and democracy

The leximin rule introduces a notion of equity which defines the social choice according to the choice of the less satisfied agent. This leads some authors (Roberts [1980], Kolm [1973]) to say that this rule corresponds to a k-rank dictatorship. This k-dictatorship is binary and based on interpersonal comparisons of utility. The two following theorems, that we simultaneously introduce, determine a *democratical limit* which can be identified by the two axioms of minimal equity and monotonicity.

THEOREM 3: *If the SWF W satisfies [P3], [P4], [P5] and [P6], W is the leximin principle :* $W = W^L$.

The demonstration of this theorem is quite simple ; it is enough to check that W^L satisfies [P6] because [P1] and [P2] are implying [P3] (lemma 1) and [P3], [P4] and [P5] are defining W^L (theorem 2). (see Annex 3.)

THEOREM 4 (May's Theorem) : *If the SWF W satisfies [P3], [P4] and [P6], W is a SWF such that* :$\forall(x,y) \in X^2$, $\forall u(.) \in \mathcal{U}(X)$: $\mathcal{P}_S(x,y) > \mathcal{P}_S(y,x) \Leftrightarrow$ *the two following coalitions* $An = \{i \in S \ / \ u_i(x) < u_i(y)\}$ *and* $Pr = \{j \in S \ / \ u_j(x) > u_j(y)\}$ *satisfy* : $| An | < | Pr |$.

This theorem expresses the axioms under which the *binary* principle of the majority rule allows to produce a coherent collective decision. This one is based on the comparisons of cardinals $| An |$ and $| Pr |$. It is a fuzzy generalization of Deschamps & Gevers [1978] presentation for May's theorem.

The difference between the two process (theorem 3 (leximin) and theorem 4 (majority rule)) clearly deals with the axiom [P5] of minimal equity which does not appear in May's theorem. If we consider the majority rule as a kind of democracy archetype, we obtain two results ; the first one paradoxical and the other one more natural.

1- Democracy can be antinomic with justice not only when the agents' preferences are fuzzy, but also when they are usual.

2- Democracy badly deals with interpersonal comparisons of satisfaction. In other words, a social representation of individual preferences would only take the agents into consideration, not their levels of satisfaction.

II.2. Generalized theorem : Arrow versus May

II.2.1. Fuzzy coalitions, anti and pro

We saw that May's theorem was based on the definition of two usual coalitions, An and Pr : the agent i *totally* belongs to $An(x,y)$ if he considers the relative qualities of x to be *lower* than y's ones ; this is exactly what we were pointing out in note 2 of last paragraph, noting on one hand that democracy badly fits with interpersonal comparisons and on the other, that it only takes the agents into account and not their levels of satisfaction. Now, it is quite intuitive to consider the membership of an agent to a decisive coalition, Pro or Anti, to depend on the relative qualities he assigns to the object he prefers. Hence, preferring a socialist to a communist does not mean the same thing as being a *member* of the socialist party. However, according to May's theorem, both agents, the one who *prefers* and the one who *joins* the party, belong in a like manner, i.e. in the same level, to the coalition $Pr(socialist, communist)$. The logic of May's theorem is electoral : it means "*a man, a vote*". However, the aggregation topics apparently do not have any reason to be solved thanks to the voting theory (see Moulin [1979]). In other words, what happens if the agents' membership to coalitions Anti and Pro is no more defined on the single Boolean pair $\{0,1\}$ but on the Zadeh interval $[0,1]$?

Let us consider a pair (x,y), belonging to X. Each agent i, member of society S has its own relation of preference $\mathcal{P}_i(.,.)$.

Axiom [P1] of binary independence also allows to order individual preferences on a scale from zero to one, giving a zero level of relative qualities to the less satisfying (or incomparable) object and a level of one to the most satisfying object. We admit the i's membership level to the coalitions to be given by his degree of strong preference. So let us consider the agent j as follows : $\mathcal{P}_j(x,y) > \mathcal{P}_j(y,x)$.

Hence, $pr(j) = \mathcal{P}_j(x,y)$ and $an(j) = 0$, where $pr(.)$ and $an(.)$ are the membership functions of the coalitions $\mathcal{Pr}(x,y)$ - Pro - and $\mathcal{An}(x,y)$ - Anti. The coalitions are fuzzy subsets of S, defined as follows :

$$\mathcal{Pr}(x,y) = \{i \in S;\ \mathcal{P}_i(x,y) \geq \mathcal{P}_i(y,x) \text{ with } pr(i) = \mathcal{P}_i(x,y)\}. \qquad (def.1)$$

$$\mathcal{An}(x,y) = \{i \in S;\ \mathcal{P}_i(x,y) \leq \mathcal{P}_i(y,x) \text{ with } an(i) = \mathcal{P}_i(y,x)\}. \qquad (def.2)$$

The indifferent agents are those who belong in the same level to $\mathcal{Pr}(x,y)$ and to $\mathcal{An}(x,y)$. They define the coalition $I(x,y)$ of indifferent agents :

$$\begin{aligned} I(x,y) = \mathcal{Pr}(x,y) \cap \mathcal{An}(x,y) &= \text{Min}[pr(i), an(i)] \\ &= 0 \text{ if } i \in \mathcal{Pr}(x,y) \text{ as } an(i) = 0 \\ &= 0 \text{ if } i \in \mathcal{An}(x,y) \text{ as } pr(i) = 0 \\ &= pr(i) = an(i) \text{ else.} \end{aligned}$$

II.2.2. The leaders of coalitions

The valuation of membership to Anti and Pro coalitions implies that it is possible to ordinally compare the different agents, members of a same coalition. There are agents who belong more than others to the Pro (or Anti) coalition. This means that the level of satisfaction established from the relative qualities of the object they prefer (in a binary comparison), leads them to defend more or less the coalition which backs up their preference. The agent whose preference is the *greatest* is called the *leader*.

$\forall (x,y) \in X^2$, we call *leader-pro*, the agent d_p who belongs to the fuzzy coalition $\mathcal{Pr}(x,y)$ such that the other agents have a membership degree to the coalition $\mathcal{Pr}(x,y)$ which is *lower or equal* :

$$\forall (x,y) \in X^2, \exists d_p \in \mathcal{Pr}(x,y) \,/\, \forall i \in \mathcal{Pr}(x,y) : pr(d_p) \geq pr(i). \qquad (def.3)$$

The *leader-anti* is symmetrically defined as follows :

$$\forall (x,y) \in X^2, \exists d_a \in \mathcal{An}(x,y) \,/\, \forall i \in \mathcal{An}(x,y) : an(d_a) \geq an(i). \qquad (def.4)$$

We assume :

[C1] : a leader of coalition - $\mathcal{A}n(x,y)$ or $\mathcal{P}r(x,y)$ - does not belong to $I(x,y)$: ($d_p \notin I(x,y)$, $d_a \notin I(x,y)$).

[C2] : $pr(d_p)$ is never equal to $an(d_a)$.

The first condition combined with the second one intuitively means that a coalition leader cannot be at the same time leader of the Anti and the Pro coalitions. However, these conditions do not prevent from social indifference because nothing forbids a coalition to have several leaders, which then corresponds to situations of *binary oligarchies* (Bordes [1980] defines them in a different manner).

II.2.3. Generalized theorem of preferences aggregation

We have to consider some agents of society to show too insignificant preferences. Their level of membership corresponds to their strong preference degree. Hence, a weak membership level means a weak involvement in the choice.

The planner can decide to take the opinions of agents into consideration when the two given objects seem to have a great interest for them, i.e. a great level of relative qualities ; the other agents are *forgotten* by the planner. If the latter is very demanding, the number of agents who are concerned in the choice is very little. This notion of planner's requirement corresponds to the mathematical principle of the α-cut of a fuzzy subset. If the planner decides to require a level α, $\alpha \in [0,1]$, of membership to coalitions in order to take part in the choice, we have :

$$\underline{Pr(x,y)}_\alpha = \{i \in \mathcal{P}r(x,y) \,/\, pr(i) \geq \alpha\} \text{ and}$$

$$\underline{An(x,y)}_\alpha = \{i \in \mathcal{A}n(x,y) \,/\, an(i) \geq \alpha\}.$$

THEOREM 5 (generalized) : *Let α be the minimal step chosen in* [0,1] *by the planner. If the SWF W satisfies [P1], [P2], [P4] and [P6], then,* $\forall u(.) \in \mathcal{U}(X)$, *where X is a connected referential set of objects and the preferences are continuous,* $\forall (x,y) \in X^2 : u_S(x) \geq u_S(y) \Leftrightarrow |\,\underline{Pr(x,y)}_\alpha\,| \geq |\,\underline{An(x,y)}_\alpha\,|$.

Remarks :

1- If $\alpha = 0$, $\underline{Pr(x,y)}_\alpha = Pr(x,y)$, and $\underline{An(x,y)}_\alpha = An(x,y)$; theorem 5 is the same as May's theorem (theorem 4).

2- If $\alpha = \text{Max}_S\,\{[pr \cup an]\,(i)\}$; theorem 5 is a theorem of binary dictatorship.

Proof : If $\alpha = 0$, $\underline{Pr(x,y)}_0 = \{i \in \mathcal{P}r(x,y) \,/\, pr(i) \geq 0\}$. In others words, we find all agents such that : $\mathcal{P}_i(x,y) \geq \mathcal{P}_i(y,x)$, which means, if *X* connected and the preferences are continuous : $u_i(x) \geq u_i(y)$.

In the same way, $\underline{An(x,y)}_0 = \{i \in \mathcal{An}(x,y) \, / \, an(i) \geq 0\}$, which means that any agent for which $\mathcal{P}_i(y,x) \geq \mathcal{P}_i(x,y)$, belongs to $\underline{An(x,y)}_0$; we are in the case of May's theorem. Hence, the conclusion is the same : $u_S(x) \geq u_S(y) \Leftrightarrow |\underline{Pr(x,y)}_0| \geq |\underline{An(x,y)}_0|$.

If $\alpha = \mathrm{Max}_S \{[pr \cup an](i)\}$, this means that we have previously built up the union of two coalitions. Classical algebra for fuzzy subsets (see Kaufmann [1974], Prevot [1977], Zimmermann [1985]) teaches that the union of two fuzzy subsets to be defined by taking the maximum of each level of membership. Here, except the indifferent agents, for whom this maximum indifferently corresponds to $pr(.)$ or $an(.)$, the other agents have a level of membership to $\mathcal{Pr} \cup \mathcal{An}$ that is identical to the one they have for $\mathcal{Pr}(x,y)$ if they are *for x against y* or the one they have for $\mathcal{An}(x,y)$ if they are *for y against x*. The maximum of the membership levels to $\mathcal{Pr} \cup \mathcal{An}$ therefore corresponds to the degree of the leader for which the level of membership is the greatest. In other words, if $\alpha = \mathrm{Max}_S \{[pr \cup an](i)\}$, this means that $\forall i \in S$:

$$\begin{aligned} [pr \cup an](i) &= \mathrm{Max}[pr(i),\, an(i)] \\ &= pr(i) \text{ if } i \notin \mathcal{An}(x,y) \\ &= an(i) \text{ if } i \notin \mathcal{Pr}(x,y) \\ &= pr(i) = an(i) \text{ else.} \end{aligned}$$

On the basis of the two conditions which rule the *leadership*, we can establish for the coalition $\mathcal{Pr}(x,y)$ as for $\mathcal{An}(x,y)$:

$$\begin{aligned} \mathrm{Max}_S \{[pr \cup an](i)\} &= \mathrm{Max}_S[\mathrm{Max}_{\mathcal{Pr}}\, pr(i),\, \mathrm{Max}_{\mathcal{An}}\, an(i)] \\ &= \mathrm{Max}[pr(d_p),\, an(d_a)] \\ &= pr(d_p) \text{ if } pr(d_p) > an(d_a) \\ &= an(d_a) \text{ if } an(d_a) > pr(d_p). \end{aligned}$$

Anyhow, if $\alpha = \mathrm{Max}_S[pr \cup an(i)]$, α corresponds to the membership level of the two leaders whose strong preference was the greatest. This implies the cardinal of the α-cut to be equal to zero for the coalition whose leader's preference is the weakest and equal to the number of leaders for the other coalition.

If $pr(d_p) > an(d_a)$: $|\underline{Pr(x,y)}_\alpha| \geq 1$ while $|\underline{An(x,y)}_\alpha| = 0$,

from which we can imply that $u_S(x) \geq u_S(y)$, which corresponds to the binary dictator's choice (the leader of $\mathcal{Pr}(x,y)$). All the intermediate situations, $\alpha \in]0,\, \mathrm{Max}_S \{[pr \cup an](i)\}[$, correspond to situations of *binary oligarchies* : a group of agents which are considered as significant dictates its choice to the whole society.

□

Before analyzing this result, we should make some remarks.

1- The leximin principle leads to a fortuitous dictatorship of the less satisfied agent (the first of the less satisfied nonindifferent agents). The *leximax* principle implies the fortuitous dictatorship of the most satisfied agent (see Sen [1974], Kolm [1973], Hammond [1976] and Harsanyi [1973]), which implicitly corresponds to a binary dictator. This means that the agents having fuzzy preferences allow an aggregation process which is not dependent on interpersonal comparisons. Actually, the planner's action consists in excluding some agents whose membership is *ordinally* compared to a given exogenous step and not to other preferences. Therefore, it does not concern the membership levels of the other agents.

2- If the referential set is connected and the agents preferences continuous, the minimal step of implication α can continuously *describe* [0,1], taking the risk to lead to situations without collective solutions beyond $\mathrm{Max}_S\,\{[pr \cup an]\,(i)\}$.

3- The generalized theorem assigns a social situation to each value of step α, i.e. a welfare function *SWF*, which varies from the leximax principle ($\alpha = \mathrm{Max}_S\,\{[pr \cup an]\,(i)\} \leq 1$) to the majority rule ($\alpha = 0$), passing by democratically intermediate situations, in particular the binary oligarchies. A reversal of the membership functions $(1 - pr(i),\, 1 - an(i))$ would permit to vary from the majority rule to the leximin principle.

4- The planner's requirement, represented by α, is an increasing function of the iniquity of collective decisions.

Final Remarks

What does it mean ?

First, the stronger the planner's requirement is, the more democracy is badly treated. If this requirement is considered as a minimal involvement step, the generalized theorem means the majority rule to lead to a collective decision which is independent of the interest the agents assign to the choice. It is an electoral rule since an identical power of decision corresponds to each agent. Next, the minimal involvement step given by the planner leads to determinant sets (or power-decisive coalitions) : in other words, the minimal involvement step reveals those agents whose preferences are so significant that they can form a p-decisive coalition while Arrow's theorem assumes the existence of these p-decisive coalitions without justifying their constitution.

However, the generalized theorem does not ensure the planner to choose a particular step rather than another. Hence, the antinomy between justice and democracy, based on interpersonal comparisons of satisfaction, is not justified any more if the agents' preferences are fuzzy, since the only comparison which is made deals with the minimal step and not with the other agents' preferences. Finally, we can say that if the fortuitous dictatorship of an agent corresponds to a planner's strong requirement, it is not necessarily built up in terms of justice.

CHAPTER 3

Fuzzy Games

The first part of our work was devoted to the *new* agent that we desired to consider in an economical and social *situation.* We then tried to define his behaviour, his rationality and the insertion of his decision in a larger social structure where he would be considered no more like a lone Robinson but just like one of the agents of the social decision. The intersection of both first chapters was the preference theory. Henceforth, to define equilibria inside a theory of fuzzy preferences, we introduce a new concept ; the conflict. By trying to model it, we enter the domain of game theory.

Shapley & Shubik, in their 1972 paper, tried to distinguish some social categories related to a particular kind of individuals whose group can help the economist to describe the world he is trying to explain. They showed five different categories : citizens, industrials, financiers, politicians and bureaucrats. It becomes obvious that the interests of each group are different : the concept of conflict belongs to the economic world. Nevertheless, the conflict can rise between *individuals* or *groups*. Hence, we can have two different analyses, deriving from this distinction ; the first one dealing with the non-cooperative game theory and the second with the cooperative game theory.

If we consider the *normal form* of a game, the decision power is completely and precisely shared between the agents. However, if we consider the *characteristic form* of a game, it implies a cooperative rationality that allows cooperative solutions. If the game theory, in its normative aspect, gives an answer to the question "how must we play ?", it permits to explain the different kinds of possible behaviours, *prudent*, *sophisticated*, *passive* and *threatening*.

A *non-cooperative* game is a *mathematical object* that models a conflict between different agents (players). For example, when competing on a market where substituable goods are supplied, firm managers are *typically* players. A *cooperative* game is a conflict model where the agents have the possibility to gather themselves in order to protect their own interests. Cooperation is just a tool for players to defend themselves. The process that leads to cooperative equilibria formally models the control of coalitions upon the game results.

However, this approach is not economically neutral from a historical point of view. Some fundamental concepts of classic economics were already leading to these ideas of equilibrium. Smith's invisible hand, Walras' general equilibrium, Cournot's and Stackelberg's duopolies are as many historical notions that yet defined the main *concepts* that the game theory finally uses. Debreu will later prove that a Walrasian general equilibrium is a non-cooperative equilibrium, that they are equivalent in terms of social efficiency when the agents' cooperation is forbidden : the functions of reaction studied by Stackelberg correspond to the famous "*response-map*" of non-cooperative games ; Edgeworth's box generates equilibria which deal with saddle points of the first theorem of the theory. Nevertheless, Von Neumann & Morgenstern's work could not be summed up as a systematic *mathematization* of already existing results whose foundations would be exclusively economical. The genesis of game theory is related to a fruitful dialectic movement between economics and pure mathematics.

First, we are going to present the fuzzy literature devoted to non-cooperative games (mostly composed of Butnariu's works [1979;1982;1985] on fixed points in a fuzzy universe, Bose & Sahani [1987], Heilpern [1981], Weiss [1975], Chitra & Subrahmanyam [1987], Kaleva [1985] on cardinal fuzzy games and finally Ponsard [1986] on Nash-equilibrium in a fuzzy spatial universe). On the other hand, we present some results issued from a continuous representation of the lexicographic preorder under a condition of fuzziness.

We must note that most of the theorems (except in Ponsard's articles) need a referential space with a metric topological structure. In a purely economic context, this implies a cardinal representation of preferences.

Nevertheless, the theory of fuzzy games (particularly fuzzy non-cooperative games) can be summed up in a set of specific fixed points theorems and in a few cardinalistic models. In the first section, we present some generalizations of Kakutani's theorem and an application to Nash-equilibria. Then, in a second section, we come back to fuzzy behaviours, in order to generate ordinal strategic utility functions. Finally, we define some solutions for cooperative models when the usual conditions are not satisfied.

SECTION ONE : FIXED POINTS AND NASH-EQUILIBRIUM

"Dans une partie, il faut ce point fixe ; une conscience, non pas immuable, mais qui s'analyse et qui évolue, en ne perdant ni sa tradition, ni le sens de sa tradition."

Maurice Barrès - Les Déracinés.

We are going to explain fixed point theorems when the considered universe is fuzzy. Usual fixed point theorems concern the invariance of an element when the set is transformed either by a function (Brouwer [1912]) or a correspondence (Kakutani [1941]).

I.1. Fixed points and fuzzy universe

What do the usual results become when any element can partially belong to the initial set ?

I.1.1. Definitions of a fuzzy Correspondence and a fuzzy fixed point

I.1.1.1. A fuzzy correspondence

Definition 1 : A fuzzy correspondence on the referential set X is a mapping $\mathcal{R}(.)$ of X towards $\mathcal{L}(X)$, where $\mathcal{L}(X)$ is the powerset of all fuzzy subsets[1] of X (cf Zadeh [1965]). We note $a(.)$ the membership function of the fuzzy subset $\mathcal{A}$ of X. If $\mathcal{R}(.)$ is a fuzzy correspondence on X, we also note $\mathcal{R}_X$ the fuzzy subset of X^2 which has a membership function $r(x,y) = r_x(y)$, for any (x,y) of X^2 (cf Goguen [1967] for the lattice structures). We note $\mathcal{M}(X)$ the set of fuzzy correspondences defined on X.

I.1.1.2. A fixed point of fuzzy correspondence

Definition 2 : A fixed point of a fuzzy correspondence $\mathcal{R}(.)$ defined on X is an element x^0 of X such that $\forall x \in X : r(x^0,x^0) \geq r(x^0,x)$. (i.e. $\forall x \in X,\ r_{x^0}(x^0) \geq r_{x^0}(x)$.)

Therefore, we can see that the problem of existence for a fixed point in the case of a fuzzy correspondence $\mathcal{R}(.) \in \mathcal{M}(X)$ is not a simple generalization of the very classic problem of the existence of a fixed point (cf. Kakutani) for a usual correspondence (Dixmier [1981], Eaves [1971], Todd [1976], Debreu [1956], Arrow & Hahn [1971] for the applications of fixed point

---

1 Fixed point theorem in an imprecise universe that we shall later prove (theorem II) is totally independent of the membership set M if this one is convex and preordered.

theorems to Walrasian economics). Actually, if we define a classic correspondence (CC) $F(.)$ of X towards $P(X)$ (where $P(X)$ is the powerset of usual subsets of X), then the element x^0 of X is a fixed point for $F(.)$ (namely $x^0 \in F(x^0)$) if and only if x^0 is a fixed point of the fuzzy correspondence $\mathcal{F}(.) \in \mathcal{M}(X)$ defined such that :

$$\forall x \in X, f_x(.) = \mathrm{f}_x(.),$$

where $\mathrm{f}_x(.)$ is the characteristic function of a usual subset $F(x)$ of X where $\mathcal{F}_{x^0} \neq \varnothing$.

I.1.2. Notions and results of convex analysis

(Let us consider that the convexity in this paragraph corresponds to the usual notion of convexity. In the following section, this convexity becomes fuzzy to generate more or less strong conditions for theorems of nonemptiness of the core.)

Definition 3 : Let $\mathcal{A}$ be a fuzzy subset belonging to $\mathcal{L}(X)$. We say that $\mathcal{A}$ is a convex fuzzy subset if and only if its membership function is quasi-concave :

$$\forall \mathcal{A} \in \mathcal{L}(X), \forall t \in [0,1], \mathcal{A} \text{ is a convex fss } \Leftrightarrow$$

$$\forall (x,y) \in X^2, a[tx + (1-t)y] \geq \mathrm{Min}[a(x), a(y)].$$

Definition 4 : The fuzzy correspondence $\mathcal{R}(.)$ is *convex* if for the vector topological space X, locally convex and Hausdorff-separated[2] and C a subset of X, nonempty, compact and convex, the fuzzy subset $\mathcal{R}_x \in \mathcal{L}(X)$ is a convex fuzzy subset of X.

Definition 5 : The fuzzy correspondence $\mathcal{R}(.)$ is *closed* if and only if the membership function $r_x(.)$ is upper semicontinuous.

Note : If $\mathcal{R}(.)$ is a fuzzy correspondence on a nonempty, compact and convex subset C, we consider $\mathcal{R}(.)$ to be defined on X with : $\mathcal{R}_x = \varnothing$ if $x \notin C$.

We should note that a topological space is Hausdorff-separated if it verifies the separation properties (it is the *canonical* form of the definition) establishing that for any two points in the considered space, there exists at least two disjoint open sets containing respectively both points. The metric spaces (topology associated to a distance) always verify this separation property. It is not systematically true for pure topological spaces. One of the important corollaries of this separation property is that any single element is closed, i.e. the intersection of all closed neighbourhoods (cf Berge [1959] and Gerard-Varet, Prevot & Thisse [1976], Chap.3).

---

2 A topological space is *Hausdorff-separated* if for any $x \in X$, the intersection of all the closed neighbourhoods of X is the single element $\{x\}$.
A topological space X is *locally convex* if $\forall x \in X$, any neighbourhood of X is convex.

I.1.3. Fixed point theorems

The following theorem includes two classic results by Brouwer and Kakutani (Butnariu [1982] from Berge [1959]).

THEOREM I : *Let X be a real vector topological space, locally convex and Hausdorff-separated. If $C \in P(X)$ is a compact, convex and nonempty subset of X and $F(.)$ a usual correspondence of C towards $P(C)$, having the two following properties : (1) $\forall x \in X, F(X)$ is convex, compact and nonempty, (2) the graph set $F = \cup_{x \in C}(\{x\} \times F(x))$ is a closed set in $X \times X$, then, $\exists x^0$; $F(x^0) \ni x^0$.*

We can see (Todd [1976], Rosenmüller [1981]) that if $X = R^m$ and $F(x) = \{f(x)\}$ with f(.) a continuous function of C into itself, we find Brouwer's theorem, which means that any continuous function on a subset of R^m passes through the diagonal. If $X = R^m$ and $F(.)$ is a usual upper semicontinuous correspondence, it is Kakutani's theorem (see Border [1985], Chap.6 and 15).

The general theorem with the help of which we prove the existence of a fixed point in a fuzzy universe deals (Butnariu [1980;1982;1985], Bose & Sahani [1987], Chang [1985] and Kaleva [1985]) with the application of theorem I to the usual correspondence $R(.)$ associated to the fuzzy correspondence $\mathcal{R}(.)$. Each fuzzy correspondence $\mathcal{R}(.)$ defined on X where $\mathcal{R}_x = \emptyset$ if $x \notin C$ (the compact, convex and nonempty subset of X) can be associated to a usual correspondence $R(.)$ of C towards $P(C)$ such that :

$$\forall x \in C, R(x) = \{y \in C \ ; r_x(y) = \text{Max}_{z \in C}\, r_x(z)\}.$$

THEOREM II : *Let X be a real vector topological space, locally convex and Hausdorff-separated ; let C be a nonempty, compact and convex subset of X. If $\mathcal{R}(.)$ is a convex fuzzy correspondence, closed in C, then $\mathcal{R}(.)$ has a fixed point in C.*

Proof: We are going to use theorem I in order to prove that the usual correspondence associated to $\mathcal{R}(.)$, that we note $R(.)$, has a fixed point in C. This only means that we must prove the conditions of theorem I to hold.

α- convexity of $R(.)$.

Let us consider any three elements $\{x, y, z\}$ of the referential set C, and $t \in [0,1]$. If $(y, z) \in R(x) \times R(x)$, this means from the definition of $R(.)$, because $\mathcal{R}(.)$ is convex :

$$r_x[ty + (1-t)z] \geq \text{Min}[r_x(y), r_x(z)] = \text{Sup}_{w \in C}\, r_x(w).$$

Hence, $[ty + (1-t)z] \in R(x)$ and therefore $R(.)$ is convex.

β- nonemptiness of $R(.)$.

Since $r_x(.)$ is upper semicontinuous (by the closure of the fuzzy correspondence $\mathcal{R}(.)$ on C, def.5), it implies for the compact set C, that $r_x(.)$ reaches its maximum on C. Let us consider y as this maximum. Therefore :

$$r_x(y) = \text{Max}_{z \in C}\, r_x(z),$$

which means that y belong to $R(x)$. Hence, $R(x) \neq \emptyset$.

γ- compactedness of $R(x)$, $\forall x \in X$.

If $(x_a)_{a \in J}$ (J the ranking set) is a sequence in $R(x)$ and x^0 the limit point of this sequence, we can write :

$$r(x, x_a) \geq r(x, y) \text{ (i.e. } r_x(x_a) \geq r_x(y)).$$

This is true for any y of X and any a of J ; moreover : $r_x(x^0) = \lim_{a \in J}[\text{Sup}\, r_x(x_a)] \geq r_x(y)$, for any y belonging to C, because of the upper semicontinuity of $r_x(.)$. Hence, $r_x(x^0) = \lim_{a \in J}[\text{Sup}\, r_x(x_a)]$ means, following the definition of $R(x)$, that x^0 belongs to $R(x)$: then, $R(x)$ is closed. Since C is compact, C is bounded, hence $R(x)$ is also bounded. In conclusion, $R(x)$ is compact.

δ- the closure of graph $R = \cup_{x \in C}(\{x\} \times R(x))$.

If $(x_a)_{a \in J}$, $(y_a)_{a \in J}$ are two sequences of C with the couple (x_a, y_a) included in graph R, for any a, $a \in J$, we can write : $\forall y \in C, \forall a \in J, r(x_a, y_a) \geq r(x_a, y)$, or again, $r_{x_a}(y_a) \geq r_{x_a}(y)$. Let us assume the limit of x_a to be x^0 while y_a leads to y^0, in X. Then :

$$\forall y \in C,\, r_{x^0}(y^0) = \lim_{a \in J}[\text{Sup}\, r_{x_a}(y_a)] \geq \lim_{a \in J}[\text{Sup}\, r_{x_a}(y)].$$

Since $r(., y)$ is also upper semicontinuous (by the closure of $\mathcal{R}(.)$ in C), we can write :

$$\forall y \in C,\, r_{x^0}(y^0) \geq r_{x^0}(y).$$

This means that (x^0, y^0) belongs to graph R, since by compactedness of $R(x^0)$, $x^0 \in C$ and $y^0 \in R(x^0)$, where $\forall y \in C$, $r_{x^0}(y^0) \geq r_{x^0}(y)$. Therefore : $r_{x^0}(y^0) = \text{Max}_{y \in C}\, r_{x^0}(y)$, : $x^0 \in R(x^0)$.

The four conditions of theorem I are satisfied ; the usual correspondence $R(.)$ has a fixed point in C. We must now prove that if $R(.)$ has a fixed point, then $\mathcal{R}(.)$ also has one, in C.

ε- $\exists x \in C$; $\mathcal{R}_x \ni x$.

This proof is quite simple : if $R(.)$ is a CC admitting a fixed point, denoted x^0, this means :

$$\exists x^0 \in C ; R(x^0) \ni x^0.$$

The definition of $R(x^0)$ leads to :

$$R(x^0) = \{y \in C ; r_{x^0}(y) = \text{Max}_{z \in C}\, r_{x^0}(z)\}.$$

Therefore, $\forall y \in C, r_{x^0}(x^0) \geq r_{x^0}(y)$. Hence, we can write : $\forall y \in C, r(x^0, x^0) \geq r(x^0, y)$ which exactly corresponds to the definition of a fixed point for a fuzzy correspondence.

□

We can notice theorem II, generalized by Brouwer and Kakutani to be exclusively based upon a topological structure which is not necessarily metric. Butnariu's generalized theorem [1982] (the proof we gave is adaptated from Butnariu's one and recovered by Bose & Sahani [1987] as Chitra & Subrahmanyam [1987]) implies - when we shall apply these results to the cooperative games - cardinal payoffs and utility functions that do not respect the independence axiom. Nevertheless, this theorem is an exception with Kaleva [1985] and Heilpern [1981] which are also founded on topological structures, but f-topological in the meaning of Chang [1968], namely founded upon the two particular notions of f-continuity and f-topology. There also exists fixed points theorems for fuzzy numbers (Badard [1984]) but these have nothing to do with our analysis and rely upon *fuzzy arithmetic*, based on possibility distributions (see Billot [1987b], Chap.1).

The extensions of theorem II, realized by Bose & Sahani [1987], correspond to more particular *specifications*, related to a particular choice of metric ; Hausdorff is one of them as Heilpern's one in his 1981 paper, which is a mix of a metric - usual distance - and a membership function. It is the same for Chitra & Subrahmanyam [1987] or Liu [1985] and that is why we have concentrated our efforts on Butnariu's theorem which remains valid for any topological structure, metric or not.

I.2. Nash-equilibria for fuzzy non-cooperative games

This approach essentially consists in generalizing Nash's [1950] contribution for the characterization of the conditions under which a non-cooperative game has a balanced issue, namely satisfying everyone, or at least, satisfying enough players so that they *continue* to choose the same strategy. Actually, the reason why economic models (in their normative and microanalytic development) often need fixed point theorems, derives from the fact that a fixed point of an application or a correspondence describes an *invariance* situation, i.e. a state that always remains even if the mapping (that application or the correspondence) is mathematically active. If the mapping contains a particular discourse - which is the case in economics - for example related to the agents' rational behaviour (consumers optimizing their utility, producers maximizing their profit as in a Walrasian economy), this invariance becomes the *keeping* symbol of a particular chosen state ; this means a sufficiently satisfying situation for the agents to decide them not to change it.

In this case, the agents are players, i.e. decision-makers whose choices are *interactive*. They have a set of strategies - prices, quantities, goods, etc... - into which they choose. We say a game to be *fuzzy* when players have fuzzy preferences.

I.2.1. Preliminary notions

We consider a game with *n* players. We say that the cardinal of the set of players is *n* (i.e. if *S* is a society of *n* players : $|S| = n$). This game is - as Butnariu [1979] said it - "*a set of rules allowing the formal information exchange*" between the participants, namely the elements of *S*. It becomes obvious that looking for "*the best exchange rule of information*" depends on the nature of information but also on the subjective perception of each player, perception of the exchange rules or objects of the exchange.

It was implicit, since the beginning of this work that $\underline{M} = [0,1]$ (even if theorem II is independent of $\underline{M}$). Following Butnariu [1978], we denote *U* the universe of informations or the set of the objects. In the same way as in chapter one, $a(x)$ denotes the membership level of object $x \in U$ to the fuzzy subset $\mathcal{A}$ of *U*. By definition (Kaufmann [1973], Prevot [1977]), the product of two fuzzy subsets $\mathcal{A}$ and $\mathcal{B}$ is a fuzzy subset defined such that :

$$[a \times b](x) = a(y) \times b(z) \text{ if } x = (y,z) \in U$$
$$= 0 \text{ else.}$$

Let us note that this definition of the product of two fuzzy subsets allows the multiplication (therefore the addition) of membership levels. This definition is necessary to define the non-cooperative game model that we present (cf. Butnariu [1979], [1982]).

α- Let $\mathcal{R}(.,.)$ be a fuzzy relation between $\mathcal{A}$ and $\mathcal{B}$ and $\mathcal{S}(.,.)$ be another fuzzy relation between $\mathcal{B}$ and $\mathcal{C}$. Then $\mathcal{S} \circ \mathcal{R}(.,.)$ describes a fuzzy relation between $\mathcal{A}$ and $\mathcal{C}$ defined as follows :

$$\mathcal{S} \circ \mathcal{R}(x,t) = \text{Sup}\{\mathcal{R}(x,y) \times \mathcal{S}(y,t) \,;\, y \in U\} \text{ if } (x,t) \in U$$
$$= 0 \text{ else.}$$

β- If $\mathcal{X} \in \mathcal{L}(\mathcal{A})$ (where $\mathcal{L}(\mathcal{A})$ is the set of all the fuzzy subsets included in $\mathcal{A}$), then the image of $\mathcal{X}$ by $\mathcal{R}(.,.)$ in a fuzzy subset $\mathcal{R}(\mathcal{X})$ whose membership function $r_{\mathcal{X}}(.)$ is defined as follows :

$$r_{\mathcal{X}}(y) = \text{Sup}\{x(x) \times \mathcal{R}(x,y) \,;\, x \in U\}.$$

Here, we propose an additive form of membership function. We must say that if this function derives - not from the agents' subjective evaluation, but - from an objective measure of the model, the reluctance that we have related about cardinalism disappears.

I.2.2. Fuzzy non-cooperative games

I.2.2.1. The model

The concept of a *n-person fuzzy cooperative game* can be mathematically described as a data set :

$$G = \{ST_1, \dots, ST_i, \dots, ST_n; Y_1, \dots, Y_i, \dots, Y_n; \mathcal{E}_1, \dots, \mathcal{E}_i, \dots, \mathcal{E}_n\},$$

where N is the set of players ($|N| = n$; i:1,...,n), such that for any player $i \in N$, the four following definitions (we call them the *4D*) are satisfied.

1- $ST_i = \{st_1^i, \dots, st_{n(i)}^i\}$ ($n(i) \in N$) is the player i's set of pure strategies.

2- Y_i is a usual subset of $R^{n(i)}$. Its elements are called "the player i's *strategic arrangements*".

If $w^i = \{w_1^i, \dots, w_{n(i)}^i\} \in Y_i$, then w_j^i is called the *weight* assigned by player i to the pure strategy st_j^i.

A n-dimension vector w, $w = \{w^1, \dots, w^n\} \in Z = \prod_{i \in N} Y_i$ is called *strategic choice in G*.

3- $\mathcal{E}_i \in \mathcal{L}(Z)$ and $\forall w \in Z$, $e_i(w)$ is the *possibility level* of the strategic choice w evaluated by the player i (see Billot [1987b], Chap.1).

4- $Z_i = \prod_{j \in N - \{i\}} Y_j$, $W_i = \mathcal{L}(Z_i) \times Y_i$, and $s_i = (\mathcal{A}_i, w^i)$ is called the player i's *strategic conception* in G.

The following axiom becomes necessary :

AXi : If $\mathcal{A}_i \in \mathcal{L}(Z_i)$ and $\mathcal{A}_i \neq \emptyset$, then $e_i[\mathcal{A}_i] \neq \emptyset$, i.e. : $\exists s_i \in W_i$; $e_i[\mathcal{A}_i](w_i) \neq \emptyset$.

Let us comment on these definitions.

1- The first proposition means that each player i has a set of pure strategies. Its cardinal can vary from an agent to another.

2- The second proposition allows player i to mix different pure strategies. This permits the game to become convex, by going from ST_i to Y_i convex.

3- Each player i assigns a level of possibility deriving from his belief on the strategic choice to the *defined strategic choice*, namely the vector of pure strategic combinations. This means, that their is no rigid relation (of an *exclusive* type, as it happens with probabilistic beliefs) between the player i's believes about all the strategic choices belonging to Z. In other words, $e_i(w)$ just measures the membership level of possibility (*I believe that it is very possible that...*) of w and not the probability of appearance of w. This possibility is purely subjective and does not influence the possibility that i assigns to the other strategic choices, what we sum up by saying that there is no mass-unity constraint ; in other words, the sum of possibilities is not necessarily equal to 1 even though e_i is defined on [0,1].

4- The fourth proposition explains the player i's conception to be well defined with the fuzzy subset $\mathcal{A}_i$ issued from his possibility distribution upon the strategies chosen by the other players, acknowledging the fact that i had chosen w^i as mixed strategy. This intuitively corresponds to the *best answer* notion, even though it means here *more or less* good answers.

As a conclusion, let us recall that the axiom AXi means for any information set dealing with the other players' behaviour, that i is always able to build up a strategy - in Butnariu's words [1978], [1979], a *regular strategy* -, namely a strategic conception that may be used as an answer to fuzziness (actually, not well-known) of the other players' behaviour.

I.2.2.2. Definition and player's preferences

Definition 6 : Let G be a n-person fuzzy non-cooperative game satisfying the $4D$ and AXi. A *play* is a vector $s = (s_1, \ldots, s_n) \in W = \prod_{i \in N} W_i$.

Let us note that solving the problem of the best information exchange in G is equivalent to find the best play in G, since a play s in G is a mathematical representation of information exchanges inside the game.

Definition 7 : Let $s_i = (\mathcal{A}_i, w^i)$ and $s_i' = \left(\mathcal{A}_i', w'^i\right)$ be two i's strategic conceptions. We say that s_i is a *better strategic conception* than s_i' (we write $\mathcal{R}(s_i, s_i') > \mathcal{R}(s_i', s_i)$) if and only if : $e_i[\mathcal{A}_i](w^i) > e_i[\mathcal{A}_i'](w'^i)$.

This means that the strategic conception s_i is better than s_i' if the first one is considered as more possible than the second.

Definition 8 : Let $s = (s_1, \ldots, s_n)$ and $s' = (s_1', \ldots, s_n')$ be two plays of a game where $\forall i \in N$, $s_i' = \left(\mathcal{A}_i', w'^i\right)$. We say that s is *socially preferred* to s' (i.e. $\mathcal{R}(s, s') > \mathcal{R}(s', s)$) if and only if : $\forall i \in N$, $e_i[\mathcal{A}_i](w^i) > e_i[\mathcal{A}_i'](w'^i)$.

What does it all mean ? Let us consider that the players have received some information. Each player i belonging to N can build up a fuzzy subset $\mathcal{A}_i \in \mathcal{L}(Z_i)$ and choose $w^i \in Y_i$ to define his strategic conception $s_i = (\mathcal{A}_i, w^i)$ (def.4 of the $4D$). Each player does the same thing at the same time ; the game is therefore based on a play s composed of the n strategic conceptions s_i. But all of them are *more or less* possible because of the rules of the game G. We can naturally consider as rational, the players who prefer strategic conceptions that are the *most possible*, therefore, the *best possible* plays. It is what Butnariu calls a *regular play*. The *regularity* of the play derives from the transition of the strategic choice possibility towards the individual conception and finally towards the play.

Let us now consider $\mathcal{A}_i^*$, $i \in N$, to be defined by two players from their exchanges of information ; a kind of *non-constraining cooperation* (see for this concept Moulin [1977] and [1979]) which then implies each player i to define the best relative strategic conception ($s_i = s_i^*$).

It then becomes easy to consider that rational players choose s_i^* such that s^* forms the best possible play, i.e. the *the socially most preferable* play that can be reached by using the given information deriving from $\prod_{i \in N} \mathcal{A}_i^*$.

Definition 9 : A possible solution (*PS*) of the game G is a play $s^*, s^* = (s_1^*, \ldots, s_n^*)$, where $\forall i \in N$, $s_i^* = \left(\mathcal{A}_i^*, w^{*i}\right)$, such that for any other play s, $s = (s_1, \ldots, s_n)$, where $\forall i \in N, s_i = (\mathcal{A}_i^*, w^i)$, the play s cannot be *socially preferable* to s^*, i.e. : $\forall w^i \in Y_i, \forall i \in N, e_i[\mathcal{A}_i^*](w^{*i}) \geq e_i[\mathcal{A}_i^*](w^i)$.

The rules defining the fuzzy games may allow the players to collaborate (that is to exchange some information) without inducing a *formal* coalition. In other words, this game structure, based on the individual and social comparisons of strategic conceptions, allows a description of the agents' collaboration without modifying the non-cooperative nature of the game. This *non-constraining collaboration* - we must insist on this concept since it greatly differs from the cooperation one that is related to interest *groups* - must be considered as a pure information exchange which does not imply the *collaborating* players's decisions to be consistent with the ones that would derive from direct cooperation.

Mathematically, a *non-constraining* collaboration of the players in a non-cooperative game consists in playing as described below :

$$s^* = (s_1^*, \ldots, s_n^*) \text{ where } \forall i \in N, s_i^* = \left(\mathcal{A}_i^*, w^{*i}\right) \text{ with}$$

$$a_i^* = (w^1, \ldots, w^{i-1}, w^{i+1}, \ldots, w^n) = 1 \text{ if } \forall j \in N - \{i\}, w^j = w^{*j},$$

$$= 0 \text{ otherwise.}$$

We must now define the equilibrium.

Definition 10 : An *equilibrium point* of the game G is a possible solution (*PS*) , $s^* = (s_1^*, \ldots, s_n^*)$ where $s_i^* = \left(\mathcal{A}_i^*, w^{*i}\right), \forall i \in N$, if the play s^* satisfies the *non-constraining condition* written above .

As in the traditional approach, the non-cooperative fuzzy game equilibrium corresponds to the fixed point of a correspondence defined from the individual preferences. We now define on one hand the individual fuzzy preference (according to Butnariu [1979]) and on the other, the social fuzzy preference.

Definition 11 : The *individual fuzzy preference* of a player $i \in N$ is the fuzzy relation $\mathcal{E}_i(.,.)$ on $\mathcal{L}(W \times W)$ (with W corresponding to $\mathcal{L}(Z) \times Y$) defined as follows :

$$\mathcal{E}_i(s, \bar{s}) = \text{Max}\{e_i[\mathcal{A}_i](\overline{w^i}), e_i[\mathcal{A}_i](w^i)\} \cdot \prod_{j \in N - \{i\}} e_j[\mathcal{A}_j](\overline{w^j}),$$

for two plays $s = (s_1, \ldots, s_n)$ and $\bar{s} = (\bar{s}_1, \ldots, \bar{s}_n)$ where s is *preferred* i : $\Leftrightarrow$ $\mathcal{E}_i(s, \bar{s}) > \mathcal{E}_i(\bar{s}, s)$.

We can notice $\mathcal{E}_i(.,.)$ to be a cardinal measure of i's preference. This preference evaluates which strategic conception is most possible according to the other players' ones.

Definition 12 : The *social preference* is a fuzzy relation $\mathcal{E}_S(.,.)$ on $\mathcal{L}(W \times W)$ defined as follows :

$$\mathcal{E}_S(s, \bar{s}) = \prod_{i \in N} \mathcal{E}_i(s, \bar{s}), \forall (s, \bar{s}) \in W \times W \text{ (where } W = \mathcal{L}(Z) \times Y \text{).}$$

In the same way, we can notice $\mathcal{E}_S(.,.)$ to be a cardinal measure of preference.

I.2.3. Existence theorem of an equilibrium for a non-cooperative fuzzy game

THEOREM III : *Let* $\overline{s} = (\overline{s}_1, \ldots, \overline{s}_n)$ *be a play of* G *where* $\overline{s}_i = (\overline{\mathcal{A}}_i, \overline{w}^i)$, $\forall i \in N$. *If* $\overline{\mathcal{A}}_i \neq \emptyset$, *for any* $i \in N$, *then both following propositions are equivalent : (1)* $\overline{s}$ *is a PS of* G, *(2)* $\overline{s}$ *is a fixed point in* $\mathcal{E}_S(.,.)$.

Proof : α:(1) $\Rightarrow$ (2) :

Let us consider a player $i \in N$. If $\overline{s}$ is a *PS* of G (def.7) :

$$\Rightarrow \mathcal{E}_i(\overline{s},\overline{s}) = \mathrm{Max}\{e_i[\overline{\mathcal{A}}_i](\overline{w}^i), e_i[\overline{\mathcal{A}}_i](\overline{w}^i)\} \cdot \Pi_{j \in N-\{i\}} e_j[\overline{\mathcal{A}}_j](\overline{w}^j)$$
$$= e_i[\overline{\mathcal{A}}_i](\overline{w}^i) \cdot \Pi_{j \in N-\{i\}} e_j[\overline{\mathcal{A}}_j](\overline{w}^j)$$
$$= \Pi_{i \in N} e_i[\overline{\mathcal{A}}_i](\overline{w}^i).$$

We can write, since $\overline{s}$ is a *PS* of G :

$$\forall s \in W, \mathcal{E}_i(\overline{s},s) = \mathrm{Max}\{e_i[\overline{\mathcal{A}}_i](\overline{w}^i), e_i[\overline{\mathcal{A}}_i](w^i)\} \cdot \Pi_{j \in N-\{i\}} e_j[\overline{\mathcal{A}}_j](w^j),$$

since $\forall j \in N$, $e_j[\overline{\mathcal{A}}_j](\overline{w}^j) \geq e_j[\overline{\mathcal{A}}_j](w^j)$ which implies :

$$\Pi_{j \in N-\{i\}} e_j[\overline{\mathcal{A}}_j](\overline{w}^j) \geq \Pi_{j \in N-\{i\}} e_j[\overline{\mathcal{A}}_j](w^j).$$

Now, we must multiply each side by $e_i[\overline{\mathcal{A}}_i](\overline{w}^i)$:

$$e_i[\overline{\mathcal{A}}_i](\overline{w}^i) \cdot \Pi_{j \in N-\{i\}} e_j[\overline{\mathcal{A}}_j](\overline{w}^j) \geq e_i[\overline{\mathcal{A}}_i](\overline{w}^i) \cdot \Pi_{j \in N-\{i\}} e_j[\overline{\mathcal{A}}_j](w^j) \text{ i.e.}$$
$$\Pi_{i \in N} e_i[\overline{\mathcal{A}}_i](\overline{w}^i) \geq e_i[\overline{\mathcal{A}}_i](\overline{w}^i) \cdot \Pi_{j \in N-\{i\}} e_j[\overline{\mathcal{A}}_j](w^j).$$

i.e. : $\mathcal{E}_i(\overline{s},\overline{s}) \geq \mathcal{E}_i(\overline{s},s)$.

Since, $\mathcal{E}_S(\overline{s},\overline{s}) = \Pi_{i \in N} \mathcal{E}_i(\overline{s},\overline{s})$, we can write : $\forall s \in W$, $\mathcal{E}_S(\overline{s},\overline{s}) \geq \mathcal{E}_S(\overline{s},s)$, which corresponds to the definition of a fixed point for the relation $\mathcal{E}_S(.,.)$.

β:(2) $\Rightarrow$ (1) :

If $\overline{s}$ is a fixed point of $\mathcal{E}_S(.,.)$, this means :

$\forall s \in W$, $\mathcal{E}_S(\overline{s},\overline{s}) \geq \mathcal{E}_S(\overline{s},s)$,

i.e. $\Pi_{i \in N} \mathcal{E}_i(\overline{s},\overline{s}) \geq \Pi_{i \in N} \mathcal{E}_i(\overline{s},s)$.

The definitions of $\mathcal{E}_i(\overline{s},\overline{s})$ and $\mathcal{E}_i(\overline{s},s)$ which appeared in α) stay valid. Hence, we have just to prove : $\forall w^i \in Y_i$, $\forall i \in N$, $e_i[\overline{\mathcal{A}}_i](\overline{w}^i) \geq e_i[\overline{\mathcal{A}}_i](w^i)$.

Let us define for any player the following play :

$$s^{(i)} = (s_1^{(i)}, \ldots, s_n^{(i)}) \text{ where } s_j^{(i)} = (\overline{\mathcal{A}}_j, w_{(i)}^j) \text{ with,}$$

$$w_{(i)}^j = \overline{w^j} \text{ if } j \neq i \text{ and } w_{(i)}^j = w^j \text{ if } j = i.$$

Hence, we rewrite our condition of individual preference while assuming the opposite hypothesis of which we need, i.e. $\forall j \in N$, $e_i[\overline{\mathcal{A}}_i](\overline{w^i}) < e_i[\overline{\mathcal{A}}_i](w^i)$, and let us show that it leads to a contradiction.

$$\mathcal{E}_i(\overline{s}, s^{(i)}) = \text{Max}\{e_i[\overline{\mathcal{A}}_i](\overline{w^i}), e_i[\overline{\mathcal{A}}_i](w_{(i)}^i)\} \cdot \Pi_{j \in N-\{i\}} e_j[\overline{\mathcal{A}}_j](w_{(i)}^j)$$

$$= e_i[\overline{\mathcal{A}}_i](w^i) \cdot \Pi_{j \in N-\{i\}} e_j[\overline{\mathcal{A}}_j](\overline{w^j}).$$

Let us calculate $\mathcal{E}_j(\overline{s}, s^{(i)})$ for any $j \neq i$:

$$\mathcal{E}_j(\overline{s}, s^{(i)}) = \text{Max}\{e_j[\overline{\mathcal{A}}_j](\overline{w^j}), e_j[\overline{\mathcal{A}}_j](w_{(i)}^j)\} \cdot \Pi_{t \in N-\{j\}} e_t[\overline{\mathcal{A}}_t](w_{(i)}^t)$$

$$= \text{Max}\{e_j[\overline{\mathcal{A}}_j](\overline{w^j}), e_j[\overline{\mathcal{A}}_j](\overline{w^j})\} \cdot e_i[\overline{\mathcal{A}}_i](w^i) \cdot \Pi_{t \in N-\{i,j\}} e_t[\overline{\mathcal{A}}_t](\overline{w^t})$$

$$= e_j[\overline{\mathcal{A}}_j](\overline{w^j}) \cdot e_i[\overline{\mathcal{A}}_i](w^i) \cdot \Pi_{t \in N-\{i,j\}} e_t[\overline{\mathcal{A}}_t](\overline{w^t})$$

$$= e_i[\overline{\mathcal{A}}_i](w^i) \cdot \Pi_{j \in N-\{i\}} e_j[\overline{\mathcal{A}}_j](\overline{w^j}).$$

It follows :

$$\forall i, j \in N, \ \mathcal{E}_j(\overline{s}, s^{(i)}) = e_i[\overline{\mathcal{A}}_i](w^i) \cdot \Pi_j e_j[\overline{\mathcal{A}}_j](\overline{w^j}).$$

This allows to say :

$$\mathcal{E}_S(\overline{s}, s^{(i)}) > \mathcal{E}_S(\overline{s}, \overline{s}) \qquad (A)$$

since, $\forall j \in N$, $\mathcal{E}_j(\overline{s}, \overline{s}) = \Pi_{j \in N} e_j[\overline{\mathcal{A}}_j](\overline{w^j})$, and, $e_i[\overline{\mathcal{A}}_i](w^i) > e_i[\overline{\mathcal{A}}_i](\overline{w^i})$.

Equation (A) contradicts the proposition defining $\overline{s}$ as a fixed point of $\mathcal{E}_S(.,.)$, which was the starting proposition. Hence, it is necessary for $\overline{s}$ to be a fixed point of the fuzzy relation $\mathcal{E}_S(.,.)$:

$$\forall i \in N, \ e_i[\overline{\mathcal{A}}_i](\overline{w^i}) \geq e_i[\overline{\mathcal{A}}_i](w^i).$$

It follows that $\overline{s}$ is by definition a PS of G. We have proved the formal equivalence between a fixed point of the $\mathcal{E}_S(.,.)$ relation and a possible solution of the fuzzy game.

□

Remark : theorem I is no more true when one of the players (noted i) is such that $e_i[\overline{\mathcal{A}}_i](\overline{w^i}) = 0$. Thus, it is necessary to exclude this occurrence.

LEMMA : *There exists no agent i, $i \in N$, such that if $\overline{s}$ is a fixed point of $\mathcal{E}_S(.,.)$, then for $\overline{s}_i = (\overline{\mathcal{A}}_i, \overline{w^i})$: $e_i[\overline{\mathcal{A}}_i](\overline{w^i}) = 0$.*

Proof : Let us assume the player i, $i \in N$, to be such that :

$$e_i[\overline{\mathcal{A}}_i](\overline{w^i}) = 0.$$

Since $\forall j \in N$, $\mathcal{E}_j(\bar{s},\bar{s}) = \prod_{j \in N} e_j[\bar{\mathcal{A}}_j](\overline{w^j})$, this means that :

$$\forall j \in N,\ \mathcal{E}_j(\bar{s},\bar{s}) = 0 \Rightarrow \mathcal{E}_S(\bar{s},\bar{s}) = 0.$$

Since $\bar{s}$ is a fixed point of $\mathcal{E}_S(.,.)$, this means that : $\forall s \in W$, $\mathcal{E}_S(\bar{s},\bar{s}) = \mathcal{E}_S(\bar{s},s) = 0$.
If $\mathcal{E}_S(\bar{s},s) = 0$, and this for any play s of W, then : $\forall s \in N$, $\prod_{j \in N} \mathcal{E}_j(\bar{s},s) = 0$.

If this last equation is true for any play s of W, it is true for any play s', $s' \in W$, with $s_j' = (\bar{\mathcal{A}}_j, w_j')$.

Let us calculate $\prod_{j \in N} \mathcal{E}_j(\bar{s},s')$.

$$\mathcal{E}_i(\bar{s},s') = \text{Max}\left\{ e_i[\bar{\mathcal{A}}_i](\overline{w^i}), e_i[\bar{\mathcal{A}}_i](w'^i)\right\} \cdot \prod_{j \in N-\{i\}} e_j[\bar{\mathcal{A}}_j](w'^j)$$

$$= e_i[\bar{\mathcal{A}}_i](w'^i) \cdot \prod_{j \in N-\{i\}} e_j[\bar{\mathcal{A}}_j](w'^j) \text{ because } e_i[\bar{\mathcal{A}}_i](\overline{w^i}) = 0$$

$$= \prod_{j \in N} e_j[\bar{\mathcal{A}}_j](w'^j) \qquad (A)$$

$$\mathcal{E}_j(\bar{s},s') = \text{Max}\left\{ e_j[\bar{\mathcal{A}}_j](\overline{w^j}), e_j[\bar{\mathcal{A}}_j](w'^j)\right\} \cdot \prod_{t \in N-\{j\}} e_t[\bar{\mathcal{A}}_t](w'^t)$$

$$= e_j[\bar{\mathcal{A}}_j](\overline{w''^j}) \cdot \prod_{t \in N-\{j\}} e_t[\bar{\mathcal{A}}_t](w'^t) \qquad (B)$$

where $\overline{w''^j}$ means the two strategic conceptions to be possible ($\neq 0$) without knowing *a priori* which one is *most possible*.

If $\prod_{j \in N} \mathcal{E}_j(\bar{s},s') = 0$ since $\forall j \in N-\{i\}$, $e_j[\bar{\mathcal{A}}_j](w'^j) \neq 0$, this means that $e_i[\bar{\mathcal{A}}_i](w'^i) = 0$ is necessary (with equations (A) and (B)). Axiom AXi ensures for a given information set, $\bar{\mathcal{A}}_i$, the existence of a strategic conception such that its *possibility* always differs from 0 (that is, for a given $\bar{\mathcal{A}}_i$, there exists w'^i, $w'^i \in Y_i$; $e_i[\bar{\mathcal{A}}_i](w'^i) \neq 0$). By knowing s' to be any play of W, with the only particularity of being based upon the same information set for i, we can easily conclude that there is no player who estimates a strategic conception which corresponds to a fixed point of the social relation of preference as *impossible*.

□

Before commenting this result, let us remember this model to be firmly inspired by Butnariu [1979], [1982] for the very notion of a *strategic conception* and basic assumptions. For the other concepts, we free ourselves from Butnariu's works because the individual relations of preference like the fundamental sets of the game G are different. Nevertheless, the originality of such an approach and especially the introduction of the *non-constraining cooperation* into non-cooperative games, (often noticed, Rosenmüller [1981], Owen [1982], Schleicher [1979] and Moulin [1981] but never explicitly introduced into usual games) are contained as a whole in Butnariu's papers devoted to fuzzy non-cooperative games.

The theorem that ends this section - which we do not prove since it is identical to the proof of theorem I - classically associates an equilibrium point to a fixed point of a correspondence.

Theorem I allows to characterize the possible solutions of the game G by the set of fixed points of the social relation of preference. Henceforth, the possible solutions are equilibria if they verify the following property (def.8) : $\bar{s}$ is a Nash-equilibrium of G if and only if : $\bar{s} = (\bar{s}_1,\ldots,\bar{s}_n)$, $\bar{s}_i = (\bar{\mathcal{A}}_i, \bar{w}^i)$,

$$\bar{a}_i = (w^1,\ldots,w^{i-1},w^{i+1},\ldots,w^n) = 1 \text{ if } \forall j \in N-\{i\},\ w^j = \bar{w}^j,$$

$$= 0 \text{ else.}$$

Let us remark $\overline{W}$ the set of all plays $\bar{s}$ of G to satisfy this property (which cancels the fuzzy aspect of the information sets). Such a game - reducing W into $\overline{W}$ - is called *with perfect information.* This is obvious because the information becomes Boolean (i.e. $\underline{M} = \{0,1\}$ and $\forall i \neq j, \bar{\mathcal{A}}_i = \bar{\mathcal{A}}_j$). The fuzzy aspect of the game just dealing with the plausibility - the *possibility* - of strategic conceptions belonging to $\overline{W}$ and the individual relations of preference, we can conceive a concept of *balanced solution* which corresponds to a Nash-equilibrium.

A play of G with perfect information is then totally defined by the following vector of strategic choices, $\bar{w} = (\bar{w}^1,\ldots,\bar{w}^n) \in Z = \prod_{i \in N} Y_i$.

Definition 13 : We call *reduced social preference*, the fuzzy relation $\mathcal{E}_S^*(.,.) \in \mathcal{L}(Z \times Z)$ such that : $\mathcal{E}_S^*(w,w') = \mathcal{E}_S(s,s')$, where s and s' are plays with complete information respectively determined from vectors w and w'.

THEOREM IVa : *Let* $\bar{w} = (\bar{w}^1,\ldots,\bar{w}^n)$ *be a vector of* Z *and* $\bar{s}$ *a play with perfect information determined by* $\bar{w}$. *It is equivalent to write : (1)* $\bar{s}$ *is a Nash-equilibrium of* G, *(2)* $\bar{w}$ *is a fixed point of the reduced social preference* $\mathcal{E}_S^*(.,.)$ *of* G.

The existence of a Nash-equilibrium for a non-cooperative fuzzy game depends on the characteristics of the fuzzy correspondence $\mathcal{E}_S^*(.,.)$. Under the same conditions as in theorem II (§I), we obtain the following existence theorem :

THEOREM IVb : *Let* Z *(* $Z = \prod_{i \in N} Y_i$ *) be a real convex topological space, Hausdorff-separated, nonempty and compact. If* $\mathcal{E}_S^*(.,.)$ *is a convex fuzzy relation, closed in* Z, *then* G *has a Nash-equilibrium.*

The proof is equivalent to the one of theorem II.

I.2.4. Analysis and comments

By examining the preceding theorems, we clearly see that the method used for analyzing equilibria for non-cooperative fuzzy games is identical to the one of a usual game. It is based on the equivalence between a fixed point and a Nash-equilibrium, the correspondence being fuzzy or not. The application of theorem IVb to fuzzy economic games (Ponsard [1986], [1987]) really concludes by relevant results according to the concept of *non-constraining collaboration.* Nevertheless, we can regret theorem IVb to need, in order to be proved, a modification of the assumptions of fuzzy games that were described in paragraph I.2.2.1. In particular, the assumption of complete information suggests a question with no answer : does there exist an equilibrium for a fuzzy game if the set of strategic choices remains fuzzy ? The second section, by differently defining fuzziness (the fuzzy relations of preference were, here, cardinal as in Butnariu's works) thanks to a new assumption, we modify players' behaviour in a fuzzy game.

We know (Owen [1982], Aubin [1986]) the standard behaviour of a rational player in a non-cooperative game not to be as precise as what we call a *cautious behaviour* (minimizing losses) or a *sophisticated one* (based on the successive elimination of dominated strategies). Actually, the rules which define the game allow the appearance of Nash-equilibrium to be plausible. But, we are not necessarily able to deduce what strategy is going to be chosen by each player. This means that when a game has many (nonequivalent) Nash-equilibria, a player can rationally choose an equilibrium strategy if and only if he knows which equilibrium the other players have chosen.

If we try to create a *symbolic* scenario explaining a non-cooperative game process, we must delimit two different steps. First, the players have to agree on the choice of an issue (a *play* would write Butnariu), this would constitute a formal agreement. Then, all effective communication between players would be cut off. Finally, they decide their strategic choice (or their strategic conception) without being committed by the promise they made to play this strategy. If there are many chances for the n-tuple of strategies to be a Nash-equilibrium, there are also many chances for this issue to be effectively realized. It is the same in a fuzzy game when plays issued from the conceptions only depend on strategic choices, which corresponds to the case of perfect information (i.e. $\overline{\mathcal{A}}_i = \overline{\mathcal{A}}_j, \forall i \neq j$).

Nevertheless, it is clear that these kinds of scenarii, explaining the process of a non-cooperative game solution, are related with an evident step of *non-constraining collaboration* (what Border [1985] calls *secret cooperation*). We can sum up the very nature of this equilibria - more largely the non-cooperative games - by pointing out that non-cooperative game models have a descriptive aspect more important than normative one.

The advantage of Butnariu's non-cooperative fuzzy games is to precise the influence of the information structure on the existence of an equilibrium. Actually, only perfect information allows the existence of a fuzzy correspondence fixed point into the game, i.e. an equilibrium. Hence, the *non-constraining collaboration* - which is necessary in a usual game without being directly modelled - corresponds, in a fuzzy game, to a modification of $\overline{\mathcal{A}}_i$, fuzzy subset of $\mathcal{L}(Z_i)$, by exchanging some information. The existence of a Nash-equilibrium entirely depends on these exchanges. If they are sufficient, the information becomes the same for everyone. Otherwise, only possible solutions exist. Hence, in a fuzzy non-cooperative game, the step of *non-constraining collaboration* is more than contingent to the equilibrium ; it completely determines the plausibility of existence of a Nash-equilibrium.

SECTION TWO : PRUDENT BEHAVIOUR AND EQUILIBRIA

We have seen, during the first section of this chapter, that we could define a fuzzy game from the notion of a strategic conception which permits to sum up the information and the agent's choices according to his preferences. One of the most well-known corollaries of Nash-equilibrium theorem corresponds to the minimax theorem (von Neumann & Morgenstern [1944], ed.1970) which model the prudent behaviour of a rational player in a zero-sum game with two-players (i.e. the gains of one player are the losses of the other). Here, we are going to prove that any prudent player can define a functional utility that ordinally translates his preferences in regard to strategies. It becomes obvious that the *non-constraining collaboration* is no more pertinent as an operational concept because each agent can maximize his strategic utility without knowing what the other player does. Nevertheless, this strategic utility function does not a priori exist. Actually, the preference preorder which precisely corresponds to a prudent approach of the game is the lexicographic preorder which is not continuous and prevents any utility function to translate it in a satisfying way (there exist *weak* types of representations for the lexicographic preorder, Moulin [1981], Fenchel [1956], and also Kannai [1974] and Mas-Colell [1974]). Thus, it is necessary to add an assumption, that we call *Local-non-Discrimination* (*LD*), in order to get a satisfying representation of the fuzzy lexicographic preorder thanks to a continuous utility function.

II.1. Lexicographic preorder and continuity

II.1.1. Definitions

Definition 14 : We call *usual lexicographic preorder*[3], noted *ULP*, the ordinal product of a totally preordered set by itself; $\forall((a,b),(a',b')) \in X^2$: $(a,b)ULP(a',b') \Leftrightarrow (1) a > a'$ or $(2) a = a'$ and $b > b'$.

3 We note *ULP* the *strict* preference and *ULPI* the *nonstrict* (*indifference*) preference.

We see this decomposition not to lead to a partition of X^2.

So, if we consider the structure $(R^2, ULPI)$ and if we suppose that there exists a utility function $u(.)$, we can write for any x of R :

$$J_x = [\inf_{y\in R} u[(x,y)], \sup_{y\in R} u[(x,y)]].$$

Because of the *ULPI* definition, J_x is not a *hole*[4]. Let us now consider $x' \in R - \{x\}$. We have : $J_x \cap J_{x'} = \varnothing$. If $x' < x$, we must only show that :

$$\inf_{y\in R} u[(x',y)] > \sup_{y\in R} u[(x,y)].$$

As $(x',y)ULP(x,y)$ because $x' > x$, this means $\forall y \in R, u[(x,y)] < u[(x',y)]$; hence, we can write : $\sup_{y\in R} u[(x,y)] < \inf_{y\in R} u[(x',y)]$, therefore : $J_x \cap J_{x'} = \varnothing$.

This shows that there would be, following the definition of $u(.)$, a bijection between R (*convex*) and a *countable* set of two by two disjoint intervals in R that would not be holes ; which is absurd. This conclusion is the reason why $u(.)$ cannot be a real-valued continuous utility function representing the *ULPI* lexicographic preorder.

To sum up, the usual lexicographic preorder is not a preorder satisfying the assumption of preference continuity which is the basis of the existence of a continuous utility function preserving the preorder.

II.1.2. The fuzzy lexicographic preorder

Definition 15 : We call *fuzzy lexicographic preorder* noted $\mathcal{F}lp(.,.)$, the ordinal product of a usual preordered set X, (reflexive (A.s.)[5] and f-transitive) by itself : $\forall((a,b),(a',b')) \in X^2$;

$$\mathcal{F}lp((a,b),(a',b')) > \mathcal{F}lp((a',b'),(a,b)) \Leftrightarrow (1) a > a' \text{ or } (2) a = a' \text{ and } b > b'.$$

The assumption of fuzzy preference continuity is trivially not satisfied. Nevertheless, there is a condition that allows this assumption to hold.

II.1.3. The assumption of Local-non-Discrimination

II.1.3.1. Topology

Let X be any given set. A topology T is a family of open sets of X such that :

---

4 An interval $[x,y]$ of $(X, ULPI)$ such that $yULPx$ and $]x,y[= \varnothing$ is a *hole* for *ULPI*.

5 A fuzzy preorder $\mathcal{R}(.,.)$ is reflexive (A.s.) if and only if $\forall x \in X$, $\mathcal{R}(x,x) = 1$.

(i) X and $\varnothing$ are open sets : $X \in T, \varnothing \in T$,

(ii) The union of any family of open sets of X is an open set of X.

(iii) The intersection of a finite family of open sets is an open set.

II.1.3.2. Definition of a neighbourhood

Let (X,T) be a topological space and $x \in X$. A part V of X is called *a neighbourhood of x in X* if there exists an open set $O \in T$ such that $x \in O \subseteq V$.

We can notice that an open neighbourhood (resp. closed) is an open part (resp. closed) of X containing x.

II.1.3.3. The Usual Local-nonDiscrimination (*ULD*)

Let Π be a usual preorder (Preference, Indifference) on X, let V_x be the set of all the neighbourhoods of x ;

$$\forall x \in X, \forall V(x) \in V_x : \exists y \in X \cap V(x) ; yIx.$$

This assumption, in the usual case, means that for any element x of X, there exists another element y of X, always belonging to the intersection of X with any neighbourhood of x (especially the smallest) such that x and y are indifferent.

If *ULD* is satisfied, this means that *ULD* holds for *all the neighbourhoods* of x *except* x itself[6]. Therefore, y can be as *close* of x as possible according to the topology T. We notice this *infinite proximity* (which reminds the principle of local-nonsatiation) to be implicitly based on the existence of an element y which belongs to the smallest neighbourhood of x.

We remark also that *ULD* is satisfied for any x of X. This means, by transitivity of indifference (this is particularly clear if X has a minimum), that we are in a generalized indifference situation. It looks like an assumption of *short-sightedness* because the agents hardly discriminate between two proximate objects and this bad ability of discrimination conveys from element to element.

II.1.3.4. The Fuzzy Local-nonDiscrimination (*FLD*)

Let $\mathcal{R}(.,.)$ be any fuzzy preorder on X and V_x the set of all the neighbourhoods of x ;

---

6 If X is included in R, the natural topology of R prevents $\{x\}$ to be an open set therefore a neighbourhood of itself.

$$\forall x \in X, \forall V(x) \in V_x : \exists y \in X \cap V(x) ; \text{Min}[\mathcal{R}(x,.) = \mathcal{R}(.,x)] = \text{Min}[\mathcal{R}(y,.) = \mathcal{R}(.,y)].$$

Remark : we are here in a fuzzy topological system, namely a structure based on a fuzzy topology I and a usual referential. It does not change the meaning of the assumption even though fuzzy neighbourhoods derive from the existence of fuzzy open sets in the topology I (see Chang [1968]).

Each agent has fuzzy preferences corresponding to $\mathcal{Flp}(.,.)$ and considers two very close objects (x,y) as indifferent (in the sense of *FLD*) but this indifference is not of a unique type. It can vary in intensity between 0 and 1, even though in the usual case, it is conveyed in level 1 since the usual indifference means $[I(x,y) =_{(y,x)} = 1]$. Actually, in the fuzzy case, the transmission of indifference that implies a generalized indifference leads to a *multivalued indifference* which is not necessarily related to a single level of utility.

Let us show that the fuzzy preorder $\mathcal{Flp}(.,.)$ under the assumption of Fuzzy Local-non-Discrimination does not induce any more a contradiction between a countable set and a convex set (as noticed by Debreu [1959], chap.4, footnote n°2).

II.1.4. From lexicographic preorder to utility function

Thanks to $\mathcal{Flp}(.,.)$, we buld up a fuzzy subset $\mathcal{X}$, associated to the referential X such that :

$$\mathcal{X} = \{x \in X; \chi(.)/\forall x \in X, \chi(x) = \text{Min}_y[\mathcal{Flp}(x,y) = \mathcal{Flp}(y,x)]\}.$$

Generally, x is only indifferent to itself for $\mathcal{Flp}(.,.)$. From now on, under *FLD*, there exists another element $y \neq x$ that is indifferent in terms of membership level, i.e. in terms of utility level. The membership level is the minimum of the indifference levels $\{\mathcal{Flp}(x,x), \mathcal{Flp}(x,y)\}$ where $\mathcal{Flp}(x,y)$ depends on x and y.

This derives from the difference between local and global preferences. The agents are supposed to be always irrational and this irrationality is dominated by the *anti*-projector Min. We also know the utility function to be directly assimilated to the membership function $\chi(.)$ of the fuzzy subset $\mathcal{X}$ of X. We are going to prove that the assumption of Fuzzy Local-nonDiscrimination when applied to the fuzzy lexicographic preorder allows to cancel the absurd *biunivoque correspondence* between a countable set of disjoint and nonempty intervals and a convex set.

LEMMA 1 : *Let $(R^2, \mathcal{Flp}(.,.))$ be a structure. The set I_a is defined for $a = (x,y)$ as follows :*

$$I_a = [\inf_{y \in R} \chi(x,y), \sup_{y \in R} \chi(x,y)].$$

Under FLD, $\exists a' = (x',y)$ with $\mathcal{Flp}(a,a') = \mathcal{Flp}(a',a)$, such that $I_a \cap I_{a'} \neq \varnothing$.

Proof: If a is a point of R^2, this means that there exists a point a' of R^2 such that :

$$\mathcal{Flp}(a,a') = \mathcal{Flp}(a',a).$$

Under *FLD*, we suppose $x < x'$. We assimilate s to $\sup_y \chi(x,y)$ and i to $\inf_y \chi(x',y)$. If we consider R^2 when structured by its natural topology, the sets $\{s\}$ and $\{i\}$ are trivially closed, by Hausdorff's property of separation. Let us now show that there exists a' such that the proposition $I_a \cap I_{a'} = \emptyset$ is absurd.

I_a and $I_{a'}$ are closed. So, $I_a^c \cap I_{a'}^c$ is a nonempty open set if $I_a \cap I_{a'} = \emptyset$ where $I_a^c, I_{a'}^c$ are the complement sets of $I_a, I_{a'}$ in R^2. Let us consider $\hat{a} \in R^2$ such that $\chi(\hat{a})$ belongs to $]s,i[$ and a^* such that $\chi(a^*)$ belongs to $]\leftarrow, i[$. Let us define the closed set $[\chi(a^*), \chi(\hat{a})]$. s belongs to $[\chi(a^*), \chi(\hat{a})]$ which is then a neighbourhood of s because there already exists an open set $]\chi(a^*), \chi(\hat{a})[\ni s$. It is obvious that $i \notin [\chi(a^*), \chi(\hat{a})]$. This is a contradiction with the fact that there exists a' belonging to the intersection of X with any neighbourhood of a such that a and a' are indifferent for $\mathcal{Flp}(.,.)$. We can conclude that under *FLD*, the interval $]s,i[= \emptyset$, i.e. $s = i$ which means :

$$\sup_y \chi(x,y) = \inf_y \chi(x,y), \text{ i.e. } I_a \cap I_{a'} \neq \emptyset.$$

□

This lemma shows that *FLD* thickens the indifference classes, even if the preorder is lexicographic. The condition of membership to the intersection of any neighbourhood with X introduces a supplementary notion of proximity which allows to link the maximum and the minimum of any set. This condition means that each element x is indifferent to another element y, belonging to the intersection of X with any neighbourhood of x. Hence, there exists y which is infinitely close of x, and the agent cannot discriminate them.

This demonstration implies the following theorem :

THEOREM 1 : *Under the Fuzzy Local-nonDiscrimination, the fuzzy lexicographic preorder can be represented by a continuous utility function, defined on a real connected referential.*

We do not need to prove this theorem since the precedent lemma ensures the continuity of the preorder $\mathcal{Flp}(.,.)$. Under *FLD*, the general existence theorem holds.

II.2. Non-cooperative fuzzy ordinal game

From now on, we are in a general case usually called "games with decentralized non-cooperative behaviours" (Schotter & Schwodialler [1980], Owen [1982]). In other words, we only specify a fuzzy game thanks to preferences. The term *decentralized* derives from the fact that each player must choose lonely his strategy (and not a strategic conception). All communications are forbidden, there is no initial issue nor history (or memory) of the game.

II.2.1. The game model

We consider a non-cooperative n-person game in a normal form. Each player i (i:1,...,n) can choose into a convex set of strategies, X_i - this set is a usual set - and knows his payoff-function $P_i(.,.)$, defined on the Cartesian product of the n sets of strategies, $\prod_{i=1}^{n} X_i$. We consider X_i to be a real set and $P_i(.,.)$ to be continuous on $\prod_{i=1}^{n} X_i = X$. The game in its normal form corresponds to : $(X_1,\ldots,X_i,\ldots,X_n;P_1,\ldots,P_i,\ldots,P_n)$.

We are in the case where each agent i ignores everything of the $(n-1)$ other players' P_j. This means that i considers that all the $(n-1)$-tuple of strategies could be used by the other players. The *prudent* agent's rationality consists in *forecasting the worst* and being *cautious.*

II.2.2. Prudent behaviour and rationality

Let us consider an application $t(.)$ that *arranges* the different n-tuple of strategies. In fact, for any agent i, the choice of the strategy $x_i \in X_i$ leads to a payoffs vector associated to this strategy and related to the different strategies chosen by the $(n-1)$ other players. In other words, x_i *is identical* to the vector $P_i(x_i,x^*)$ where the $(n-1)$-tuple $x^* \in \prod_{i=1}^{n-1} X_i$. The application $t(.)$ lets the vector $\vec{x}_i$ components be *ordered* in the increasing way.

$$t : X_i \to X_i$$

$$\vec{x} \to t(\vec{x}_i) = \vec{x}_i^t \text{ where } P_i^o(x_i,x^*) > P_i^q(x_i,x^*) \Leftrightarrow o > q.$$

From now on, any vector x_i is an *arranged* vector $\vec{x}_i^t$. We therefore decide to keep on noting it x_i.

It is obvious that the agent's prudent behaviour corresponds to the lexicographic fuzzy preorder $\mathcal{F}lp(.,.)$.

II.2.3. Individual preference and fuzzy lexicographic preorder

An arranged strategy x_i is preferred by i to another strategy y_i if and only if :

$$\forall t < q, P_i^t(x_i,x^*) = P_i^t(y_i,x^*) \text{ et } P_i^q(x_i,x^*) > P_i^q(y_i,x^*).$$

The properties of the individual preorder are :

1- Fuzzy reflexivity (A.s.) : $\forall x_i \in X_i$; $\mathcal{F}lp(x_i,x_i) = 1$.

2- f-transitivity :

$$\forall(x_i, y_i, z_i) \in (X_i)^3 \text{ ; if } \mathcal{F}lp(x_i, y_i) > \mathcal{F}lp(y_i, x_i)$$
$$\text{and } \mathcal{F}lp(y_i, z_i) > \mathcal{F}lp(z_i, y_i)$$
$$\text{then } \mathcal{F}lp(x_i, z_i) > \mathcal{F}lp(z_i, x_i).$$

II.2.4. The assumption of Fuzzy Local-nonDiscrimination

$$\forall x_i \in X_i, \forall V(x_i) \in V_{x_i} : \exists y_i \in X \cap V(x_i), \text{ Min}[\mathcal{F}lp(x_i,.) = \mathcal{F}lp(.,x_i)] = \text{Min}[\mathcal{F}lp(y_i,.) = \mathcal{F}lp(., y_i)].$$

Each player i considers two very close strategies x_i and y_i as indifferent. The eventual difference of the associated payoffs is such that i is not able to discriminate them. Even though mathematically different, both strategies lead to the same *satisfaction*. For example, let us consider two strategies which would be different only at the smallest payoff level. A prisoner (the dilemma) will not discriminate a fifteen year penalty from a fifteen year + *1 second* penalty, even though the usual lexicographic preorder would make that difference.

II.3. Strategic utility function

Theorem 1 allows - under (*FLD*) - to represent $\mathcal{F}lp(.,.)$ with a continuous strategic utility function (*strategic* because it is defined on X_i). We note it $s(.)$:

$$\forall(x_i, y_i) \in (X_i)^2 \text{ ; } s(x_i) \geq s(y_i) \text{ iff Min}[\mathcal{F}lp(x_i,.) = \mathcal{F}lp(.,x_i)] \geq \text{Min}[\mathcal{F}lp(y_i,.) = \mathcal{F}lp(., y_i)].$$

Each player's program consists in maximizing $s(.)$ on X_i. The only question that we can ask is : does the strategy that maximizes $s(.)$ really exist ? In the case of theorem 1, we need the referential to be connected. We must give a supplementary condition.

The set X_i of individual strategies is a compact set (closed and bounded).

THEOREM II : $\forall i, \exists x_i \in X_i \text{ ; } [Arg\{\text{Max}_{X_i} s(x_i)\}] \neq \varnothing$.

Proof : All we have to do is using the classic theorem of Weierstrass : if $s(.)$ is a continuous function on X_i and if X_i is compact and nonempty, then $s(.)$ reaches its maximum on X_i.

□

Instead of directly studying the conditions of a Nash-equilibrium, we work here on the most important corollary of Nash's theorem, namely von Neumann's theorem which gives the sufficient conditions for a particular kind of non-cooperative games - 2-person zero-sum games - to admit at least a balanced solution. We know (Moulin [1981], Sugden [1986], Bernheim, Peleg & Whinston [1987a] and [1987b]) that a saddle point (maximin) - or game value - is nothing else than a Nash-equilibrium of a zero-sum game.

However, *FLD* by thickening the indifference classes of the lexicographic fuzzy preorder, increases the set of feasible equilibra. Henceforth, the balanced issues deriving from a careful behaviour prevent any *non constraining collaboration* : the agents decide in a decentralized way. Nevertheless, we are going to prove that this kind of rationality can generate Nash-equilibria when the agents' behaviour is fuzzy.

II.4. Prudent equilibria and fuzzy Nash-equilibria

We call *2-person zero-sum game*, a game in a normal form such that :

$$(X_1,X_2;P_1,P_2=-P_1).$$

The first player's gains are the second player's losses. The strategic utility functions obtained under *FLD* are ordinal even though the payoffs are cardinal.

THEOREM III : *In the game* $(X_1,X_2;P,-P)$ *where* X_1 *and* X_2 *are the connected and compact sets of strategies and P continuous, under FLD, the set :* $\{[Arg\{\text{Max}_{X_1} s_1(x_i)\}], [Arg\{\text{Max}_{X_2} s_2(x_i)\}]\}$ *contains the usual saddle point of the game.*

Proof : If a strategy $\bar{x}$ belongs to $[Arg\{\text{Max}_{X_1} s_1(x)\}]$, then, $\forall y \in X_1$, $s_1(x) \geq s_1(y)$. We can also deduce from the definition of the fuzzy subset $\mathcal{X}_1$ (defined in I.1.4.) associated to the usual referential X_1, $\mathcal{X}_1 = \{x \in X_1\,;\, \chi_1(.)/\chi_1(x) = \text{Min}_y[\mathcal{F}lp(x,y) = \mathcal{F}lp(y,x)]\}$,that $\forall x \in X_1$, $\forall y \in X_2$, $\text{Min}_y P(\bar{x},y) \geq \text{Min}_y P(x,y)$, and this because of the fuzzy lexicographic preorder. We can conclude that $\text{Min}_y P(x,y) = \text{Max}_y[-P(x,y)]$, $\text{Min}_y P(\bar{x},y) \geq \text{Max}_y[-P(x,y)]$.

Hence, we can write :

$$\forall x \in X_1, \forall y \in X_2\,;\, P(\bar{x},y) \geq -P(x,y). \tag{1}$$

And, for the second player :

$$\forall x \in X_1, \forall y \in X_2\,;\; -P(x,\bar{y}) \geq P(x,y), \tag{2}$$

where $\bar{y} \in [Arg\{\text{Max}_{X_2} s_2(x)\}]$.

Let us now combine both equations (1) and (2) :

$$-P(x,\bar{y}) \geq P(x,y) \Leftrightarrow P(x,\bar{y}) \leq -P(x,y)$$

$$\Rightarrow P(x,\bar{y}) \leq -P(x,y) \leq P(\bar{x},y).$$

Hence :

$$\forall x \in X_1, \forall y \in X_2\,;\, P(x,\bar{y}) \leq -P(x,y) \leq P(\bar{x},y)$$

$$\Leftrightarrow P(x,\bar{y}) \leq P(\bar{x},y). \tag{3}$$

We know X_1 and X_2 to be compact and therefore by Weierstrass's theorem, $P(.,y)$ to reach its maximum on X_1. i.e. : $\exists x^* \in X_1/\forall x \in X_1$, $P(x^*,\bar{y}) \geq P(x,\bar{y})$.

If this is true for any x of X_1, it is particularly true for $\bar{x}$, therefore :

$$P(x^*,\bar{y}) \geq P(\bar{x},\bar{y}). \tag{4}$$

In the same way, we can prove :

$$P(\bar{x},y^*) \leq P(\bar{x},\bar{y}). \tag{5}$$

Because of (3), we can write :

$$\text{if, } \forall x \in X_1,\ \forall y \in X_2,\ P(x,\bar{y}) \leq P(\bar{x},y) \Rightarrow P(x^*,\bar{y}) \leq P(\bar{x},y^*). \tag{6}$$

With (4) and (5) :

$$P(\bar{x},y^*) \leq P(\bar{x},\bar{y}) \leq P(x^*,\bar{y}) \Rightarrow \text{ with (6),}$$

$$P(x^*,\bar{y}) \leq P(\bar{x},y^*) \leq P(\bar{x},\bar{y}) \leq P(x^*,\bar{y}),$$

which is consistent with : $P(x^*,\bar{y}) = P(\bar{x},y^*) = P(\bar{x},\bar{y}) = P(x^*,\bar{y})$, i.e. : $(\bar{x},\bar{y}) = (x^*,y^*)$.

By using (3), (4) and (5), we can find the usual equation defining the saddle point :

$$P(x,\bar{y}) \leq P(\bar{x},\bar{y}) \leq P(\bar{x},y).$$

Hence, the couple (x^*,y^*) belongs to the set : $\{[Arg\{\text{Max}_{X_1} s_1(x_i)\}], [Arg\{\text{Max}_{X_2} s_2(x_i)\}]\}$.

□

Because the usual saddle point belongs to the subset of the non dominated optimal points of X, it follows an increase of the set of game equilibria.

For any decentralized game equilibrium (without *non constraining collaboration*) to correspond to a Nash-equilibrium, implies the game to be *inessential*. This is the case of the 2-person zero-sum games. It means (Bernheim, Peleg & Whinston [1987a]) that the issue is Pareto-optimal. We can now establish the following theorem :

THEOREM IV : *In an inessential game* $(X_1,\ldots,X_n;P_1,\ldots,P_n)$, *where* X_i *is a convex and connected set and* $P_i(.,.)$ *a continuous function, under FLD, the set of* $[Arg\{\text{Max}_{X_i} s_i(x)\}]$ *contains the usual set of Nash-equilibria.*

In such an inessential game, there are no other balanced solutions than the Pareto-optimal ones. The prudent behaviour only leads to Pareto-optimal solutions. Actually, a player using another strategy than prudent may be threatened. To be optimal, strategies must ensure the optimal payoff - i.e. $Arg\{\text{Max}\, s(x)\}$. They correspond to prudent strategies in an inessential game. Because an inessential game means that the issue based on these optimal strategies is Pareto-optimal, hence, this means any Pareto-optimal issue to be prudent, i.e. to correspond to a Nash-equilibrium.

Final remarks

It is clear that the goal of non cooperative fuzzy games *à la* Butnariu and the one we presented afterwards are very different. In the first case, there is a modelling of the *non constraining collaboration*, in the second case, the players' behaviours are completely *decentralized*. There is therefore an implicit measure of non-cooperation. The results obtained from fuzzy games (of Butnariu's type) essentially consist in describing rules for the information exchange untill it converges towards a Nash-equilibrium. It is obvious that these fuzzy games when completely decentralized do not have a balanced solution but only possible solutions (P.S.). Instead, in the decentralized and ordinal approach that we present, the *inessential* game condition is sufficient to make the issue balanced. However, the main contribution in this chapter is to show on one hand the *non constraining collaboration* to be fundamental in the convergence process towards balanced solutions. On the other hand, by continuity of the fuzzy lexicographic preorder and the satisfying representation of this preorder with an associated continuous function, we substitute a n-maximisation for any *decentralized* game (and any inessential game).

At the beginning of the book, we showed that a system of fuzzy preferences was not in contradiction with a numerous representation of the individual satisfaction. Here, in a conflict situation, the player remains optimizer ; he does not *"recontract"* according to the other players choices. However, for a particular class of games, the *inessential* one, the set of Nash-equilibria is wider because the agents do not make the difference between two very close issues. In other words, under *FLD*, the cost of discrimination between two theoretical objects - whatever they are - is more important than the eventual differential of utility. If we observe the mathematical process which lets $\mathcal{F}lp(.,.)$ continuous , we see that only a fuzzy preorder could do it, because it allows a mulitivalued indifference.

Now, the group is placed in a conflict situation. What does the core notion become if players preferences are fuzzy ? Is a fuzzy core empty or not ?

SECTION THREE : COOPERATIVE FUZZY GAMES

The notion of cooperation (Ichiishi [1981;1982], Scarf [1967;1971;1973], Shapley [1973], Schleicher [1979]) deals with *super-players* ; namely groups of players who are going to behave in the same way a single player does. This means that players are able to *depute* a collective institution to represent them. These institutions are theoretical entities which symbolize all union forms, trade unions (syndicates), trusts and the other diverse associations. Even if the analysis of a syndicate in terms of game theory distinguishes a simple *coalition* from a *syndicate* (see Dreze & Gabszewicz [1971]), it is only justified by a theoretical willing to reduce the number of feasible coalitions that can improve their satisfaction according to a given imputation and thus to increase the cardinal of the core associated to the cooperative game (see Rosenmüller [1981] and Cornwall [1984], chap. 5).

Literature on cooperative fuzzy games is not very large. Two specific poles are Aubin [1974;1979;1981;1986] and Butnariu [1979;1980;1985;1986; 1987].

Butnariu goes on with his work devoted to non-cooperative fuzzy games. He develops the notions of *strategic conception* and *research on the optimal rule of information exchange.* He generalizes the concept of Shapley value to a fuzzy game and studies its stability in terms of *individual structure of information.*

On the other hand, Aubin defines a cooperative fuzzy game as a game where the membership[7] to coalitions is fuzzy. This approach is very close to ours even if the used concepts are not the same. Here, we transform the usual cooperative game model and use some principles of convex analysis.

Classic theorems of nonemptiness of the core (Scarf [1967], Munier [1973], Ischiishi [1981], Rosenmüller [1981], Border [1982], Cornwall [1984]) deal with a condition of convexity for the fundamental sets (set of mixed strategies for pure games, consumption one in exchange economies) and also for the individual functions (quasi-concave payoffs and convex preorders). Each balanced game is based on this condition. Without it, the core is empty. We define the *core* to be the set of all undominated issues, imputations or allocations.

Economists thought that the *idea of threat* could be formally explained according to the concept of core (Schotter & Schowdialler [1980]). The eventual betrayal of a given coalition can be immediately *counteracted* by other players' reactions. These reactions then prevent all players belonging to the *betrayal* coalition to benefit from their membership to that coalition and, at least, dissuade them from participating. The notion of threat leads us to a concept of *arbitrage.* The core is finally the set of all the acceptable arbitrages.

In economics, we can consider the agents to have the possibility of *recontract* all engagements. This argument (explained by Edgeworth [1881]) corresponds to the fact that all contracts could always be cancelled after words if other contracts, proved to be better, would appear. The contracts are described here by issues, imputations or allocations. This assumption of *recontracting* is exactly the same (Malinvaud [1975], Negishi [1962]) as the Walrasian condition of existence of an auctioneer. One of the *miracles* of game theory is to have gathered

7 Aubin writes : "*At first, cooperative games theoricians ran into difficulties deriving from the fact that the set of coalitions is finite. The structure of the set is too poor and the results too trivial. Many attempts to increase the set of players had been originated ; for example, one consisted in taking the interval* [0,1], *called "players continuum", as set of players. We defend here another proceeding consisting in keeping a finite number of players and taking a continuum of coalitions, called "set of fuzzy coalitions"*". Thus, for Aubin, a cooperative fuzzy game is a game where fuzzy coalitions are introduced.

the problem of nonemptiness of the core and convexity of the model (sets and functions). This condition of convexity can be easily interpreted. In fact, the question we ask is : what happens if the agents' fuzzy preferences are not convex ?

III.1. f-Convexity and fuzzy preorders

III.1.1. The mathematical model

We consider a referential set X of any objects. Let us suppose the set to be convex and thus connected. Let us consider a fuzzy relation of preference $\mathcal{R}(.,.)$ be defined upon the Zadeh set [0,1]. The agent arranges the different elements of X thanks to $\mathcal{R}(.,.)$, a f-transitive and reflexive (F.s.) fuzzy relation. i.e. :

$$1\text{- } \forall(x,y,z)\in X^3, \text{ if } \mathcal{R}(x,y)\geq\mathcal{R}(y,x) \text{ and } \mathcal{R}(y,z)\geq\mathcal{R}(z,y)$$

$$\text{then } \mathcal{R}(x,z)\geq\mathcal{R}(z,x).$$

$$2\text{- } \forall x\in X,\ \mathcal{R}(x,x)\in[0,1].$$

We assume that if $\forall(x,y)\in X^2$, $\mathcal{R}(x,y)\geq\mathcal{R}(y,x)$, then $\mathcal{X}(x)\geq\mathcal{X}(y)$, in order to generate a preordered fuzzy subset, noted $\mathcal{X}$: the agent's local preference ($\mathcal{R}(.,.)$) does not contradict his global preference ($\mathcal{X}(.)$). There is no locally irrational agent ($\mathcal{R}(.,.)$ is always f-transitive).

If $\mathcal{R}(.,.)$ is f-transitive and reflexive (F.s.), then $\mathcal{R}(.,.)$ is a fuzzy preorder (F.s.). We also know that if the referential set X is connected, $\mathcal{X}(.)$ is a continuous function of utility on X under the assumption of fuzzy preference continuity[8]. So, we suppose this assumption of continuity to be satisfied.

III.1.2. Basic propositions

P1 : $[\forall\alpha\in]0,1[: \mathcal{X}(\alpha x+(1-\alpha)y)=0]$. *No convex combination of x and y belongs to X.*
P2 : $[\exists\alpha\in]0,1[: \mathcal{X}(\alpha x+(1-\alpha)y)=0]$. *There exists a convex combination of x and y that does not belong to X.*
P3 : $[\mathcal{X}(x)\neq 0]$. *x belongs to X.*

By convention, we note :

- $X(1)$, the set of objects of X that satisfy P1 for all y of X :

8 The two following sets are fuzzy closed sets : $\forall x'\in X$,

$$\mathcal{X}^+=\{x\in X\ ;\ \mathcal{X}(x)\geq\mathcal{X}(x')\} \text{ and } \mathcal{X}^-=\{x\in X\ ;\ \mathcal{X}(x)\leq\mathcal{X}(x')\}.$$

$$X(1)=\{x \in X;\ \forall y \in X, \forall \alpha \in]0,1[\ /\ \chi(\alpha x+(1-\alpha)y)=0\}.$$

• $X(2)$, the set of objects of X that satisfy P2 for all y of X :

$$X(2)=\{x \in X;\ \forall y \in X, \exists \alpha \in]0,1[\ /\ \chi(\alpha x+(1-\alpha)y)=0\}.$$

• $X(3)$, the set of objects of X that satisfy P3. Actually, it corresponds[9] to the exclusive support of $\mathcal{X}$:

$$X(3)=supp\,\mathcal{X}.$$

We assume the *exclusive support* of $\mathcal{X}$ to be *convex* and thus connected.

III.1.3. Simple propositions

For $x \in X$,

a- It is obvious that :

$$\text{if } [\forall \alpha \in]0,1[\text{ and } \forall y \in X, \chi(\alpha x+(1-\alpha)y)=0]$$

$$\Rightarrow [\exists \alpha \in]0,1[, \forall y \in X, \chi(\alpha x+(1-\alpha)y)=0].$$

We can also conclude :

$$\underline{X(1) \subseteq X(2)}.$$

b- We know also[10] :

$$\text{if [it does not exist } \alpha \in]0,1[\,;\ \forall y \in X, \chi(\alpha x+(1-\alpha)y)=0]$$

$$\Rightarrow [\forall \alpha \in]0,1[, \forall y \in X, \chi(\alpha x+(1-\alpha)y)\neq 0].$$

Since the exclusive support of $\mathcal{X}$ is convex :

$$\forall \alpha \in]0,1[, \forall y \in X, \chi(\alpha x+(1-\alpha)y)\neq 0].$$

Then, the complement set of $X(2)$ in X and $X(1)$ are disjoint. If we note $X(2)^c$ the complement set of $X(2)$ in X, we can write :

$$\underline{X(2)^c \cap X(1)=\varnothing}.$$

III.1.4. Complex propositions

c- $\underline{X(1) \subseteq X(3)^c}$.

9 Do not always assimilate the exclusive support of $\mathcal{X}$ and the set X itself. Nothing prevents an element from X to have a zero level of membership to $\mathcal{X}$: $supp\,\mathcal{X}=\{x \in X;\chi(x)>0\}$. A non-exclusive support of $\mathcal{X}$ is: $supp_{nex}\mathcal{X}=\{x \in X;\chi(x)\geq 0\}$. It corresponds trivially to X.

10 Simple propositions a) et b) allow to write $X(2)$ and $X(1)$ as being the same set ; this result appears explicitly in the complex proposition e).

Proof: If $[\forall \alpha \in]0,1[, \forall y \in X, \varkappa(\alpha x + (1-\alpha)y) = 0]$, then, for a given $x, x \in X$, since $\varkappa(.)$ is continuous on X : $\lim_{\alpha \to 1^-}[\varkappa(\alpha x + (1-\alpha)y)] = 0$, i.e. $\varkappa(x) = 0 : x \notin X(3)$. Hence, if $x \in X(1)$ $\Rightarrow x \notin X(3)$; it corresponds to : $X(3)^c \supseteq X(1)$, i.e. $X(1) \subseteq supp\, X^c$.

$\square$

d- $X(3)^c \subseteq X(2)$.

Proof : If $\varkappa(x) = 0$, this means since $\varkappa(.)$ is a continuous function on X :

$$\lim_{\alpha \to 1^-}[\varkappa(\alpha x + (1-\alpha)y)] = 0.$$

In other words, $\exists \alpha \in]0,1[$ such that, $\forall y \in X : \varkappa(\alpha x + (1-\alpha)y) = 0$, i.e. : $x \in X(3)^c \Rightarrow$ $x \in X(2)$; $X(3)^c \subseteq X(2)$.

$\square$

e- $X(2) = X(1) = X(3)^c$.

Proof : Proposition d) and proposition c) mean : $X(2) \supseteq X(3)^c \supseteq X(1)$.

We also know $X(1) \subseteq X(2)$ and $X(2)^c \cap X(1) = \varnothing$. If $X(1) \subseteq X(2)$, then :

$$X(2)^c \subseteq X(1)^c \Rightarrow X(2) \cap X(1)^c = \varnothing.$$

But, $X(2)^c \cap X(1) = \varnothing$ (with b)) ; i.e. $X(2)^c \cup X(1) = X$ and $X(2) \cup X(1)^c = X$. Hence : $X(2)^c \cup X(1) = X(2) \cup X(1)^c$.

We have just shown $X(2) \cap X(1)^c = \varnothing$. By definition $X(2) \cap X(2)^c = \varnothing$, so we can conclude :

$$X(2) = X(1).$$

If $X(2) = X(1)$ and $X(2) \supseteq X(3)^c \supseteq X(1)$, it is obvious that :

$$X(2) = X(1) = X(3)^c \text{ or } X(2)^c = X(1)^c = X(3) = supp\, X.$$

$\square$

(For all detailed proofs, see Quine [1972], chap. 18, 19 and 20)

What have we shown ? If $X(2)^c = X(1)^c = supp\, X$, it means that if x belongs to the support of X, then : $[\forall \alpha \in]0,1[, \forall y \in X, \varkappa(\alpha x + (1-\alpha)y) = 0]$.

As soon as two objects x and y have a membership degree to X which is superior to 0, there exists a convex combination which *also* has a membership degree superior to 0.

The usual convexity means that if x and y belong to the usual set X, and if X is connected, then all the convex combinations of x and y belong to the usual set X. Intuitively, the notion of *weak fuzzy convexity* means : *if two elements of the referential set belong to the exclusive support of the fuzzy subset, then there is a convex combination of these two elements which also belongs to the exclusive support of the fuzzy subset*. When the membership function is continuous, the complex proposition e) implies any exclusive support to be *weak convex*.

Definition 16 : A fuzzy subset $\mathcal{X}$ of a convex referential set X is *weak f-convex* iff :

$$\forall(x,y) \in (supp\,\mathcal{X})^2, \exists\alpha \in]0,1[\,; (\alpha x + (1-\alpha)y) \in supp\,\mathcal{X}.$$

Definition 17 : A fuzzy subset $\mathcal{X}$ of a convex referential set X is *strong f-convex* iff :

$$\forall(x,y) \in (supp\,\mathcal{X})^2, \forall\alpha \in]0,1[\,; (\alpha x + (1-\alpha)y) \in supp\,\mathcal{X}.$$

Another way in presenting the strong *f*-convexity is by considering the two following propositions as equivalent :

$$[\forall\alpha \in]0,1[, \chi(\alpha x + (1-\alpha)y) > 0] \Leftrightarrow [\chi(x) > 0 \text{ and } \chi(y) > 0].$$

When proving the complement set of $X(2)$ in X to be the exclusive support of $\mathcal{X}$, $supp\,\mathcal{X}$, we prove the following lemmas :

LEMMA 3a : *Let X be a convex referential and $\mathcal{X}$ any fuzzy subset of X. If $\chi(.)$, the membership function is continuous, then $\mathcal{X}$ is weak f-convex.*

LEMMA 3b : *Let X be a convex referential and $\mathcal{X}$ any fuzzy subset of X. If $\chi(.)$ is continuous and $supp\,\mathcal{X}$ convex, then $\mathcal{X}$ is strong f-convex.*

This *f*-convexity is quite different from convexity that is generally used in fuzzy literature (Liu [1985], Weiss [1975], Kaufmann [1973], Prevot [1977], Zimmermann [1985], Ponsard [1980] and Chang [1968]). Actually, the more general definition of fuzzy convexity simply comes out of properties of an epigraph (see Moulin, Fogelman-Soulie [1979]).

If we consider a function $f(.)$ defined from a space E, towards R, we call *epigraph* of $f(.)$, noted $epi(f)$, the following set : $\{(x,\lambda) \in E \times R; f(x) \leq \lambda\}$.

The epigraph of $f(.)$ is convex if the function $f(.)$ is also convex. On the other hand, the non-exclusive complement set $\overline{epi(f)}_\lambda$, defined as follows $\overline{epi(f)}_\lambda = \{(x,\lambda) \in E \times R; f(x) \geq \lambda\}$,, is convex if and only if for E convex : $f(\alpha x + (1-\alpha)y) \geq \text{Min}\{f(x), f(y)\}$. It means that $f(.)$ is quasi-concave. In other words, a fuzzy subset $\mathcal{X}$ is convex (for the usual literature) if the membership function $\chi(.)$ is quasi-concave.

The membership function $\chi(.)$ derives directly from preorders. The fuzzy subset derives from the individual preferences and it is convex only if the membership function is quasi-concave. This implies the fuzzy subset $\mathcal{X}$, preordered by $\mathcal{R}(.,.)$, to be convex if the membership function $\chi(.)$ is quasi-concave, i.e. if preorders are convex. That way, there is a relation between the convexity of the fundamental set (which concerns the referential) and the convexity of associated preorders : this relation is basic for nonemptiness of the core in the cooperative games approach.

Our goal is simple. We try to work with the only *f*-convexity, immediately acquired if $\chi(.)$ is continuous, i.e. if the referential set X is connected and individual preorders continuous. The *peripheral core* (P.C.), is not identical to the usual core or Aubin's fuzzy core. To define it, we need two references : a planner interested in nonemptiness of the peripheral core and the ε-cores of the non fuzzy literature (Weber [1979], Wooders [1983]).

III.2. Nonemptiness of the peripheral core

III.2.1. ε-cores, game planner and coalitions

First, we must explain, using a more intuitive analysis, what the *peripheral core* is. If the usual core (we call it *intra-muros core* because always included in the peripheral one) is empty - namely the game is not balanced - what is *practically* happening ? In our approach, if individual preorders are not convex, the intra-muros core is empty. Actually, we try to suggest some original results in terms of equilibrium when individual fuzzy preorders are no more *convex*.

III.2.1.1. ε-cores

If the game is not balanced - i.e. the preorders are not convex -, the intra-muros core is empty. In an exchange economy, the concept of *approached core* allows new conditions which guarantee its nonemptiness (see Wooders & Zame [1984]). One of the possible modellings of the notion of an approached core is the ε-core introduced by Shapley & Shubik in their [1969] paper ; using an extension of balanced structure from Scarf[11] [1967], Weber [1979] shows that a lot of games admit nearly nonempty cores when a players continuum in the sense of Aumann is introduced.

The analysis of the approached core for games with a players continuum and without a balanced structure was made by Wooders [1983] who uses an assumption of replication of the economy.

Aubin's works (with fuzzy coalitions) showed the evident relation between the *extension of the players set* - by assumption or replication -, and the *condition of a balanced game*. In other words, we can expect balanced results for a cooperative game - without convexity for preorders - if we extend the cardinal of society from finite to infinite. Nevertheless, in such an economy (or such a game), the core is ε-approached. In terms of utility, the agents accept to loose an ε of satisfaction and thus they do not block up allocations which balance the game ; hence, we can deduce an approached-core, noted ε-core. One of the interpretations of this *short-sightness* proposed by Shapley and Shubik explains "ε" as an organisational tax that coalitions deduct.

---

11 or *balancedness*, see Bondavera [1963] and Shapley [1973], deriving from the convexity of preorders in a game without utility compensations and without side payments, which corresponds to the case of an exchange economy where individual utilities are ordinal.

However, these approached-cores are based on a principle which consists in transforming society in order to *convexify* it (by replication or direct continuum as Aumann did) and putting convexity of society in place of convexity of individual preorders. What happens if one do not replicate an economy with a finite number of players ? The answer that we propose is based, on one hand, on the *f*-convexity of the fuzzy subset associated to the player's preorder and on the other hand, on a game planner.

III.2.1.2. The game planner

In Walras' works, there is an agent, the auctioneer, whose satisfaction increases with the decrease of excess demand or excess supply. Here, the *game planner* is a twin brother of the Walrasian auctioneer. Under constraint of nonemptiness of the peripheral core, his satisfaction increases with the decrease of the *gap* between the peripheral core and the intra-muros one.

The last peripheral core (i.e. the one which maximizes the planner's utility under constraint of nonemptiness) belongs to the same family as Owen's Least-Core [1982], implied by regression upon the ε-cores in a replicated economy.

III.2.1.3. Coalitions

In an exchange economy, what does "*participate to a coalition*" mean ? An economic coalition (i.e. related to an exchange economy with or without production) is based on the individual interest. Therefore, this interest is defined according to a rationality that leads the individuals to research for a maximum of satisfaction in a given environment, even if this satisfaction results from a fuzzy approach of the preferences. Apart from *endogeneousing* the membership of agents to the coalitions, nothing let us economically explain the reason why agents belong to different levels to the present coalitions.

However, the agent can think that he is *more or less* represented by coalitions. This means that the agent gives a *fraction of representativity* to each coalition to which he participates. The difference between the standard approach and the fuzzy one is the following : I completely belong to my university as well as my apartment house but I am a professor and a roomer, a teacher and a proprietor. So to perfectly describe myself, I must tell that a part of me is explained by my university and another by the apartment house in which I am living. It does not contradict the fact of totally belonging to my university and totally inhabiting my apartment. However, a system of fuzzy coalitions means "*I belong to X university in* 0,4" or "*I am an inhabitant of the Y apartment house in* 0,5". Nevertheless, the economic entities (trade unions, association) cannot compose fuzzy subsets.

In other words, we must not assimilate a coalition that can share some economic variable (internal market as in the labour theory) and a coalition directly issued from individual choices. The target of the last is just to generate a collective decision. This conception brings us to throw out the assumption of fuzzy coalitions. Aubin's assumption implied a restriction of the intra-muros core under a necessary condition of convexity for individual preorders. Our goal is not to restrain the core but, on the contrary, to allow some results in situations where it is naturally empty.

III.2.2. The concept of peripheral core

Let us remember the different assumptions of our model.

III.2.2.1. The economic model

1- Let S be a finite set of players (or economic agents). Its cardinal $|S| = n$.

2- We call any usual subset of S a *coalition of agents*. We can deduce that 2^n coalitions are feasible.

Any coalition is *a priori* feasible. However, we can intuitively suppose that some of the 2^n coalitions are not really active. That is the reason why the set of active coalitions, noted AC, is a usual subset of $P(S)$, the powerset of S. One calls AC a *structure of coalitions* where $AC \subseteq P(S)$ (hence, $\emptyset \in P(S)$ but trivially $\emptyset \notin AC$).

3- For any agent i belonging to C, a family of coefficients (α_c^i) corresponds to each active coalition C, $C \in AC$. α_c^i describes the i's individual *fraction* that he estimates *represented* by C (while belonging to C in a usual degree of membership, i.e. 1). That way, a member of X family, professor of Y university, supporter of Z union, has 3 coefficients α_X, α_Y and α_Z, which *perfectly* describe him. In other words, for this agent i :

$$\alpha_X^i + \alpha_Y^i + \alpha_Z^i = 1.$$

4- Each active coalition C, $C \in AC$, represents any member in the same way. Assistant-professors or full-professors are represented by university Y (in which there is two different ranks) in an identical way :

$$\forall C \in AC, \forall (i,j) \in C^2, i \neq j \; ; \alpha_C^i = \alpha_C^j.$$

4bis- The satisfaction of assumptions 3) and 4) implies what we call a *balanced structure*.

5- For any subset C from S - especially any element of AC - we note R^C, the set of vectors of components u_i, where u_i is the utility level of the agent i, (for a given allocation). From this definition, we deduce[12] : $R^n = R^S$.

6- Let the application π be an operator such that for any vector $u = (u_i)_{i \in S}$ of R^S, $\pi(u)$ corresponds to the only components that concern the members of a coalition C ; it generates a vector of R^C :

$$\pi : R^S \to R^C$$

$$(u_i)_{i \in S} \to \pi(u) = (u_i)_{i \in C}.$$

We call C-*imputation* any vector of R^C. A n-person cooperative game corresponds to the data - for any nonempty coalition from S - of a nonempty subset of R^C, noted $V(C)$ where :

$$V(C) - R^C \subset V(C). \quad (1)$$

III.2.2.2. The exchange economy

One considers an exchange economy. Let us consider agents (in a finite number $n = |S|$) in a game situation. They have to share their initial endowments, noted $\vec{D}$, composed with l goods divided between n individuals (i.e. $\vec{D} \in R^l_+$). We assume the initial detention of endowments (A1) and selfishness (A2).

We call *allocation* any vector x of R^{ln}_+. If the allocation x is such that : $\Sigma^n_{i=1} x_i = \vec{D}$, the allocation x is *feasible*.

A. The agents' specification

This is where we find again fuzzy preferences. Each agent i, $i \in S$, has a fuzzy preorder of preference (F.s.), i.e. $\mathcal{P}_i(.,.)$, is f-transitive and reflexive (F.s.). We suppose the fuzzy preorder to be continuous and each consumption set X_i, $X_i \subset R^l_+$, to be convex (therefore connected). It allows the existence of a continuous fuzzy utility function on X_i, defined on [0,1]. We note $fu_i(.)$ this fuzzy utility function.

We say the coalition C (of AC) to totally block the allocation $x \in R^{ln}_+$, if there exists another feasible allocation $y \in R^{ln}_+$, such that :

$$\alpha\text{-} \vec{D} = \Sigma_{i \in S} y_i$$

$$\beta\text{-} \pi_C[fu_{(y)}] \gg \pi_c[fu_i(x)]. \qquad (\gg \text{ means } \textit{per component})$$

We note $IFA(C)$ the set of internal feasible allocations :

---

12 This writing is a convention which avoids to distinguish the coalition and its cardinal, when defining the referential field of internal utility vectors.

$$IFA(C) = \{y \in R_+^{ln}; \forall i \in C, y_i \in R_+^l \text{ and } \Sigma_{i \in C} y_i = \Sigma_{i \in C} d_i\}.$$

We note $FU(C)$, the set of fuzzy utility levels that C can simultaneously ensure to its members, i.e. :

$$FU(C) = \{[fu_i(y_i)]; y \in IFA(C)\}.$$

B. The agents' behaviour

The set $IFA(S)$ is the set of all feasible allocations. By definition, we suppose that $IFA(S) \subseteq \Pi_{i \in S} X_i$. Thus $IFA(S)$ is convex and connected. We assume it to be compact. Each agent, member of the society S, is going to generate a fuzzy subset $\mathcal{IFA}_i(S)$ - that *we assume the exclusive-support to be convex* - implied by his fuzzy preorder (F.s.) : $\forall (x, y) \in [IFA(S)]^2$, if i considers the relative qualities of allocation x (restricted by A2 to x_i) to be greater than the ones of y, we have : $ifas_i(x_i) > ifas_i(y_i)$, where $ifas_i(.)$ is the membership function of the fuzzy subset $\mathcal{IFA}_i(S)$ included in the referential set $IFA(S)$. Since $\forall i \in S$, $\mathcal{P}_i(.,.)$ is a continuous preorder (F.s.) and $IFA(S)$ is connected, the membership function $ifas_i(.)$ is continuous[13].

LEMMA 4 : $\forall i \in S$, *$\mathcal{IFA}_i(S)$ is strong f-convex.*

Proof: It is obvious since $ifas_i(.)$ is continuous and *supp* $\mathcal{IFA}_i(S)$ convex. One has only to apply lemma 3b.

□

C. The definition of the peripheral core

"The reader will find that it will pay well to absorb these definitions at the outset to avoid the temptation to treat them as empty formalism. It is important to be in a balanced frame of mind for this section !"

Werner Hildenbrand & Alan Kirman

Introduction to Equilibrium Analysis

By defining a fuzzy utility function $ifas_i(.)$ on $IFA(S)$, each agent restrains his satisfaction to only feasible allocations. The possibilities of blocking are just of one type. In a given coalition,

13 It is obvious that if $\Pi_{i \in S} X_i = IFA(S)$ then $ifas_i(.)$ and $fu_i(.)$ are identical. We assume here to be in that case. That is the reason why we can use indifferently $ifas_i(.)$ or $fu_i(.)$.

if the allocation x is always less satisfying than another internal feasible imputation, x is totally blocked. An allocation x belongs to the intra-muros core if no coalition blocks it. We can define the intra-muros core (IMC) as follows :

$$IMC = \{x \in IFA(S);\ \forall C \in AC, \exists i \in C;\ \forall y \in IFA(C),\ ifas_i(x_i) \geq ifas_i(y_i)\}.$$

We know IMC to be a usual set, that is :

$\forall x \in IMC;\ imc(x) = 1.$

But the intra-muros core only describes allocations which are totally unblocked. This corresponds to a unitary membership degree. Let us now consider allocations that are *a priori* blocked but with a *more or less* level of satisfaction. If a feasible allocation x' is blocked, it does not belong to the intra-muros core :

$$imc(x') = 0 \Leftrightarrow \exists C \in AC;\ \forall i \in C, \exists y \in IFA(C) : ifas_i(x_i) < ifas_i(y_i).$$

As soon as a member of each allocation prefers a feasible *external* allocation, this allocation belongs to IMC.

However, by introducing ordinal interpersonal comparisons of utility, because of the game planner, there are some rejected allocations that imply a level of satisfaction which is very closed but inferior to the level of utility corresponding to the elements of IMC. To sum up this information, the best tool is the intersection and/or the union of the different fuzzy subsets $\mathcal{IFA}_i(S)$. Actually, taking the intersection of the different fuzzy subsets $\mathcal{IFA}_i(S)$ is equivalent to confer the *minimum level of maximum levels* of satisfaction to the rejected allocation. Of course, it just concerns members of coalitions that belong to the AC structure. We assume furthermore :

A3 : We can make interpersonal ordinal comparisons of utility.

A4 : $\forall i \in C, \forall C \in AC, fu_i(d_i) > 0.$

We can now define the Peripheral Core as follows :

Definition 18 : We call *Peripheral Core* the fuzzy subset of $IFA(S)$ such that :

$$\mathcal{PC} = \{x \in IFA(S),\ pc(.) \in \underline{M} = [0,1];\ pc(x) = \text{Min}_{C \in AC}[\text{Max}_{i \in C}\ ifas_i(x_i)]\}.$$

It is obvious that any element of $\mathcal{IFA}_i(S)$ belongs to $\mathcal{PC}$ ($\forall i \in S$).

THEOREM I : *Whatever is the nature of the agents' fuzzy preferences (convex or not) under A4, the exchange economy is balanced if,* $\forall i \in S, X_i$ *is convex,* $\mathcal{R}_i(.,.)$ *continuous and supp* $\mathcal{IFA}_i(S)$ *convex (i.e.* $\mathcal{PC} \neq \varnothing$ *).*

Proof : α- Let us consider a balanced structure of coalitions, noted E and the allocation[14] $\vec{0}$ trivially satisfying $\pi(\vec{0}) \in V(C), \forall C \in AC$. For every coalition C of E, there exists internal allocations $y^C \in IFA(C)$ such that, $\forall i \in C : ifas_i(y_i^C) \geq 0$.

14 $\vec{0}$ is the n-null vector $(0,0,0,\ldots,0)$.

These conditions define the *internal core of the coalition* C, in other words, feasible allocations that increase the minimum level of satisfaction. Because the structure E is balanced, we can associate a coefficient $\alpha_C > 0$ to each coalition C of E such that $\forall i \in S : \sum_{C \in E_i} \alpha_C = 1$, where E_i is the set of the different coalitions belonging to E which contains i. Let us define an allocation z as follows : $\forall i \in S, \sum_{C \in E_i} \alpha_C \cdot y_i^C = z_i$.

It means that z_i is a convex combination of several y_i^C, $C \in E_i$. Because of the convexity of any X_i, if it contains y_i^C, it contains z_i. X_i is convex and therefore connected, hence, the fuzzy individual preorder $\mathcal{P}_i(.,.)$ is continuous and each $\mathcal{IFA}_i(S)$ has a convex exclusive support (i.e. $fu_i(.)$ is continuous on X_i). Then, the fuzzy subset of $\vec{x} \in R_+^l$ such that $ifas_i(x_i) > 0$ is strong f-convex. If we call $\mathcal{X}$ this fuzzy subset[15] of X_i, then if two allocations belong to it, every convex combination of these two allocations also belongs to it. By definition, $\chi(y_i^C) > 0$. Thus, $z_i = \sum_{C \in E_i} \alpha_C \cdot y_i^C$ is such that $\chi(z_i) > 0$. Finally, we obtain that if $ifas_i(y_i^C)$ is greater than 0, then $ifas_i(z_i)$ is also greater than 0. So, we have just to prove z to belong to $IFA(S)$ in order to obtain the existence of an equilibrium of such an exchange economy.

β- By summing the second member for any (i, C) of $S \times E$, it follows :

$$\sum_{i \in S} z_i = \sum_{C \in E} \sum_{i \in C} \alpha_C \cdot y_i^C = \sum_{C \in E} \alpha_C . [\sum_{i \in C} y_i^C] = \sum_{C \in E} \alpha_C . [\sum_{i \in C} d_i]$$

$$= \sum_{C \in E} \sum_{i \in C} \alpha_C \cdot d_i = \sum_{i \in S} \sum_{C \in E_i} \alpha_C \cdot d_i = \sum_{i \in S} d_i . \left[\sum_{C \in E_i} \alpha_C \right] = \sum_{i \in S} d_i .$$

That proves $z \in IFA(S)$.

γ- As, $\forall C \in E$, $y^C \in IFA(S)$, $z \in IFA(S)$, $IFA(S)$ convex and each $\mathcal{IFA}_i(S)$ strong f-convex, we just have to start again α) in order to obtain : $\forall i \in S$, $ifas_i(z_i) > 0$.

By observing the definition of $\mathcal{PC}$, we immediately have : $pc(z) > 0 \Rightarrow \mathcal{PC} \neq 0$.

□

We have showed that an exchange economy is always balanced even though the agents' fuzzy preferences are not convex. In order to do this, there must exist, at least, one allocation of $\prod_{i \in S} X_i$ such that the coalitions members have levels of fuzzy utility greater than 0. This constraint is explained by A4 which is not so restrictive. It means that the agents assume initial endowments to have a non-null level of utility. (Another way is defining fuzzy subsets on a membership set $\underline{M} =]0,1]$).

THEOREM Ibis : *Under A1, A2, A3 and A4, if* $IFA(S)$ *is convex, and* $\forall i \in S, X_i$ *convex and* $\mathcal{R}_i(.,.)$ *continuous, the peripheral core of the exchange economy is nonempty.*

---

15 If $x \in \mathcal{X}$, $\chi(x) = ifas_i(x) > 0$. If $x \notin \mathcal{X}$, $\chi(x) = 0$. It means, in fact, that $\forall i \in S : \mathcal{X} \equiv \mathcal{IFA}_i(S)$. Since lemma 4 defines $\mathcal{IFA}_i(S)$ as a f-convex fuzzy subset, it is obvious that $\mathcal{X}$ is also f-convex.

However, the peripheral core contains any allocation of $IFA(S)$ that satisfies A4. But, we can compare allocations of the peripheral core by looking at function $pc(.)$.

If IMC is empty, there exists "*approximately balanced*" allocations that can solve the exchange problem in a given economy. To find a f-balanced[16] solution, it is just necessary to find an internal allocation which is considered by any member of each coalition as defining a non-null level of utility. It seems natural to assimilate this allocation to individual endowments. If we have a nonempty fuzzy subset that contains all the f-balanced solutions, we must choose the f-balanced allocations that most approach IMC. Because of the definition of $\mathcal{PC}$, it implies a membership degree deriving from the utility of the less satisfied agent of the most satisfied agents (Def.3), for each allocation of $\mathcal{PC}$.

Because of A3, a game planner can compare elements that compose $\mathcal{PC}$. The principal tool used by the planner is α-cutting. First, we must prove two results.

LEMMA 1 : *If* $\mathcal{PC} \neq \varnothing$ *and* $IMC \neq \varnothing$, *then* : $IMC \subset supp\,\mathcal{PC}$.

Proof: If $IMC \neq \varnothing$, this means : $\exists x \in IFA(S)\,;\, x \in IMC$, i.e. :

$$\forall C \in AC, \exists i \in C, \forall y \in IFA(C) : ifas_i(x_i) \geq ifas_i(y_i).$$

Hence, we have : $\forall y \in IFA(C)$: $\mathrm{Max}_{i \in C}\, ifas_i(x_i) \geq \mathrm{Min}_{i \in C}\, ifas_i(y_i)$. $\mathcal{PC}$ is nonempty, A4 is satisfied and thus, $\forall i \in S : ifas_i(d_i) > 0$. It follows, $\forall C \in AC$:

$$\mathrm{Max}_{i \in C}\, ifas_i(x_i) \geq \mathrm{Min}_{i \in C}\, ifas_i(d_i) > 0.$$

It means : $\mathrm{Min}_{C \in AC}\, \mathrm{Max}_{i \in C}\, ifas_i(x_i) > 0$.

Hence, we can conclude : $pc(x) > 0 \Rightarrow x \in supp\,\mathcal{PC}$.

□

Here, we assume any internal allocation in any given coalition not to generate *a maximum of satisfaction which can be superior* to the maximum of satisfaction generated by any allocation belonging to IMC. We call this assumption *Postulate of Internal Satisfaction.*

PIS : $\forall C \in AC, \forall y \in IFA(C), \forall x \in IMC : \mathrm{Max}_{i \in C}\, ifas_i(y) \leq \mathrm{Max}_{i \in C}\, ifas_i(x)$.

LEMMA 2 : *Let* $x \in IMC \neq \varnothing$ *be any allocation. Under PIS*, $\forall x' \in \mathcal{PC}'$ *(where* $\mathcal{PC}'$ *is such that* $supp\,\mathcal{PC}' = supp\,\mathcal{PC} - IMC$ *)* : $pc(x') < pc(x)$.

Proof: If $x' \in \mathcal{PC}' : \exists C' \in AC\,;\, \forall i \in C', \exists y' \in PR(C')$ such that : $ifas_i(x') < ifas_i(y')$.

Then : $\mathrm{Max}_{C'}\, prs(x_i') < \mathrm{Max}_{C'}(y_i')$.

We know that $x' \in \mathcal{PC}' \Rightarrow \forall C \in AC - C' : \forall y \in IFA(C)$,

16 We note f-balanced allocation, any *approximately balanced* allocation.

$\exists i \in C;\ ifas_i(y) \leq ifas_i(x')$

and $\forall j \in C - \{i\};\ ifas_j(y) > ifas_j(x')$.

And, $\forall C \in AC - C'$, $\text{Max}_{i \in C}\, ifas_i(x') \geq \text{Min}_{i \in C}\, ifas_i(y)$. Hence, we obtain :

$1 - \exists C' \in AC, \exists y' \in PR(C');\ \text{Max}_{i \in C'}\, ifas_i(x') < \text{Max}_{i \in C'}\, ifas_i(y')$.

$2 - \forall C \in AC - C', \forall y \in IFA(C) : \text{Max}_{i \in C}\, ifas_i(x') \geq \text{Min}_{i \in C}\, ifas_i(y)$.

This means : $\text{Min}_{C \in AC} \text{Max}_{i \in C}\, ifas_i(x') < \text{Max}_{C \in AC}[\text{Max}_{i \in C'}\, ifas_i(y'), \text{Min}_{i \in C}\, ifas_i(y)]$.

i.e. : $pc(x') < \text{Max}_{C \in AC}[\text{Max}_{i \in C'}\, ifas_i(y'), \text{Min}_{i \in C}\, ifas_i(y)]$.

Let us show, $\forall x \in IMC$:

$$pc(x) \geq \text{Max}_{C \in AC}[\text{Max}_{i \in C'}\, ifas_i(y'), \text{Min}_{i \in C}\, ifas_i(y)].$$

Let us suppose an allocation x belonging to IMC, such that :

$$pc(x) < \text{Max}_{C \in AC}[\text{Max}_{i \in C'}\, ifas_i(y'), \text{Min}_{i \in C}\, ifas_i(y)].$$

This means : $\text{Min}_{C \in AC} \text{Max}_{i \in C, C'}\, ifas_i(x) < \text{Max}_{C \in AC}[\text{Max}_{i \in C'}\, ifas_i(y'), \text{Min}_{i \in G}\, ifas_i(y)]$.

It implies two alternative situations :

1- $\exists C \in AC - C' : \text{Max}_{i \in C}\, ifas_i(x) < \text{Min}_{i \in C}\, ifas_i(y) \Rightarrow \forall i \in C : ifas_i(x) < ifas_i(y)$.

Hence, we have : $\exists C \in AC;\ \forall i \in C, \exists y \in IFA(C) / ifas_i(x) < ifas_i(y)$.

Thus, the coalition C blocks x. It implies : $x \notin IMC$, which is inconsistent with the beginning assumption.

2- $\text{Max}_{i \in C'}\, ifas_i(x) < \text{Max}_{i \in C'}\, ifas_i(y')$.

This case is inconsistent with PIS. In conclusion, we have :

$\forall x \in IMC,\ pc(x) \geq \text{Max}_{C \in AC}[\text{Max}_{i \in C'}\, ifas_i(y'), \text{Min}_{i \in C}\, ifas_i(y)]$.

Hence : $\forall x \in IMC, \forall x' \in \mathcal{PC}$:

$$pc(x) \geq \text{Max}_{C \in AC}[\text{Max}_{i \in C'}\, ifas_i(y'), \text{Min}_{i \in C}\, ifas_i(y)] > pc(x') \Leftrightarrow pc(x) > pc(x').$$

□

III.2.3. The α-approached cores[17]

17 Do not assimilate this notion with the one of α-core, issued from the introduction of external effects, (utility of coalitions depending on the utility of other coalitions). See Rosenthal [1971].

Theorems I and Ibis lead to consider any solution of $\mathcal{PC}'$ as *approximately balanced*, i.e. the allocations of the peripheral core when *IMC* is empty. However, even if it is not empty, the membership function of $\mathcal{PC}$ can discriminate between all of the allocations of *IMC* (because of A3). So, we can exhibit balanced solutions which are *most preferable*.

Lemma 2 means that the game planner can search for a social allocation which is more satisfying in the sense that social utility (i.e. $pc(.)$) increases when, on one side, we *approach* *IMC* (if it exists), and on the other side, when we *order* the allocations of $\mathcal{PC}$. This social utility, $pc(.)$, must be a continuous function defined on [0,1]. It means that $\mathcal{PC}$ is weak f-convex (lemma 3).

Let us recall what is an α-cut : $\forall \mathcal{A}$ a fuzzy subset of X, we call, A_α, "α-cut of $\mathcal{A}$" in α level, $\alpha \in]0,1]$, the following usual set : $A_\alpha = \{x \in X;\ a(x) \geq \alpha\}$.

Definition 19 : We call *α-approached core*, noted PC_α, every α-cut of the peripheral core $\mathcal{PC}$.

We can notice that the greater α is, the smaller the cardinal of the obtained usual set is : let $(\alpha, \alpha') \in]0,1]^2$ with $\alpha > \alpha'$, then $|PC_\alpha| < |PC_{\alpha'}|$.

The game planner is going to search for the level α^* such that $\forall \alpha > \alpha^*$, $|PC_\alpha| = 0$ where $|PC_{\alpha^*}| \neq 0$, i.e. the *last*[18] *α-cut of the peripheral core* that is nonempty.

Definition 20 : We call *Last Core*, noted *LC*, the α^*-approached core.

LEMMA 3 : *if* $IMC \neq \emptyset$, *under PIS*, $LC \subseteq IMC$.

Proof: If $IMC \neq \emptyset$, we know that for $x' \in IMC$, $\forall x \in \mathcal{PC}' : pc(x) > pc(x')$; hence, for $\bar{\alpha}$ defined as follows : $\bar{\alpha} = \mathrm{Max}_{x \in \mathcal{PC}'}\, pc(x)$, it is obvious that $\forall \alpha > \bar{\alpha} : |PC_\alpha| \leq |IMC|$. If it is true for every α, $\alpha > \bar{\alpha}$, it is also true for α^*, which is, by definition, greater than $\bar{\alpha}$, since $IMC \neq \emptyset$. Hence, it follows : $|PC_{\alpha^*}| \leq |IMC|$ i.e. $LC \subseteq IMC$.

□

LEMMA 4 : *If* $IMC = \emptyset : \Rightarrow LC = PC_{\alpha^*}$ *where* $\alpha^* = \mathrm{Max}_{x \in \mathcal{PC}}\, pc(x)$.

Proof: If $IMC = \emptyset \Rightarrow \mathcal{PC}' = \mathcal{PC}$. Thus, the maximum of α such that $|PC_\alpha| \neq \emptyset$ where $\forall \beta > \alpha$, $|PC_\beta| = \emptyset$, is obviously defined as follows : $\alpha^* = \mathrm{Max}_{x \in \mathcal{PC}}\, pc(x)$. Then, it implies : $LC = PC_{\alpha^*}$.

□

LEMMA 5 : *If* $supp\, \mathcal{PC} \neq \emptyset \Rightarrow LC \neq \emptyset$.

Proof: If $supp\, \mathcal{PC} \neq \emptyset \Rightarrow \exists x \in IFA(S)$; $pc(x) > 0$, hence $\exists \alpha, \alpha = pc(x) \Rightarrow LC \neq \emptyset$.

□

---

18 To be sure of the existence of α^*, it is necessary to define $pc(.)$ as a continuous function on a compact set ; that is the case, since $\mathcal{PC}$ is weak f-convex and $IFA(S)$ compact.

Lemma 3 means the Last Core to be included or equal to *IMC* when individual preorders are convex. Lemma 4 explains the fact that the upper degree of the membership function *pc*(.) defines the Last Core if *IMC* is nonempty. Lemma 5 assures nonemptinessness for the Last Core as soon as *supp* $\mathcal{PC}$ is nonempty.

We can conclude by the following theorem which sums up the analysis of the peripheral core :

THEOREM II : *The conditions under which the Last Core of an exchange economy is nonempty are : 1- the set of feasible allocations is compact and convex, 2- the Peripheral Core is nonempty and weak f-convex, 3- PIS is satisfied.*

Final Remarks

The introduction of α-approached cores is not here related to the concept of a replicated economy and/or a continuum of agents. The set of agents is finite. That explains the necessity of assumption A3 of interpersonal comparison of utility.

We wanted to weaken the assumption of convexity and we have reached our goal thanks to the *f*-convexity of a fuzzy subset. By definition, the peripheral core contains any socially feasible allocation for which the less satisfied of the most satisfied agents of society has a positive fuzzy utility. However, in any given coalition which is nonblocking, the most satisfied agent must prefer it to any internal allocation. Then, the most satisfied agent of the blocking coalition must not prefer it to any other internal allocation. In other words, a socially feasible allocation belongs to *IMC* under the condition of nonexistence of one internal allocation in at least one coalition that is preferred to it by every member of this coalition.

For the peripheral core, we find these two steps. Each coalition considers every social feasible allocation. Then we deduce *n* possible levels of membership deriving from the most satisfied agents. Finally, we attribute to the considered allocation the level of satisfaction deriving from the less satisfied agent of the *preselected* agents. These different notions deal with the concepts of union and intersection of the $\mathcal{IFA}_i(S)$, thanks to the fuzzy subsets algebra (Zimmermann [1985]). In other words, if we are under usual conditions (convex preorders of preference), the game planner generates a *perfectly balanced solution* which has a better (or equal) social level than allocations of *IMC*.

CHAPTER 4

Fuzzy General Equilibrium

Here, we are going to assume preferences to be fuzzy in the case of an exchange economy with production. Hence, we introduce factors or inputs and the associated markets. The former influence individuals' choices (especially in terms of labour) and modify the structure of models by generating some new markets (of factors) and new agents (the producers).

We focus the analysis on labour because the assumption of fuzzy preference only deals with the agent's arbitrage between labour and leisure.

First, we try to set up the notion of *task*. Then, we prove the double consistency of fuzzy behaviours and quasi-markets of task with a *standard* Walrasian general equilibrium.

Traditionally, in microeconomics, an assistant-professor in finances of Duke University does not make the same job than its colleague in finances of Stanford University. In the same way, a doctor making an appendectomy on January 12, 1991, and another doctor making another appendectomy on January 13, 1991 do not make the same job. This method of differentiation - which allows to include the spatio-temporal characteristics - implies a hyperspecification of labour in date, location and description which induces a great increasing of potential labour markets. Therefore, we must theoretically reconsider each service as a pure commodity. One of the contingent problems is to explain the reason why the demand is going to be broke down on all markets of service by including same parameters as the supply.

It is necessary to introduce a principle of differentiation based on a qualitative distinction rather than a quantitative one : in a firm, a farm, a university, for an executive officer as well as an employer, a professor or a doctor, each work can be defined as a set of particular tasks. A commercial assistant trades contracts, takes care of the administrative work, searches for information, aims to invest on new markets ; a teacher teaches but makes also researches, participates to conferences, writes papers...

SECTION ONE : TASKS AND QUASI WAGE-RATES

Most of the recent works in unemployment theory, up to Malinvaud [1986], emphasizes the following phenomenon : in each industrialized country, the probability of being unemployed is decreasing with professional qualifications. This is directly related to the rarity of supplied tasks. The more an individual is qualified, the more the tasks he supplies are rare, the less he risks to be unemployed.

The relation between *qualification* and tasks profile leads us to briefly analyze the literature which has studied the notion of "ability", i.e. skills, qualification, competence...

I.1. The different approaches of ability

I.1.1. The "skills" approach

One of the best known criticisms of the Walrasian model is the indirect introducing of labour in the utility function (see Pagano [1985], chapter I, p. 5-15). This method implies the ability not to be directly introduced into the individual goals (the agents try to maximize their time of leisure under their budget constraint for consumption). Arrow [1979] studied the problem of ability under the classical smithian assumption of labour division and severely concludes that on the contrary of what Adam Smith thought, the diversity of abilities is not an empirical evidence. Therefore this division is not the only optimal mechanism of coordination. The criticism of the smithian sketch of the pin factory, even though others did it before Arrow (for example Giola [1815] or Babbage [1832]), allowed to bring up to date this concept and to attract new authors towards an attempt of integration of the ability notion into balanced models.

Most of Rosen's papers [1978;1982;1983] tries to introduce the individual abilities thanks to the human capital approach, and shows that it is optimal for agents to *reveal* their skills. Pagano [1985] uses the notion of *ability (skills) as an agent's initial endowment* and introduces it into a general equilibrium model. The main results consists in evaluating the level of collective welfare (under a group of traditional axioms) by the level of skills utilization.

I.1.2. The "hedonic" approach

What recalls the modern labour approach consists essentially in introducing an *estimative* analysis of labour which forbids a space-time specification. It looks like Lancaster's approach applied to labour. Lucas [1972] defines the *Hedonic Price Functions* by introducing the idea according to which the observed prices are a direct function of the intrinsic qualities of commodities (with an eventual deviation). For the labour market, it means : wages are a direct function of the intrinsic qualities of labour.

The question to be asked is : how can we model these characteristics ? Thanks to skills ? No, since labour characteristics are independent from the agent's skills (see Hahn's model introducing the *general ability*, or Mookherjee [1986]). Thanks to wages ? No, because if a wage expresses these characteristics, the causal relation is inverted.

The way we estimate the most efficient to model these characteristics is to *break down each work into a tasks vector* - each task being precisely defined. Therefore, we obtain two new concepts : the *task* one (and contingent ones of *quasi-market* and *wage quasi-rate*) and the *partial competition* one.

I.2. Task, quasi wage-rate and partial competition

I.2.1. The task notion

Pagano defined the term *"task"* as *"the way to use labour force"*. In other words, a task is an answer to the questions "how" and "how long" using labour force. In Pagano's works, like in most authors' papers of what is called the Italian labour school (Zamagni or Nuti), the considered concept of *task* leads to an asymmetrical definition. In the model presented by Pagano [1985] (chapter VII, p. 122-126), labour demand is very classically satisfied on the labour market. Next, inside the firms, labour is transformed into tasks. The agents maximize their utility functions and thus choose the optimal leisure time and consumption. Hence, they supply labour in a undifferentiated manner. On the contrary, in a second model (Pagano [1985], chapter VII, p. 116-124), there is a symmetrical definition but tasks are introduced as direct arguments of the utility function thanks to *skills* which symbolize the agents' initial endowments.

However, the analysis in terms of market which leads to the notion of *partial competition* needs to deepen the concept of task. When a worker enters a particular market, he has already wondered what he is able to do. He knows what kinds of task he can supply. But there exists a great number of jobs, i.e. tasks vectors. To reduce this increase of labour markets, we have just to establish that more a job is "demanding", greater the required skills must be. Finally, we obtain the value of jobs to increase with the value of tasks that compose them. The idea is the same as the ones of Lucas [1972] or Rosen [1974]. Actually, such a defined task is formed of intrinsic qualities that are related : calm and experience for a surgeon, oratory talent and juridical ability for a lawyer. The task is therefore the summary of these characteristics and there is a lot of jobs that have a common task. This intersection which expresses the fact that some different jobs demand the same skills and have the same common characteristics, founds the very notion of *partial competition* and the previous ones of *quasi-market* and *quasi wage-rate.*

I.2.2. Quasi-market and quasi wage-rate

A labour supply being a supply of tasks that represent the agent's skills, there exists an aggregated supply for any particular task. In the same way, a demand of labour corresponds to a demand of tasks which are necessary for the firm and therefore, there exists an aggregated demand for any particular task : the place where this supply and this demand are confronted is called a *quasi-market*. The price that balanced the quasi-market is called a *quasi wage-rate.*

I.2.3. The notion of partial competition

In standard microeconomics, agents compete only if they are in total competition, that is their tasks supplies are such that they enter the same quasi-markets. Here, agents are sometimes in *partial competition*, that is they supply some common tasks without supplying the same job. Their partial supplies of tasks (the common ones) are aggregated and determine the quasi wage-rate on the quasi-market. But, finally, the wage-rates of agents who are in partial competition are not equal, except in some particular cases when the wage-rates are identical even though jobs are different. Let us recall that partially competitive quasi-markets corresponds to what Rosen [1974] calls "*implicit markets*".

I.3. A Labour-Commodities-Economy

The concept of a Labour-Commodities-Economy is not opposite to the one of a standard Walrasian economy. It only means that a distinction is done between *pure* commodities and *labour* units. This concept allows to distinguish the eventual disequilibria of commodity from those which are related to the quasi-markets of tasks (with null prices or null quasi wage-rates) ; the analysis of commodity disequilibria (even free) is not equivalent to the one we can do about labour disequilibrium.

I.3.1. The consumers-workers

Consumers-workers belong to S ; its cardinal is equal to n (i.e. $|S|=n$). The typical behaviour of these consumers-workers is to afford their commodities demands with wages and eventually with private incomes deriving from shares of profit.

I.3.1.1. The fundamental sets

Each consumer-worker simultaneously chooses a tasks supply and a commodities demand. There are two fundamental sets whose properties can differ (especially in the next chapter) : on one hand, an individual set of tasks, noted T_i (i as symbol of the consumer-worker), and an individual set of commodities, noted C_i.

Prices of commodities are expressed according to the unit which characterizes the commodities (weight, ton, kilogram,...). The quasi wage-rate which balances the quasi-market is expressed in a hourly way if we account for task quantities in hours.

I.3.1.2. Nature and properties of the fundamental sets

Definition 1 : The number l of tasks is a given positive whole number. A job t_i of any consumer-worker i is a point of R_-^l, the tasks space. A system of quasi wage-rates[1] $\overrightarrow{w}$ is a point of R_+^{l*}. The agent's wage expressed according to the system of quasi wage-rates $\overrightarrow{w}$ corresponds to $(-\overrightarrow{w} \cdot t_i)$.

We also consider some psychological and/or institutional constraints to prevent most workers entering all quasi-markets of tasks. T_i is a usual nonempty subset of R_-^l representing the set of tasks consistent with the agent i's abilities.

---

1 In this first model, we exclude any free disposal equilibrium. Quasi wage-rates like prices (Def.2) cannot be negative. That is the reason why the system of prices and quasi wage-rates is a point of R_+^l without the null vector that we note R_+^{l*}.

A. Properties of T_i

P1 : T_i is a nonempty, closed and convex (therefore connected) usual set.

P2 : T_i is a bounded set (therefore T_i is compact).

Definition 2 : The number m of commodities is a given positive whole number. A consumer i demands a consumption bundle c_i which is a point of R_+^m, the commodities space. However, this consumption c_i is constrained by some exogeneous criterions. We note C_i, the feasible consumption set of the agent i, a usual nonempty subset of R_+^m. For a given system of commodity prices $\vec{p}$ (point of R_+^{m*}), the expenditure associated to c_i is the number $\vec{p} \cdot c_i$.

B. Properties of C_i

P3 : C_i is a nonempty, closed and convex usual set.

P4 : C_i is a bounded set (hence C_i is compact).

C. The semivectors c_i and t_i

During this chapter, we do not use the semivectors c_i and t_i. They describe the consumer-worker's both attitudes : commodities demands, i.e. the semivector c_i, and tasks supplies, i.e. the semivector t_i. Nevertheless, these two semivectors will allow a different analysis for commodities and tasks in the next chapter. Because we are in a *LCE*, we already adopt this kind of notation.

C_i is the set of all possible consumption bundles for i and T_i is the set of all feasible tasks for the worker i. We note $(C/T)_i$, the set of allocations $(c/t)_i$ with $c_i \in C_i$ and $t_i \in T_i$. By definition, $\forall i \in S$:

H1- $C_i \cap T_i = \varnothing$

H2- $(C/T)_i \subset R^{l+m}$ and

H3- $(C/T)_i$ is convex and compact.

H1 means that no *commodity* is also a task.

I.3.2. The producers-employers

I.3.2.1. The fundamental sets

Producers-employers belong to P, which cardinal is equal to n' (i.e. $|P|=n'$). The typical behaviour of a producer-employer is to maximize profits. The jth producer-employer's product is a $m+l$-dimensional vector of commodities he produces and tasks he consumes. We note $(s/d)_j$ this vector where s_j is the commodities supply and d_j the tasks demand. We note Q_j the set of all feasible $(s/d)_j$, that is the j's production set.

I.3.2.2. Properties of Q_j

P5 : Q_j is a usual nonempty, closed and convex set.

P6 : Q_j is a bounded set (therefore compact).

P7 : Q_j contains the null vector (possibility of inaction).

P6, when associated to P7, excludes the nondecreasing returns to scale.

I.4. A fuzzy *LCE* (*à la Ponsard*)

I.4.1. The consumer-worker's behaviour

We consider each consumer-worker to have a fuzzy preference $\mathcal{P}_i(.,.)$, which corresponds here to a fuzzy reflexive (F.s.) and Max-Min transitive[2] binary relation.

$$\forall i \in S : (1)\text{- } \forall x_i \in X_i,\ \mathcal{P}_i(x_i,x_i) \in \underline{M} = [0,1]$$

$$(2)\text{- } \forall (x_i, y_i, z_i) \in X_i^3,\ \mathcal{P}_i(x_i, z_i) \geq \mathrm{Max}_{y_i}[\mathrm{Min}\{\mathcal{P}_i(x_i, y_i), \mathcal{P}_i(y_i, z_i)\}].$$

Under usual assumptions, X_i connected and $\mathcal{P}_i(.,.)$ continuous, we can represent a fuzzy relation of preference by a fuzzy utility function $u_i(.)$ such that :

---

2 In order to simplify, we consider $(C/T)_i = X_i$ and $(c/t)_i$ to be noted x_i.

$$u_i(.) : X_i \to [0,1]$$

$$x_i \to u_i(x_i) \in [0,1].$$

The agent i's usual budget set for a given system of prices and quasi wage-rates (p/w), that we here note p, and for initial endowments noted e_i, can be written as follows :

$$B_i = \{x_i \in X_i;\ \forall x_i : p \cdot x_i \leq p \cdot e_i\}.$$

We can remark the initial endowments just to concern *commodities*. On the contrary of Pagano's model [1985], skills are not quantitatively measured and next introduced into initial endowments. Hence, in a *LCE* model, initial endowments are represented by the vector $(e/0)$ where "e" corresponds to commodities endowments and "0" to the R^l null vector. There is no tasks endowments.

We assume this model (Ponsard [1982a], Ponsard [1982b]) to define the budget set as a fuzzy subset (see Billot [1987b], chapter III, p. 71-78). We assume that the more one allocation is nearby saturation of the constraint, the more its membership degree to the fuzzy budget set is high.

Therefore, allocations that saturate the usual budget set have a fuzzy membership level that is equal to 1. Allocations which overstep the limits of the budget constraint have a membership level that is equal to 0. The other allocations, which are *feasible*, i.e. that stay inside the budget constraint, have a membership level defined between 0 and 1. In other words, we define a fuzzy subset $\mathcal{B}_i$ of X_i, with :

$$b_i(.) : X_i \to [0,1]$$

$$x_i \to b_i(x_i) \in [0,1]$$

$$\text{with} : b_i(x_i) = 1 \Leftrightarrow p \cdot x_i = p \cdot e_i$$

$$b_i(x_i) \in]0,1[\Leftrightarrow p \cdot x_i < p \cdot e_i$$

$$b_i(x_i) = 0 \Leftrightarrow p \cdot x_i > p \cdot e_i.$$

We can notice the function $b_i(.)$ to depend on e_i. It is a monotonous decreasing function for increasing values of e_i.

The fuzzy utility function is defined on [0,1] and the fuzzy budget allows to sum up the consumer-worker's partial equilibrium according to two fuzzy subsets :

$$\mathcal{U}_i = \{x_i \in X_i;\ u_i(x_i) \in [0,1]\} \text{ and } \mathcal{B}_i = \{x_i \in X_i;\ b_i(x_i) \in [0,1]\}.$$

I.4.2. The producer-employer's behaviour

The jth producer-employer tries to maximize his profits. For a profile of production-employment $(s/d)_j$, we note it q_j, belonging to the production set Q_j and for a given system of prices and quasi wage-rates p, a profit can be written as follows :

$$\pi_j = p \cdot q_j.$$

In a fuzzy economy *à la Ponsard*, we must assume the producers-employers to maximize their *utility* for profit under technological constraints of *efficiency*. Hence, we define such an individual utility function for profit as follows :

$$u_j(.) : Q_j \rightarrow [0,1]$$

$$q_j \rightarrow u_j(q_j) \in [0,1]$$

with : $u_j(q_j) = 0$ if $q_j = 0$ (P7) and

$u_j(q_i) \in]0,1]$ otherwise.

Let us remark the particular case where $u_j(q_j) = 1$ to be the case for which the profile of production-employment corresponds to the maximal profit since the function $u_j(.)$ is increasing.

Moreover, any producer-employer maximizes under a technological constraint of efficiency. Therefore, we usually divide the production set into a set of efficient productions and its complement. Here, we consider productions to be more or less efficient. Hence, we can define the fuzzy subset $\mathcal{E}_j$ of efficient productions thanks to the membership function $e_j(.)$ defined as follows :

$$e_j(.) : Q_j \rightarrow [0,1]$$

$$q_j \rightarrow e_j(q_j) \in [0,1]$$

with : $e_j(q_j) = 0$ in case of losses,

$e_j(q_i) \in]0,1]$ otherwise.

The case where $e_j(q_j) = 1$ corresponds to a profile of production-employment q_j where efficiency is maximal.

Once again, we can sum up the producer-employer's partial equilibrium by defining two fuzzy subsets which one, $\mathcal{U}_j$, describes the agent's goal and $\mathcal{E}_j$, the constraint :

$$\mathcal{U}_j = \{q_j \in Q_j;\ u_j(q_j) \in [0,1]\} \text{ and } \mathcal{E}_j = \{q_j \in Q_j;\ e_j(q_j) \in [0,1]\}.$$

I.5. The method for fuzzy optimization

The problem of partial equilibrium can be summed up in defining the fuzzy subsets-goals and the fuzzy subsets-constraints. We must now explain how we can solve a fuzzy maximization problem under fuzzy constraints.

Here, we present some elements of these methods whose developments are in Ponsard [1982b] and Billot [1987b], from Tanaka, Okuda & Asai [1974] devoted to F.M.P. (*Fuzzy Mathematical Programming*).

I.5.1. General method

Let E be a usual set, $E = \{x\}$, where x is an allocation, a social state,...

Let $\mathcal{O}$ be a fuzzy subset of E, where the membership function $o(.)$ describes the satisfaction level to a given goal.

Let $\mathcal{C}$ be a fuzzy subset of E, where the membership function $c(.)$ describes the satisfaction level to a given constraint.

Definition 3 : A *fuzzy decision* $\mathcal{D}$ is the fuzzy intersection of the fuzzy subset-goal $\mathcal{O}$ and the fuzzy subset-constraint $\mathcal{C}$: $\mathcal{D} = \mathcal{O} \cap \mathcal{C}$.

Let us form the fuzzy subset $\mathcal{D}$, $\mathcal{D} = \mathcal{O} \cap \mathcal{C}$, such that :

$$d(.) : E \rightarrow [0,1]$$
$$x \rightarrow d(x) = \text{Min}[o(x), c(x)].$$

The fuzzy decision is defined according to a subset. We must look for the *supremum*, that is the best element of the fuzzy decision. This corresponds to the object whose membership level is the greatest in the fuzzy decision.

Definition 4 : The best solution for optimizing $\mathcal{O}$ under $\mathcal{C}$ is the element $\hat{d}$ such that :

$$\hat{d} = \text{Sup}_{x \in E}\, d(x) = \text{Sup}_{x \in E}\{\text{Min}[o(x), c(x)]\}.$$

Tanaka, Okuda & Asai [1974] proved that it is equivalent to search for the solution of $\text{Sup}_{x \in E}\, d(x)$ and the one of $\text{Sup}_{x \in A}\, a(x)$ where the usual set A is defined as follows :

$$A = \{x \in E;\ c(x) \geq a(x)\}.$$

The conditions under which the function $\mathrm{Sup}_{x \in A}\, a(x)$ is continuous are very weak (continuity of $a(.)$ and strict convexity of C, that is strict quasi-concavity of $c(.)$) and we analyzed them in Billot [1987b], chapter III. The assumption dealing with the set of objects is its compactedness. Under these few conditions, the existence of $\hat{a}$ is ensured.

I.5.2. The consumer-worker partial equilibrium

In order to obtain the consumer-worker's optimal demand, we must apply this result to a *LCE* model. We know the consumer-worker i's program to be defined with two fuzzy subsets $\mathcal{U}_i$ and $\mathcal{B}_i$. The fuzzy decision of i, noted $\mathcal{D}_i$, corresponds to the fuzzy intersection of both subsets $\mathcal{U}_i$ and $\mathcal{B}_i$, that is the ith consumer-worker's fuzzy subset of demand.

In applying the general result, we can say that a consumer-worker's partial equilibrium corresponds to a particular demand noted x_i such that :

$$\mathrm{Sup}_{x_i \in X_i}\, d(x_i) = \mathrm{Sup}_{x_i \in A}\, u(x_i),$$

where the usual set A is defined as follows : $A = \{x_i \in X_i;\ b_i(x_i) \geq u_i(x_i)\}$.

We must now realize the aggregation of individual demands. We note x the vector of global demand and X the global set of profiles with :

$$\Sigma_{i \in S}\, x_i = x \text{ and } X = \Sigma_{i \in S}\, X_i.$$

The *Fuzzy Mathematical Programming* associates a fuzzy subset $\mathcal{D}$ to the usual set X, such that :

$$d(.) : X \to [0,1]$$
$$x \to d(x) = Med_{x_i}\left[\mathrm{Sup}_{x_i \in X_i}\, d_i(x_i)\right],$$

where "*Med*"[3] is the aggregation operator of decisions. This aggregation derives from the "*Median*" agent. It implicitly corresponds to the traditional assumption of *representative agent*. We must now determine an individual whose behaviour can correspond to the social behaviour. Nothing *mathematically* prevents from choosing the operator "Max", or some particular strict

3 $Med(x_i)$ (resp. q_j) is the median value of the membership levels distribution to $\mathcal{D}_i$ (resp. $\mathcal{O}_j$) in the equilibrium.

or nilpotent[4] *norms* (see Dubois [1983], chap.II, p. 111).

Hence, we can summed up the aggregation of individual demands according to the total fuzzy subset $\mathcal{D}$:

$$\mathcal{D} = \{x \in X : d(x) = Med_{x_i}\left[\operatorname{Sup}_{x_i \in X_i} d_i(x_i)\right].$$

I.5.3. The producer-employer partial equilibrium

Producers-employers maximize their utility for profit under a constraint of efficiency. The fuzzy intersection of $\mathcal{U}_j$ and $\mathcal{E}_j$ corresponds to the jth producer-employer's fuzzy subset of supply noted $\mathcal{O}_j$.

We can also describe the producer-employer partial equilibrium thanks to the optimal profile of tasks and commodities supply noted q_j, as follows :

$$\operatorname{Sup}_{q_j \in Q_j} o_j(q_j) = \operatorname{Sup}_{q_j \in A'} u_j(q_j),$$

where A' is a usual set defined as follows :

$$A' = \{q_j \in Q_j : e_j(q_j) \geq u_j(q_j)\}.$$

Since the function $\operatorname{Sup}_{q_j \in A'} u_j(q_j)$ is continuous, it implies the fuzzy subset $\mathcal{U}_j$ to be strictly convex. It yields $\forall q_j \in A'$, $\operatorname{Sup}_{q_j \in Q_j} o_j(q_j)$ is strictly quasi-concave. Hence, $\mathcal{O}_j$ is strictly convex.

The individual supplies must be aggregated as were the individual demands.

We call vector of total supply, the vector q such that :

$$q = \sum_{j \in P} q_j,$$

and we also call total set, the production set Q such that :

$$Q = \sum_{j \in P} Q_j.$$

In order to associate a fuzzy subset of total production to the set Q, we must use one of the above ordinal operators. We consider, here too, the best operator to be "*Med*".

Hence we define the fuzzy subset of total production, noted $\mathcal{O}$ as follows :

---

4 We call *strict norm* an operator defined for a bijection $f(.)$ thanks to $\operatorname{Min}[1, f^{-1}(f(y) - f(x))]$ with $f(x) < 0$ if $x > 1$ and *nilpotent norm* the operator defined for an application $\Phi(.)$ thanks to $\operatorname{Min}[1, \Phi(\Phi(1) - \Phi(x) + \Phi(y))]$.

$$\mathcal{o}(.) : Q \rightarrow [0,1]$$

$$q \rightarrow \mathcal{o}(q) = Med_{q_j}\left[\mathrm{Sup}_{q_j \in Q_j}\, o_j(q_j)\right].$$

We can say :

$$\mathcal{O} = \left\{ q \in Q : \mathcal{o}(q) = Med_{q_j}\left[\mathrm{Sup}_{q_j \in Q_j}\, o_j(q_j)\right]\right\}.$$

Our goal is now to prove the existence of a general equilibrium that is consistent with $\mathcal{D}$ and $\mathcal{O}$, that is the existence of a system of prices and quasi wage-rates such that any market or quasi-market is balanced.

SECTION TWO : THE EXISTENCE OF A FUZZY GENERAL EQUILIBRIUM

The intuition of a possible consistency of individual goals, quasi-mythic for Adam Smith (the invisible hand) starts (in its modern expression) with a Cournot's remark. As Weintraub [1980] noticed it, we have to wait for Walras for this intuition to be exploited. It is still true that *modern* developments of general equilibrium analysis start with Cassel's works [1932] who proposed a simplified model of the Walrasian system and Wald [1951] who deepened the technical aspects of a system of simultaneous equations.

The technical achievement of this theory corresponds to Arrow & Debreu's works. In [1954], Arrow & Debreu improved the Wald's system by introducing topological analysis. McKenzie [1959] or Cale [1955], at the same time, also belonged to that *movement* called by Weintraub the "neoWalrasian school" which tried to define the existence of a competitive equilibrium of private ownership economy in an extremely rigourous way.

Hence, general equilibrium analysis became the heart of an important part of economic theory ; for improving the basic model or criticizing its empirical relevance (Blaug [1982]), for looking for a macroeconomic extrapolation in order to express microeconomic foundations of macro-economics (the disequilibrium School) or studying the consistency of such a concept in sequential economies (the concept of *temporary equilibrium* developed by Stigum [1969] or Grandmont [1977]).

Blaug called *neoWalrasian paradigm* those topics that are based on assumptions related to production sets and consumption ones and on a structure of behaviour describing the agent's choices when confronted to several alternatives. Basically, the object of our work is the same. But we change the structure of behaviour by introducing a new (fuzzy) behavioural standard.

II.1. A private ownership *LCE*

When presenting a *LCE*, we supposed the agent's budget to deal only with his initial endowments e_i. There is therefore no firm whose capital belongs to consumers-workers. We are now going to introduce an assumption of private ownership. This assumption concerns initial endowments and firms capital.

Each consumer-worker owns some shares. θ_{ij} represents *the shares of firm j that belong to agent i*. We can say :

$$\Sigma_{i \in S} \theta_{ij} = 1 \text{ with } \theta_{ij} \geq 0.$$

This ownership assumption for consumers-workers changes the constraints of budget since it implies any agent i to own a part θ_{ij} of firm j. This part θ_{ij} of firm j also implies a part θ_{ij} of j's profits. The agent i's new constraint, when his wealth is noted r_i, for a given system of prices and quasi wage-rates, corresponds to :

$$B_i = \{x_i \in X_i : p \cdot x_i \leq p \cdot e_i + \Sigma_{j \in P} \theta_{ij} \cdot (p \cdot q_j)\}.$$

This leads to a new fuzzy subset $\mathcal{B}_i$ with :

$$b_i(.) : X_i \rightarrow [0,1]$$

$$x_i \rightarrow b_i(x_i) \in [0,1]$$

$$\text{with : } b_i(x_i) = 1 \Leftrightarrow p \cdot x_i = p \cdot e_i + \Sigma_{j \in P} \theta_{ij} \cdot (p \cdot q_j) = r_i(p),$$

$$b_i(x_i) \in]0,1[\Leftrightarrow p \cdot x_i < r_i(p),$$

$$b_i(x_i) = 0 \Leftrightarrow p \cdot x_i > r_i(p).$$

II.2. A general fuzzy equilibrium (*à la Ponsard*)

II.2.1. The excess demand

By considering the total wealth of a Labour-Commodities-Economy to be defined as follows :

$$\Sigma_{i \in S} r_i(p) = r(p),$$

the total excess demand of *LCE*, for a given system of prices and quasi wage-rates $\overline{p}$, noted $ed(\overline{p})$ or *ed* is defined as follows :

$$ed = x - q - r.$$

It is obvious that $x \in X$ and $q \in Q$. Hence, *ed* belongs the set *ED* which corresponds to $X - Q - \{r\}$. But both partial equilibria allows to say : $x \in \mathcal{D}$ and $q \in \mathcal{O}$.

We can therefore consider *ed* to belong to a fuzzy subset $\mathcal{ED}$ of *ED* according to the membership function $\mathit{ed}(.)$ such that :

$$\mathit{ed}(.) : ED = X - Q - \{r\} \rightarrow [0,1]$$

$$ed = x - q - r \quad \rightarrow \mathit{ed}(ed) = 0 \text{ if } x - q - r = 0,$$

$$\mathit{ed}(ed) = 1 \text{ if } q = -r \text{ and}$$

$$\mathit{ed}(ed) \in]0,1[\text{ otherwise.}$$

This means that general equilibria correspond to a null membership level to the fuzzy subset $\mathcal{ED}$. The situation where the production is just equal to the opposite of resources corresponds to the highest membership level, meaning that the demand is never satisfied. This occurrence is not consistent with the assumption of irreversibility. In other words, $Q \cap (-Q) \subset \{0\}$ is not verified. Or else, the membership function will be defined on [0,1[. In usual theory, we can notice this assumption to ensure the set $X - Q$ to be closed and bounded, in order to search for equilibria in the convex closure of the economy. In Ponsard [1984], [1986], this assumption does not seem to be necessary in a fuzzy economy *à la Ponsard*, nor the free disposal assumption ($\{x \in R^{l+m} / x \leq 0\} \subset Q$).

II.2.2. The excess demand correspondence

This correspondence relates the system of prices and quasi wage-rates p to the excess demand vectors $ed(p)$. We know from definitions 1 and 2 that p is a point[5] of R_{+*}^{l+m}.

In this system, replacing p by λp where λ is a strictly positive real number, we do not modify the equilibrium conditions. We can consider a kind of restriction that leads to search for the balanced system of prices and quasi wage-rates into a usual simplex $\underline{\Pi}$, by normalizing the set :

$$\underline{\Pi} = \{\overline{p} \in R_{+*}^{l+m} : \textstyle\sum_{k=1}^{l+m} p_k = 1\}.$$

HP : The simplex $\underline{\Pi}$ is a nonempty, convex and compact set.

The demand correspondence $ed(.)$ can be defined such that :

---

5 The symbol * in (R_*) means that the null vector does not belong to R.

$$ed(.) : \underline{\Pi} \rightarrow ED$$

$$\overline{p} \rightarrow ed(\overline{p}) = x(\overline{p}) - q(\overline{p}) - r(\overline{p}),$$

where $x(\overline{p})$ represents the demand correspondence value for a system $\overline{p}$, $q(\overline{p})$ the supply correspondence value and $r(\overline{p})$ the wealth. This excess correspondence demand is continuous because of the continuity of $u_i(.)$ and $u_j(.)$.

II.2.3. The Walras' law

This law defines the system of prices as a tool for balancing some excess supplies with some excess demands, knowing that prices and quasi wage-rates are all positive and non-null. Mathematically :

$$\forall \overline{p} \in \underline{\Pi} : < \overline{p} \cdot ed(\overline{p}) > = 0.$$

We know fuzzy general equilibrium to correspond to an excess demand whose membership level to the fuzzy subset $\mathcal{ED}$ is null. This excess demand must totally satisfy the Walras' law. We can therefore infer that a fuzzy general equilibrium of a *LCE à la Ponsard* consists in a couple of a system of prices and quasi wage-rates $\overline{p}^*$ and an excess demand $ed^* \in ed(\overline{p}^*)$ such that :

$$\mathcal{ed}(ed^*) = 0 \text{ and } < \overrightarrow{p}^* \cdot ed^* > = 0.$$

II.2.4. Proof of fuzzy relevance for Walras' law (Ponsard [1986])

Let us consider the continuous function $g(.)$ defined as follows :

$$g(.) : ED \rightarrow \underline{\Pi}$$

$$ed \rightarrow g(ed) = \{\overline{p}' : \overline{p}' \cdot ed = \overline{p} \cdot ed\}.$$

LEMMA 1 : *Let $h(.)$ be a function from the simplex $\underline{\Pi}$ into itself such that : $\forall \overline{p} \in \underline{\Pi}$: $h(\overline{p}) = [g \circ ed](\overline{p})$. If $h(.)$ is continuous, then the Walras' law holds.*

Proof : $h(.)$ is defined such as :

$$\underline{\Pi} \rightarrow ED \quad \rightarrow \underline{\Pi}$$

$$\overline{p} \rightarrow ed(\overline{p}) \rightarrow \{\overline{p}' : \overline{p}' \cdot ed(\overline{p} = \overline{p} \cdot ed(\overline{p})\}.$$

Since $g(.)$ and $ed(.)$ are continuous, $h(.)$ is also continuous. Because HP guarantees $\underline{\Pi}$ to be compact, convex and nonempty, the Brouwer's theorem conditions are satisfied. $h(.)$ is a continuous mapping. Hence, it has a fixed point $\overline{p}^*$ for the $\overline{p} \rightarrow ed(\overline{p}) \rightarrow \{p'\}$.

□

II.2.5. The fuzzy excess demand correspondence

We have to define a fuzzy excess demand correspondence to prove the existence of general equilibria for a *LCE* (*à la Ponsard*). A *fuzzy excess demand correspondence*, noted $Z(.)$, is defined as follows :

$$Z(.) : (\underline{\Pi} \times ED) \rightarrow P(\underline{\Pi} \times ED)$$

$$(\overline{p}, ed) \rightarrow z(\overline{p}, ed) = \{h(\overline{p}), ed(\overline{p})\},$$

where $P(\underline{\Pi} \times ED)$ if the powerset of $(\underline{\Pi} \times ED)$.

II.3. Existence of equilibria for a *LCE* (*à la Ponsard*)

First, we recall the fixed point theorem for a fuzzy correspondence (Butnariu [1982]), next we present the existence theorem that is equivalent to Ponsard's one [1986] (even though we do not base the proof upon a F-continuous function as Ponsard did), and finally we analyze the equilibrium existence.

II.3.1. Fixed points for fuzzy correspondence

This theorem was presented in chapter three. We just recall its fundamental characteristics.

THEOREM (Butnariu [1982]) : *Let X be a real topological space, locally convex and Hausdorff-separated and C a nonempty, compact and convex subset of X. If $\mathcal{P}(.)$ is a fuzzy closed correspondence on C, then $\mathcal{P}(.)$ has a fixed point in C.*

The existence theorems proved by Ponsard [1984], [1986] are direct applications of Butnariu [1982], even though restricted to a particular economy with no free excess ; i.e. any price or quasi wage-rate is strictly positive.

II.3.2. Existence theorem of a general equilibrium for a LCE à la Ponsard

THEOREM (Ponsard [1986]) : *Let* $(\underline{\Pi} \times R^{l+m})$ *be a real topological space, locally convex and Hausdorff-separated and* $(\underline{\Pi} \times ED)$ *a subset of* $(\underline{\Pi} \times R^{l+m})$*. If* $Z(.)$*, the fuzzy excess demand correspondence is closed, with for any couple* $(\overline{p}, ed) \in (\underline{\Pi} \times ED)$*,* $z(\overline{p}, ed)$ *nonempty and convex, then there exists a system of prices and quasi wage-rates* $\overline{p}^* \in \underline{\Pi}$ *and an excess demand* $ed^* \in ed(\overline{p}^*)$ *with* $ed(ed^*) = 0$ *such that* $< \overline{p}^* \cdot ed^* > = 0$ *and* $ed(ed^*) = 0$.

Proof : α- The fuzzy correspondence $Z(.)$ is closed since its graph is the Cartesian product of two closed sets :

$$\text{graph } Z = \{([\overline{p}, ed], \mu) \in (\underline{\Pi} \times ED) \,/\, \mu \in z(\overline{p}, ed) = \text{graph } h \times \text{graph } ed\}.$$

β- In the same way, we prove $Z(.)$ to be convex on $(\underline{\Pi} \times ED)$ because deriving from the Cartesian product of two convex sets.

γ- By applying the fuzzy fixed point theorem, we know the fuzzy excess demand correspondence $Z(.)$ to have a fixed point in $(\underline{\Pi} \times ED)$. That is, $\exists (\overline{p}^*, ed^*) \in (\underline{\Pi} \times ED)$ such that :

$$(\overline{p}^*, ed^*) \in Z(\overline{p}^*, ed^*) = \{h(\overline{p}^*), ed(\overline{p}^*)\}.$$

It means : $\overline{p}^* \in h(\overline{p}^*)$ and $ed^* \in ed(\overline{p}^*)$.

By lemma 1, it yields on one hand $< \overline{p}^* \cdot ed^* > = 0$, and also $\forall \overline{p} \in \underline{\Pi} : \overline{p} \cdot ed^* = \overline{p}^* \cdot ed^*$. From these two expressions, we get : $\forall \overline{p} \in \underline{\Pi} : \overline{p} \cdot ed^* = \overline{p}^* \cdot ed^* = 0 \Rightarrow \forall \overline{p} \in \underline{\Pi} : \overline{p} \cdot ed^* = 0$. Prices are strictly positive ; it implies $ed^* = 0$ which means : $ed(ed^*) = 0$.

□

II.3.3. Analysis and comments

By analyzing this result, one can imagine some *paradoxical* equilibria.

When proving both existences of a fuzzy general equilibrium and a usual one (since the usual economy which defines $ed(.)$ also has a general equilibrium), we do not use the whole *information* that derives from fuzzy preferences (the one dealing with the intrinsic qualities of profiles) ; i.e. the one deriving from individual preferences that we have "*forgotten*" in order to utilize the fuzzy utility function by restraining the considered behaviour to a locally and globally *coherent* one. By replacing fuzzy relations of preference inside the analysis, we are going to measure their very contribution ; that is what we try to do with *paradoxical* equilibria. Nevertheless, we have first to verify the introduction of a new behaviour standard not to prevent the existence of general equilibria. That is the reason why before proving the existence of some *paradoxical* general equilibria, we prove fuzzy relations of preference to allow the existence of a *standard* general equilibrium in a pure *LCE* (which is not *à la Ponsard*).

II.4. Existence of a general equilibrium in a pure *LCE*

A *LCE à la Ponsard* differs from a pure *LCE* because of behaviours. In a pure *LCE* :

1- The consumer-worker's preferences are represented by a *fuzzy preorder*, that is a *reflexive (F.s.)* and *f-transitive fuzzy binary relation* $\mathcal{P}_i(.,.)$, or a *reflexive (F.s.) fuzzy binary relation* $\mathcal{P}_i(.,.)$ that is consistent with the principle of dominated irrationality.

2- The producers-employers are of only one type, called Arrow - Debreu type. They maximize their profits.

3- The consumer-worker's constraint is Boolean.

4- Definitions and developments of § I.3. remain true.

5- A pure *LCE* is also a private ownership economy. The initial endowments $(\vec{e})$ like firms $(\theta_{..})$ belong to the consumers-workers.

Definition 5 : We call *pure Labour-Commodities-Economy* a *LCE* defined as follows :

$$LCE = [\{(C/T)_i, \mathcal{P}_i(.,.)\}, Q_j, e_i, (\theta_{ij})],$$

satisfying points 1 to 5.

II.4.1. General equilibrium for a pure LCE

Definition 6: A *statement* of *LCE* specifies each consumer-worker's choice and producer-employers'one. It is a $(n+n')$-tuple of points of R^{l+m}, or a point of $R^{(n+n')(l+m)}$.

Definition 7: A given statement of *LCE* $[(c/t)_i, (s/d)_j]$ is a *complete equilibrium* if the total excess demand $[(c-s)/(t-d)]$ is equal to the initial endowments $(e/0)$: i.e. $c-s=e$ and $t=d$.

Definition 8 : We call general equilibrium of a pure *LCE* the triplet $[(c/t)^*, (s/d)^*, (p/w)^*]$ such that :

α- $\forall i \in S$, $(c/t)_i^*$ is the greatest element of :

$$\{(c/t) / (p/w)^* \cdot (c/t)_i^* \leq p^* \cdot e_i + \Sigma_{j \in P} \theta_{ij}[(p/w)^* \cdot (s/d)_j^*]\},$$

for $\mathcal{P}_i(.,.)$ or $Proj(.)$.

β- $\forall j \in P$, $(s/d)_j^*$ maximizes $< (p/w)^* \cdot (s/d)_j^* >$.

$\gamma 1$- $c^* - s^* = e^*$.

$\gamma 2$- $t^* - d^* = 0$.

Conditions α) and β) mean that $(c/t)_i^*$ as $(s/d)_j^*$ allow the consumers-workers like the producers-employers to be in a situation of partial equilibrium. Conditions $\gamma 1$) and $\gamma 2$) mean that the statement $[(c/t)^*, (s/d)^*]$ is a *complete* equilibrium ; for any commodity or task, supply is equal to demand. For a given system of prices and quasi wage-rates $(p/w)^*$, given initial endowments $(\vec{e})$ and parts $(\theta_{..})$ of firms and given other agents' decisions, the statement of a *LCE* is a *complete* equilibrium when any agent, consumer-worker or producer-employer, has no interest to change his decision.

II.4.2. Existence theorem of a general equilibrium for a pure LCE

Fuzzy utility functions represent fuzzy relations of preference and take their values in [0,1]. Hence, we can directly apply the Arrow - Debreu's theorem [1954], (see also Debreu [1959], [1984]).

THEOREM (of existence) : *Let a pure LCE be defined by* $[\{(C/T)_i, \mathcal{P}_i(.,.)\}, Q_j, e_i, (\theta_{ij})]$. *The LCE has a general equilibrium if and only if :*

A- $\forall i \in S$.

A1- H1, H2 and H3 hold.

A2- $(C/T)_i$ *admits a lower bound for* $\leq$.

A3- $\forall (c/t)_i \in (C/T)_i : \exists (c/t)_i'$ *such that :*

$$\mathcal{P}_i((c/t)_i, (c/t)_i') < \mathcal{P}_i((c/t)_i', (c/t)_i)$$

and/or

$$Proj[(c/t)_i'] > Proj[(c/t)_i].$$

A4- The next fuzzy subsets :

$$X^+ = \{(c/t)_i \in (C/T)_i \,/\, \chi(c/t)_i \geq \chi(b/t)_i'\} \text{ and}$$

$$X^- = \{(c/t)_i \in (C/T)_i \,/\, \chi(c/t)_i \leq \chi(b/t)_i'\},$$

are fuzzy closed with :

$\mathcal{P}_i(a,b) \geq \mathcal{P}_i(b,a) \Leftrightarrow \mathcal{U}(a) \geq \mathcal{U}(b)$ *and/or*

$Proj[a] > Proj[b] \Leftrightarrow \mathcal{U}(a) \geq \mathcal{U}(b).$

A5- $\exists c_i \in C_i$ *such that* $c_i \ll e_i$.

A6- *If* $\{(c/t)_i, (c/t)_i'\} \in [(C/T)_i]^2$, $\forall \lambda \in]0,1[$, *then if* $\mathcal{U}(c/t)_i'$ *is greater than* $\mathcal{U}(c/t)_i$, *it implies :*

$\mathcal{U}[\lambda(c/t)_i' + (1-\lambda)(c/t)_i] > \mathcal{U}(c/t)_i.$

B- $\forall j \in P$,

B1- *P5, P6 and P7 hold.*

B2- $Q_j \cap (-Q_j) \subset \{0\}$ *(irreversibility).*

B3- $\{(s/d)_j \in R^{l+m} \,/\, (s/d)_j \leq 0\} \subset Q_j$ *(free disposability).*

We do not prove this theorem (see Debreu [1959], [1984] (chap.V, p.91-96)). The demonstration is just the applied translation of Debreu [1959] to a pure *LCE*. Because fuzzy relations of preference lead to continuous fuzzy utility functions on [0,1], if the remainder of the model does not change, which is the case, the general equilibrium exists without any doubt.

CHAPTER 5

Underemployment Fuzzy Equilibrium

From the *quasi*-Walrasian theory of unemployment (Calvo [1979], Azariadis [1975], Baily [1977]) with imperfect information (Phelps [1970], Mortensen [1970] and Salop [1979]) to Hahn's [1987] paper, Shaked & Sutton's [1984] one or Rubinstein's [1981] recent works (which introduce involuntary unemployment into bargaining models), the problem of consistency between involuntary unemployment and Walrasian equilibrium is generally studied according to the search theory (with introduction of individual costs). Nevertheless, most of these authors - and especially Hahn - looked for the *precise point* of the Walrasian theory that could allow to talk about the *involuntary* aspect of unemployment when a perfect flexibility of prices and wages remained.

The problem is here the very notion of *Keynesian unemployment*. In his paper, "Was Keynes a Keynesian ?", Grossman [1972] noticed that the *real* Keynesian unemployment does not correspond to what Malinvaud [1977] called "*Keynesian unemployment*" but to one of its limit cases. When postulating the real wage to equal the marginal productivity of labour (as Keynes did), it implies the producers to be not constrained and therefore the prices can perfectly balance the commodities markets even though the nominal wage is rigid. Hence, unemployment can appear on the labour market. Is it possible to translate this idea inside a competitive economy model ?

Actually, a more precise analysis of the excess demand correspondence reveals a new conception of the Walras' law. There is another law, quite well known, called the "*law of demand*" which says that prices fall when demand rises. This law does not systematically derive from a partial equilibrium model (even with Giffen commodities) or a general equilibrium one.

Samuelson [1948], then Hicks [1956] tried to theoretically justify this law by acknowledging traditional assumptions on utility functions not to be sufficient. Hicks and Samuelson were interested by the Giffen commodities (inferior commodities for which the income term is greater than the substitution one). Even though this research is not ended (see Hildenbrand [1983]), the Sonnenschein's famous theorem [1973] for functions generalized to correspondences by Debreu [1974] and Mantel [1974] is its main result. This theorem says that the demand functions (or correspondences) resulting from a *regular* behaviour (convexity of the individual consumption sets and production ones, preferences convexity,...) can have *any form*. Therefore, the demand function (or supply in case of inputs) is not necessarily decreasing when prices increase. In other words, the correspondence of labour supply does not necessarily decrease when the wage rate decreases.

When devoted to the labour market, this theorem means any decreasing wage rate not to always imply a decreasing labour supply, hence a decreasing unemployment. In other words, the voluntary unemployed worker is the one who cancels his labour supply when estimating the wage rate to be too low. In our case, it means that an increasing wage rate would cancel this voluntary unemployment. But, according to the Sonnenschein - Debreu - Mantel theorem, *one cannot be sure* (in the *standard* Walrasian case) *that an increasing wage rate implies a decreasing unemployment*. Our conclusion is trivial ; there can be unemployed workers who *are not voluntary* inside a Walrasian model. We call them *Walrasian unemployed workers*.

SECTION ONE : EXISTENCE OF AN UNDEREMPLOYMENT EQUILIBRIUM

We are in a pure *LCE*, that is a private ownership economy where consumers-workers have fuzzy preferences in order to choose their optimal profiles of commodities and tasks. The fundamental sets are those of a pure *LCE*, and the agents are divided into two sets : the consumers-workers (S) and the producers-employers (P).

I.1. Voluntary unemployment and Walrasian involuntary unemployment

I.1.1. Basic assumptions of a pure LCE

We always note T_i ($T_i \subset R^l_-$), the tasks set of the worker i, C_i ($C_i \subset R^m_+$), the consumption set of the consumer i and Q_j ($Q_j \subset R^{l+m}$), the production set of the producer-employer j.

Assumptions P1, P2, P3, P4, P5, P6, P7, H1, H2 and H3 are still valid. We add a new assumption about commodities endowments :

H4-: $\forall i \in S, \exists c_i \in C_i : c_i \ll e_i$.

I.1.2. Voluntary and involuntary unemployment in a Walrasian economy

Definition 1 : Let $\vec{w}$ be a system of quasi wage-rates and $\vec{t}_i$ a tasks supply ; the worker is in a *Walrasian* situation of unemployment if : $<\vec{w} \cdot \vec{t}_i> = 0$, that is as soon as his earnings are null. It means that if we call t_i^k the worker i's supply of task k and w^k the quasi wage-rate that balances the kth task market, we can have : $\forall k \in \{1,\ldots,l\}, t_i^k = 0$. In this case, the agent is a *Walrasian voluntary unemployed worker* since he does not supply anything, either because the equilibrium quasi wage-rates do not satisfy him (they can be inferior to his *reservation* quasi wage-rates), or because *discouraged*, he *does not enter* the labour market.

Definition 2 : The *Walrasian involuntary unemployed worker* also corresponds to null earnings : $<\vec{w} \cdot \vec{t}_i> = 0$. But, his particular situation is such that : $\forall t_i^k, t_i^k \neq 0$ and $w^k = 0$. He only supplies tasks whose excess supplies are so important that they cannot be cancelled thanks to a simple decrease of the associated quasi wage-rates. Hence, this irreducible disequilibrium of tasks supply implies null quasi wage-rates.

If the worker i is rational in a standard manner, when getting to know of the quasi wage-rates that will pay his tasks supply, he would become a *Walrasian voluntary unemployed worker* since the usual disutility for labour makes him withdraw his supply.

We introduce now the worker's fuzzy preferences. Disutility for labour only deals with the relative preferences if those are systematically lower than the intrinsic preferences of task profiles. Hence, we can apply the model of solution for indifference that we proposed in chapter one in order to lead a decision that transforms the considered worker into a Walrasian involuntary unemployed worker.

A few remarks are necessary :

α- After reading definition 2, one may consider a *benevolent* worker to be described in such an equation. It is trivial to recall that in a usual Walrasian case, there exists one and only one *possible price* per commodity or task (on the contrary of prices systems in a competitive equilibrium with imperfect information). If benevolents also satisfy definition 2, this would mean that they do not directly appear in the model since by definition, they only supply free tasks whose quasi wage-rates are null : therefore, they would not be benevolent any more[1] !

β- The Walrasian unemployed worker is a limit case. Between the *full* worker who supplies some of the only tasks which have a strictly positive quasi wage-rate and the Walrasian involuntary unemployed worker who only supplies free tasks, there exists a lot of intermediary situations, which correspond to *partial unemployment*. Actually, it means some consumers-workers to be in the following equilibrium situation : some supplied tasks are in excess while others are not.

I.2. The consumer-worker's behaviour

I.2.1. Fuzzy preferences and dominated irrationality

The agent *i*'s preferences correspond to a reflexive (F.s.) but not necessarily f-transitive fuzzy binary relation $\mathcal{P}_i(.,.)$, defined on $(C/T)_i$. If the agent is *rational*, his relation of preference is a fuzzy preorder. If the agent is *irrational*, his relation of preference is not transitive and he utilizes the first projection to order the profiles of $(c/t)_i$. We know that in both cases, there exists a fuzzy utility function. He has local preferences between two profiles, i.e. any two elements of $(C/T)_i$, but he is not necessarily *rational*. He can contradict himself and his preferences do not always respect the f-transitivity.

What we call *dominated irrationality* consists in associating each object to its highest level of relative and intrinsic qualities when confronted to all the others. *Incoherent* fuzzy relations (with Condorcet's inconsistencies for example) must lead to an order which satisfies a condition of rationality (even weak).

In other words, if $\mathcal{P}_i(.,.)$ is not f-transitive, we define the preordered fuzzy subset $(C/\mathcal{T})_i$ of $(C/T)_i$ (where $\chi(.)$ is the membership function of $(C/\mathcal{T})_i$), such that :

equation *A*

$$\forall (c/t)_i \in (C/T)_i : \chi(c/t)_i = Proj[(c/t)_i] = \mathrm{Max}_{(c/t)_i'}[\mathcal{P}_i((c/t)_i, (c/t)_i')].$$

1 One of the Walrasian equilibrium characteristics corresponds to the fact that no transaction is possible outside the situations of equilibrium. This would imply a benevolent to supply the only tasks that are already free.

Let us take a simple example and see if an incoherent local situation allows to obtain a fuzzy preorder when applying the projection.

Example : $X = \{x, y, z\}$.

Preferences are such that :

$\leftarrow \quad \mathcal{P}_i(.,.)$

$\uparrow \quad \mathcal{P}_i(.,.)$

	x	y	z
x	0.4	0.5	0.6
y	0.6	0.5	0.8
z	0.4	0.9	0.5

Let us analyze this situation, term by term.

$$\mathcal{P}_i(x,y) = 0.5 < \mathcal{P}_i(y,x) = 0,6$$

and

$$\mathcal{P}_i(y,z) = 0.8 < \mathcal{P}_i(z,y) = 0,9.$$

If the fuzzy relation $\mathcal{P}_i(.,.)$ is f-transitive, we should have : $\mathcal{P}_i(x,z) < \mathcal{P}_i(z,x)$. But the preferences yield :

$$\mathcal{P}_i(x,z) = 0.6 > \mathcal{P}_i(z,x) = 0,4.$$

We can therefore consider the fuzzy relation $\mathcal{P}_i(.,.)$ not to be a preorder. The local preference is not *consistent* with the *global* one or the fuzzy utility defined from the principle "*equal relative preferences lead to equal satisfaction*" since there does not exist a fuzzy preordered subset $\mathcal{A}$ of $(C/T)_i$ such that (if $a(.)$ is the membership function of $\mathcal{A}$) :

$$\mathcal{P}_i(x,y) > \mathcal{P}_i(y,x) \Leftrightarrow a(x) > a(y).$$

The agent whose preferences are represented above is *locally incoherent*.

To be introduced in a competitive equilibrium model, this agent must dominate his irrationality. That is, his utility function satisfies the condition of continuity. In order to do it, the agent utilizes the first projection of his fuzzy relation of preference $\mathcal{P}_i(.,.)$. Therefore, he builds a preordered fuzzy subset $(C/\mathcal{T})_i$ of $(C/T)_i$ thanks to $Proj[.]$ which then becomes the membership function $\tau(.)$ of $(C/\mathcal{T})_i$ according to equation A.

We obtain :

$$\mathscr{X}(x) = \text{Max}[0.4,0.5,0.6] = 0.6,$$

$$\mathscr{X}(y) = \text{Max}[0.6,0.5,0.8] = 0.8 \text{ and}$$

$$\mathscr{X}(z) = \text{Max}[0.4,0.9,0.5] = 0.9,$$

i.e. $\mathscr{X}(x) < \mathscr{X}(y) < \mathscr{X}(z)$.

I.2.2. Preference continuity and fuzzy utility

The operator *Proj* is reflexive (F.s.) and f-transitive because of the properties of the "$\geq$" relation. When the consumer-worker is locally irrational and dominates this irrationality by the first projection of his fuzzy relation of preference, there exists a continuous fuzzy utility function.

Assumption of fuzzy preferences continuity (FPC) : $\forall i \in S$, the following fuzzy subsets :

$$(C/T)_i^+ = \{(c/t)_i' \in (C/T)_i \,/\, \mathscr{X}(c/t)_i' \geq \mathscr{X}(c/t)_i\} \text{ and}$$

$$(C/T)_i^- = \{(c/t)_i' \in (C/T)_i \,/\, \mathscr{X}(c/t)_i' \leq \mathscr{X}(c/t)_i\},$$

are *fuzzy closed* sets (with $\mathcal{P}_i(x,y) \leq \mathcal{P}_i(y,x) \Leftrightarrow \mathscr{X}(x) \leq \mathscr{X}(y)$ *or* $\mathscr{X}(x) = Proj[x]$).

$(C/T)_i$ is connected (since H3 defines it as a convex set). Hence, under FPC, the consumer-worker, locally rational or not, can represent his preferences with a fuzzy utility function $u_i(.)$ defined on [0,1] :

$$u_i(.) : (C/T)_i \to [0,1]$$

$$(c/t)_i \to u_i(c/t)_i \in [0,1].$$

I.2.3. The assumption of Fuzzy Local-nonDiscrimination (FLD)

This assumption is not technically necessary to the proof but realistic.

$\forall (c/t)_i \in (C/T)_i, \forall V(c/t)_i : \exists (c/t)_i' \in V(c/t)_i \cap (C/T)_i$ such that : $\mathcal{P}_i((b/t)_i,(c/t)_i') = \mathcal{P}_i((c/t)_i',(c/t)_i)$.

$V(c/t)_i$ is any neighbourhood of $(c/t)_i$.

I.2.4. The assumption of Global-nonSatiation of Preferences (GSP)

For any given profile, there always exists a better profile :

$$\forall (c/t)_i \in (C/T)_i, \exists (c/t)_i' \in (C/T)_i \,/\, \mathcal{U}(c/t)_i' > \mathcal{U}(c/t)_i.$$

We can divide this assumption into a first assumption of nonsatiation for commodities and a second one of *absence of ideal job* :

- Let $\bar{c} \in C_i : \forall t_i \in T_i, \exists t_i' \in T_i \,/\, \mathcal{U}(\bar{c}/t_i') > \mathcal{U}(\bar{c}/t_i)$.
- Let $\bar{t} \in T_i : \forall c_i \in C_i, \exists c_i' \in C_i \,/\, \mathcal{U}(c_i'/\bar{t}) > \mathcal{U}(c_i/\bar{t})$.

I.2.5. The assumption about the Quality Level of Objects (QLO)

This assumption is not explicitly used when proving the existence of an underemployment fuzzy equilibrium. Nevertheless, it is necessary when we try to interpret the tasks disequilibria that may appear. It means any object for any consumer-worker to be endowed with intrinsic qualities that are *lower* than relative ones. In other words, degrees of reflexivity are always *lower* than degrees of relative preference. This assumption implies, when dominating irrationality, any level of utility not to be influenced by the intrinsic qualities but *only by the relative ones.*

$$\forall i \in S, \forall (c/t)_i \in (C/T)_i : \mathcal{P}_i((c/t)_i, (c/t)_i) < \mathrm{Max}_{(C/T)_i}[\mathcal{P}_i((c/t)_i, .)].$$

This assumption allows to mathematically define the underemployment fuzzy equilibrium without referring to the relations between relative and intrinsic preferences. Henceforth, we must use a *memory-effect* on each agent's preferences in order to distinguish the *optimum* from the *decision.* The optimum defines the indifference class whose utility level is the highest because of the constraint of budget, and the decision is the unique allocation chosen by the agent after comparing the reflexivity degrees of allocations that belong to the optimal indifference class.

I.3. General model of a pure *LCE*

The consumer-worker's initial endowments are only composed of commodities. Tasks are considered as a typical flow that cannot be stocked. The consumer-worker's initial endowments in a pure *LCE* are represented by the vector $(e/0)_i$, where e_i correspond to commodities endowments.

Proposition : For a given system of prices and quasi wage-rates (p/w) and initial endowments $(e/0)_i$, the consumer-worker i chooses his tasks supply t_i^* and his commodities demand c_i^* such that his net expenditure $p \cdot (c_i^* - e_i)$ satisfies the budget constraint :

$$(p/w) \cdot (c/t)_i^* \leq (p/w) \cdot (e/0)_i + \Sigma_{j=1}^{n'} \theta_{ij} \cdot \Pi_j.$$

Each consumer-worker i tries to maximize $u_i(.)$ under the budget constraint. At the same time, each producer tries to maximize his profit. Therefore, a pure *LCE* is defined as follows :

$$LCE = [\{(C/T)_i, \mathcal{P}_i(.,.)\}, Q_j, e_i, (\theta_{ij})].$$

We call a *LCE* statement, any $(n'+n)$-tuple of points of R^{l+m}, i.e. a n-tuple of $(c/t)_i$ and a n'-tuple of $(s/d)_j$.

I.3.1. The definition of an underemployment fuzzy equilibrium of a pure LCE

The statement $[(c/t)_i^*, (s/d)_j^*, (p/w)^*]$ is a *possible underemployment fuzzy equilibrium* (we note *puf-equilibrium*) if and only if :

C1 : $\forall i \in S$, $(c/t)_i^*$ maximizes $u_i(.)$ on :

$$\{(c/t)_i \in (C/T)_i \,/\, (p/w)^* \cdot (c/t)_i^* = (p/w)^* \cdot (e/0)_i + \Sigma_{j \in P} \theta_{ij}[(p/w)^* \cdot (s/d)_j^*].$$

C2 : $\forall j \in P$, $(s/d)_j^*$ maximizes $[(p/w)^* \cdot (s/d)_j]$ on Q_j.

C3 : α- $\Sigma_{i \in S} c_i^* - \Sigma_{j \in P} s_j^* - \Sigma_{i \in S} e_i = 0$

β- $\Sigma_{i \in S} t_i^* - \Sigma_{j \in P} d_j^* \leq 0$ with $w^* \cdot [\Sigma_{i \in S} t_i^* - \Sigma_{j \in P} d_j^*] = 0$.

The two first conditions are usual, the third is new. C3α means the commodities markets to be balanced (that is, $\vec{p}$ belongs to R_+^{m*}) and C3β means some tasks markets to be (*possibly*) in excess supply when the associated quasi wage-rate is null (that is, $\vec{w}$ belongs to R_+^l). The Walras' law therefore holds. If such a solution is consistent with a Walrasian equilibrium, some consumers-workers can be in one of the situations that correspond to both definitions 1 and 2 of Walrasian unemployed workers. We have to prove, apart from the existence of a puf-equilibrium, that there exists a typical choice behaviour for Walrasian unemployed workers which is consistent with C1, C2 and C3.

I.3.2. Existence theorem of a puf-equilibrium

I.3.2.1. Preliminary results

We do not prove the two following lemmas (Debreu [1959;1984], Berge [1969]) :

LEMMA 1 : *Let A be a usual, nonempty and compact subset in R^{l+m} and a function f(.) defined such that :*

$$f(.) : R^{l+m} \rightarrow R$$
$$(p/w) \rightarrow f(p/w) = \text{Max}[(p/w) \cdot A]$$
$$= \text{Max}_{(c/t) \in A}[(p/w) \cdot (c/t)].$$

Then, f(.) is continuous.

The proof is based on upper-lower semicontinuity of $f(.)$ which proceeds from compactedness of A.

Definition 3 : For a given system of prices and quasi wage-rates (p/w) and for any real number α, we define each consumer-worker's demand correspondence $EC_i(.)$ such that :

$$EC_i[(p/w),\alpha] = \{(c/t)_i \in (C/T) / (p/w) \cdot (c/t)_i \leq \alpha\},$$

where α represents $[(p/w) \cdot (e/0)_i + \Sigma\theta_{ij} \cdot \pi_j]$.

Definition 4 : Since $(C/T)_i$ is convex and compact (H3), we call domain of $EC_i(.)$ noted DEC_i, the following set :

$$DEC_i = \{[(p/w) \in R^{l+m}, \alpha \in R] / \alpha \geq \text{Min}(p/w) \cdot (C/T)_i\}.$$

From lemma 1, we know the function that relates $\text{Min}(p/w) \cdot (C/T)_i$ to (p/w) to be continuous. Hence, DEC_i is a usual closed set.

LEMMA 2 : *If $(C/T)_i$ is nonempty, compact and convex and $\bar{\alpha}$ is a real number such that $\bar{\alpha} < \text{Min}(\bar{p}/\bar{w}) \cdot (C/T)_i$, then the correspondence $EC_i(.)$ is continuous at the point $[(\bar{p}/\bar{w}),\bar{\alpha}]$.*

(see Debreu [1982] in [1984], p. 134-135).

I.3.2.2. The existence theorem

THEOREM 1 : *There is a puf-equilibrium for the LCE if and only if :*

-*A*- $\forall i \in S,$

A1- $(C/T)_i$ *is a convex and compact set,*

A2- $u_i(.)$ *is continuous and quasi-concave,*

A3- $\exists c_i^\circ \in C_i : c_i^\circ \ll e_i$,

A4- FLD, GSP and QLO hold.

-B- $\forall j \in P$,

B1- Q_j *is a convex and compact set,*

B2- Q_j *contains the null vector of* R^{l+m}.

We can express this theorem according to the assumptions we used when defining a *LCE* and the properties of $(C/T)_i$.

THEOREM 1bis : *There is a puf-equilibrium for LCE if and only if H3, H4, P5, P6, P7, FLD, GSP and QLO hold and* $\forall i \in S$, $(C/T)_i$ *is a convex fuzzy subset.*

Proof: Step one : It consists in defining a *LCE feasible* statement. We say $[(c/t)_i, (s/d)_j, (p/w)]$ to be a *LCE feasible* statement if and only if :

1- $\forall i \in S : (c/t)_i \in (C/T)_i$,

2- $\forall j \in P : (s/d)_j \in Q_j$ and

3- $\sum_{i \in S}(c_i - e_i) - \sum_{j \in P} s_j = 0$ and $\sum_{i \in S} t_i - \sum_{j \in P} d_j \leq 0$.

We define a simplex of prices and quasi wage-rates noted *PW* as follows :

$$PW = \{(p/w) \in R_+^{l+m} \,/\, \textstyle\sum_{k=1}^{m} p_k + \sum_{q=1}^{l} w_q = 1\}.$$

Let $(\overline{p}/\overline{w})$ be a given system of prices and quasi wage-rates of *PW*. The producer-employer j tries to maximize his profit Π_j in Q_j. We write the maximal profit as follows :

$$\Pi_j(\overline{p}/\overline{w}) = \text{Max}(\overline{p}/\overline{w}) \cdot Q_j.$$

The consumer-worker tries to optimize his fuzzy utility function $u_i(.)$ in DEC_i :

$$EC_i(\overline{p}/\overline{w}) = \{(c/t)_i \in (C/T)_i \,/\, (\overline{p}/\overline{w}) \cdot (c/t)_i \leq (\overline{p}/\overline{w}) \cdot (e/0)_i + \textstyle\sum_{j \in P} \theta_{ij} \cdot [(\overline{p}/\overline{w}) \cdot (s/d)_j]\}.$$

It means :

$$EC_i(\overline{p}/\overline{w}) = \{(c/t)_i \in (C/T)_i \,/\, (\overline{p}/\overline{w}) \cdot (c/t)_i \leq (\overline{p}/\overline{w}) \cdot (e/0)_i$$

$$+ \Sigma_{j \in P} \theta_{ij} \cdot [\mathrm{Max}(\overline{p}/\overline{w}) \cdot Q_j]\}.$$

$(\overline{p}/\overline{w})$ is chosen by the auctioneer. The agents optimize profits and utilities in pointing out their commodities supply, tasks supply and demand. The auctioneer builds the following demand functions :

- On commodities markets :

$$\Sigma_{i \in S}(c_i - e_i) - \Sigma_{j \in P} s_j.$$

- On tasks quasi-markets :

$$\Sigma_{i \in S} t_i - \Sigma_{j \in P} d_j.$$

The auctioneer's particular utility function increases with the excess decrease. He can just influence the system of prices and quasi wage-rates. We note $a(.)$ the auctioneer's utility function :

$$a[(c/t)_i, (s/d)_j, (p/w)] = \left\langle (p/w) \cdot \frac{\Sigma_{i \in S}(c_i - e_i) - \Sigma_{j \in P} s_j}{\Sigma_{i \in S} t_i - \Sigma_{j \in P} d_j} \right\rangle.$$

Hence, we have three programs : consumers-workers maximize $u_i(.)$, producers-employers maximize Π_j and the auctioneer maximizes $a(.)$.

Step two :

- The auctioneer's set of choices is the simplex PW because for him, the only variable is the system of prices and the quasi wage-rates.

- The producer-employer j's set of choices is his production set Q_j, since on the contrary of what happens in a fuzzy *LCE* (*à la Ponsard*), producers-employers maximize their profit without constraint.

- For the consumers-workers, the problem is a little more complicated.

Let us note :

$$\alpha_i(p/w) = (p/w) \cdot (e/0)_i + \Sigma_{j \in P} \theta[(p/w) \cdot (s/d)_j].$$

This allows to rewrite the demand correspondence $EC_i(.)$ as follows :

$$EC_i(p/w) = \{(c/t)_i \in (C/T)_i \,/\, (p/w) \cdot (c/t)_i \leq \alpha_i(p/w)\}.$$

P7 implying any Q_j to contain the null vector of R^{l+m}, it leads to $(p/w) \cdot (s/d)_j \geq 0$ and this for any (p/w) of the simplex PW. Moreover H4, by assuming the existence of $c_i^* \in C_i$ such that $c_i^* \ll e_i$, implies the existence of a profile $(c/t)_i^* \in (C/T)_i$ such that $(c/t)_i^* \ll (e/0)_i$. Hence, for any (p/w) of PW :

$$(p/w)\cdot(c/t)_i^* < (p/w)\cdot(e/0)_i.$$

These two propositions yield : $\forall (p/w) \in PW$,

$$\text{Min}[(p/w)\cdot(C/T)_i] < (p/w)\cdot(e/0)_i \leq (p/w)\cdot(e/0)_i + \Sigma_{j\in P}\theta_{ij}\cdot[(\overline{p/w})\cdot(s/d)_j].$$

i.e. :

$$\text{Min}[(p/w)\cdot(C/T)_i] < \alpha_i(p/w).$$

It means $EC_i(.)$ to be nonempty and convex-valued. We must now prove it to be continuous in order to apply Kakutani's fixed point theorem.

If applying lemma 1, we know $\Pi_j(.)$ to be continuous. This implies $\alpha_i(.)$ to be also continuous. Next, lemma 2 allows to conclude that $EC_i(.)$ is continuous. Finally, we know the demand correspondence $EC_i(.)$ to be continuous and convex-valued.

Kakutani's theorem (all the conditions hold, $(C/T)_i$ compact and convex, $EC_i(.)$ continuous and convex-valued, Q_j compact and convex, $\Pi_j(.)$ continuous) implies, on one hand, the net excess demand correspondence (i.e. the difference between the demand correspondence and the supply one) to be continuous and on the other, to have a fixed point.

Step three : We are proving this fixed point to satisfy the two conditions C3α and C3β. Let us consider the definition of consumer-worker's budget. If we are in the equilibrium (for $(p/w)^*$), we can say : $\forall i \in S$,

$$(p/w)^*\cdot(c/t)_i^* \leq (p/w)^*\cdot(e/0)_i + \Sigma_{j\in P}\theta_{ij}[(p/w)^*\cdot(s/d)_j^*].$$

There are n inequalities : let us sum them up :

$$\Sigma_{i=1}^n(p/w)^*\cdot(c/t)_i^* \leq \Sigma_{i=1}^n(p/w)^*\cdot(e/0)_i + \Sigma_{i=1}^n\Sigma_{j\in P}\theta_{ij}[(p/w)^*\cdot(s/d)_j^*].$$

According to the fact that $\forall j \in P, \Sigma_{i\in S}\theta_j = 1$, which means that we are in a competitive private ownership economy ($(p/w)^*$ is exogeneous), we can write :

$$(p/w)^*\cdot\Sigma_{i\in S}(c/t)_i^* \leq (p/w)^*\cdot\Sigma_{i\in S}(e/0)_i + (p/w)^*\cdot\Sigma_{j\in P}(s/d)_j^*.$$

Hence :

$$(p/w)^*\cdot[\Sigma_{i\in S}(c/t)_i^* - \Sigma_{i\in S}(e/0)_i - \Sigma_{j\in P}(s/d)_j^*] \leq 0. \tag{1}$$

Let us note CED the commodities excess demand :

$$CED^* = \Sigma_{i\in S}(c_i^* - e_i) - \Sigma_{j\in P}s_j^*.$$

Let us note TES the tasks excess supply :

$$TES^* = \Sigma_{i\in S}t_i^* - \Sigma_{j\in P}d_j^*.$$

We can rewrite equation (1) as follows :

$$(p/w)^* \cdot (CED^*/TES^*) \leq 0 \text{ or } p^* \cdot CED^* + w^* \cdot TES^* \leq 0.$$

In the case of a pure LCE, we know that no commodity is free since $\vec{p}$ belongs to R_+^{m*}.

Hence :

$$p^* \cdot CED^* + w^* \cdot TES^* \leq 0,$$

means (with the help of the auctioneer's utility function who tries to reduce the excess) :

$$CED^* \leq 0 \text{ and } TES^* \leq 0. \quad (2)$$

GSP allows to saturate the budget constraints of consumers-workers. This implies the equation (1) to become :

$$p^* \cdot CED^* + w^* \cdot TES^* = 0. \quad (3)$$

Because ($p \in R_+^{m*}$ and $w \in R_+^l$), equations (2) and (3) yield :

$$p^* \cdot CED^* = w^* \cdot TES^* = 0, \quad (4)$$

which implies :

$$CED^* = 0 \text{ and } TES^* \leq 0.$$

This equation as (2) and (4) exactly correspond to C3α and C3β. It ends the demonstration of existence for a puf-equilibrium.

□

SECTION TWO : INVOLUNTARY UNEMPLOYMENT AND DOMINATED IRRATIONALITY

This last theorem means an underemployment equilibrium to appear in a Walrasian economy as soon as a null quasi wage-rate solves any task excess supply. But, in this model, the unemployed workers are not necessary *involuntary* because when confronted to a null quasi wage-rate, nothing allows them, up to now, to freely supply their tasks, which is the unique way to point out Walrasian involuntary unemployed workers.

In this section, we are going to explain the existence of such unemployed workers thanks to the principle of dominated irrationality, i.e. incoherent preferences *rationalized* by the first projection of fuzzy relations.

II.1. Preliminary remarks

We analyze here the relationship between GSP and FLD and the implicit microeconomic rationality of the model.

II.1.1. GSP and FLD

If preferences are not fuzzy, the agents' ability to discriminate is perfect and their budget constraints are obviously saturated by GSP. In our model, we do not know *a priori* if budget inequalities are saturated since FLD assumes any profile $(c/t)_i$ to be indifferent to another one inside each neighbourhood of $(c/t)_i$.

Thus, the optimal profile $(c/t)_i^*$ (for a given consumer-worker) is indifferent to $(c/t)_i$. Both belong to a neighbourhood of $(c/t)_i^*$. Actually, if the budget constraint is saturated by $(c/t)_i^*$, it is not always true for $(c/t)_i$, even though $\mathcal{U}(c/t)_i = \mathcal{U}(c/t)_i^*$. We can notice that this problem is only relevant for employed workers. Since unemployed workers' wage is identically null in the equilibrium ($t_i = 0$ or $t_i < 0$) , the constraint remains the same, hence $c_i^* = c_i$; the constraint is saturated.

At first, we can conclude FLD and GSP to be consistent for consumers-workers who are unemployed[2]. What about the other consumers-workers ?

Moreover, they are indifferent between two profiles but the indifference level evolves with each new profile according to the disutility function. Therefore, GSP implies the constraints to be saturated. Let us look at their preferences.

FLD leads to indifference, but this one is not always single-valued. Hence, that allows to build a utility function, $\mathcal{U}(.)$, which expresses a nonconstant satisfaction because of the operator Max that is used for the first projection of the fuzzy relation of preference. In other words, for a given consumption, indifference between two *neighbouring* profiles does not correspond to a single level.

Example : Let us consider three *neighbouring* tasks profiles t^1, t^2 and t^3, with $t^1 < t^2 < t^3$. The consumer-worker is indifferent between t^1 and t^2, then between t^2 and t^3. That is : $\mathcal{P}(t^1,t^2) = \mathcal{P}(t^2,t^1) = \alpha$ and $\mathcal{P}(t^2,t^3) = \mathcal{P}(t^3,t^2) = \beta$. But $\beta > \alpha$ because of the disutility for labour. Therefore, we have $\mathcal{U}(t^1) < \mathcal{U}(t^2) < \mathcal{U}(t^3)$. There is a unique optimum, hence GSP saturates the constraint.

2 An "easy" way to solve the problem is the following : the agents who are employed, in the equilibrium, are *crisp* consumers-workers, their preferences are not fuzzy. Those, who are unemployed workers, are also the only ones to be under FLD and to be endowed with fuzzy preferences.

II.1.2. Unemployment and rationality

The assumption of perfect divisibility for commodities and tasks - i.e. convexity of consumption sets - implies the fuzzy economic behaviour to radically differs from the usual one.

Divisibility justifies the existence of infinitely neighbouring profiles. The consumer-worker's ability to discriminate in a pure *LCE* is not perfect. Who should make difference between a kilogram of corns and the same kilogram to which we should add a supplementary weight of corns so light that any balance could measure it ? Nothing prevents an agent from being indifferent between both (if preferences are not monotonous) will answer a Boolean theoretician ! What Eubulides did with his sand pile, we can do it with a kilogram of corns. A usual coherent and rational agent has a transitive relation of preference. Transitivity is going to convey the local indifference towards the whole set and finally we are going to obtain an absurd *but coherent* indifference between an infinitely small object and an infinitely great one.

On the contrary, if the indifference is multivalued, it evolves according to quantities - thanks to the first projection. That allows to translate the utility increase without forsaking indifference between neighbouring profiles.

A Boolean theoretician cannot tell us : "But in your case, too, transitivity - even if it were "*f*" - preserves indifference !", since the consumer-worker has a fuzzy relation that can be nontransitive. Nevertheless, this nontransitive fuzzy relation does not forbid (because of the projection) the existence of a preordored fuzzy subset. Hence, a fuzzy utility function always exists for any kind of consumer-worker.

If the consumers-workers' behaviour is not coherent, they just have to dominate their irrationality in order to *decide* in their budget set.

II.2. Fuzzy preference and involuntary unemployment

The idea according to which the existence of involuntary unemployed workers is not necessarily inconsistent with a Walrasian equilibrium where prices and quasi wage-rates are flexible proceeds from Sonnenschein's [1973] theorem (and also Debreu [1974], Mantel [1974]) : as soon as the excess demand does not systematically evolve in a *natural* way when prices and quasi wage-rates change, we can assume a quasi wage-rate decrease not to automatically imply a task excess supply decrease. Nevertheless, we must suppose the rigidity of prices and quasi wage-rates (from 0) to prevent the "natural law of demand" to be verified.

Even though Sonnenschein's theorem does not allow to deduce the existence of a tasks excess supply, and thus a Walrasian involuntary unemployment, it gives the following intuition : if the particular unemployment that is consistent with a Walrasian model is *only* voluntary, there would exist a quasi wage-rate from which this tasks excess supply disappears. This is why Sonnenschein's theorem helps us in showing that we cannot prove a global demand increase to imply an unemployment decrease, since the irreducibility of excess supply necessarily contradicts the "natural law of demand".

Let us establish the following lemma :

LEMMA 3 : $\forall((c/t)_i,(c/t)_i') \in (C/T)_i^2 : \mathcal{P}_i((c/t)_i,(c/t)_i') = \mathcal{P}_i((c/t)_i',(c/t)_i)$, *is not equivalent to* $\chi(c/t)_i = \chi(c/t)_i'$.

Proof : Let us suppose :

$$\mathcal{P}_i((c/t)_i,(c/t)_i') = \mathcal{P}_i((c/t)_i',(c/t)_i) = \text{Max}_{(C/T)_i}[\mathcal{P}_i((c/t)_i,.)] = a.$$

(1)- Let us consider a profile $(c/t)_i'' \in (C/T)_i$ such that :

$$\mathcal{P}_i((c/t)_i',(c/t)_i'') = \mathcal{P}_i((c/t)_i'',(c/t)_i') = b > a.$$

We can immediately deduce :

$$\text{Max}_{(C/T)_i}[\mathcal{P}_i((c/t)_i',.)] > \text{Max}_{(C/T)_i}[\mathcal{P}_i((c/t)_i,.)],$$

hence :

$$\chi(c/t)_i' > \chi(c/t)_i.$$

(2)- If $\chi(c/t)_i = \chi(c/t)_i'$, this means :

$$\text{Max}_{(C/T)_i}[\mathcal{P}_i((c/t)_i,.)] = \text{Max}_{(C/T)_i}[\mathcal{P}_i((c/t)_i',.)], \text{ i.e. } \text{Max}_{(C/T)_i}[\mathcal{P}_i((c/t)_i',.)] = a.$$

Let us now consider that $\exists(c/t)_i'' \in (C/T)_i$ such that :

$$\mathcal{P}_i((c/t)_i',(c/t)_i'') = \mathcal{P}_i((c/t)_i'',(c/t)_i') = a.$$

Then, it yields :

$$\mathcal{P}_i((c/t)_i',(c/t)_i) \neq \mathcal{P}_i((c/t)_i,(c/t)_i').$$

□

α- Two locally indifferent profiles do not necessarily induce identical global level of satisfaction.

β- Two profiles leading to the same utility level are not necessarily locally indifferent.

β means that identical utility levels do not imply local indifferences. In other words, the satisfaction derived from a Walrasian voluntary unemployed worker's profile *can be the same* than the one deriving from an employed worker's profile, without both profiles to be *locally* indifferent. This means (independently of FLD) that an agent can locally prefer to supply tasks rather than not to supply them (and this with null quasi wage-rates in the equilibrium) without being able to deduce that the utility level assigned to both profiles are systematically coherent with local preferences. Hence, we can have a consumer-worker who *locally* behaves in a *usual* way but whose utility function differs. This type of behaviour requires (under FLD) the existence of another profile. This one, when compared to the Walrasian involuntary unemployed worker's profile, leads to at a higher level than the maximum degree of preference deriving from the comparison of the Walrasian involuntary unemployed worker's profile to all the other profiles of $(C/T)_i$.

In a puf-equilibrium, the fuzzy subset $(C/T)_i$ must be convex. In other words, the projection of $\mathcal{P}_i(.,.)$ must imply a quasi-concave membership function (which is also the utility function on $(C/T)_i$-support). Moreover, the membership function must satisfy GSP in order to saturate the constraints.

These two conditions leads to some constraints on the utility function, without assuming them to hold for the relations of preference.

QLO means intrinsic qualities of each profile to be always lower than relative ones ; therefore, the reflexivity degree of any $(c/t)_i$ is lower than $\chi(c/t)_i$. In other words, the agent can be indifferent between a null supply of tasks (and defining himself as a local voluntary unemployed worker) and a positive supply of free tasks. Nevertheless, this agent can intrinsically prefer (and only locally according to QLO) supplying free tasks : actually, a profile for which the semivector t_i is not the null vector of R^l allows the agent to point out that he *intrinsically* wants to enter the labour market.

The usual rationality implies a coherent but crisp behaviour. If the agent's associated quasi wage-rates are null, he prefers to retire from the labour market and thus to behave as a voluntary unemployed worker. It means no (intrinsic ?) satisfaction to exist for belonging to the labour market. The implicit assumption which allows to explain why some workers *persevere* in supplying free tasks, is the existence of a *local and intrinsic preference for the announcement* : the only way these workers have to demonstrate their particular status of involuntary unemployed workers is to persist in supplying tasks. And they persist because of their intrinsic preferences which assign a degree for unemployment lower than the one corresponding to employment. This behaviour derives only from a new type of rationality which is nevertheless consistent with the Walrasian one.

When a consumer-worker compares t_i to t_i', he just considers the relative qualities of the first one when compared to the second. In other words, the missing qualities in t_i and t_i' (at the same time) disappear from the agent's mind (by independence of preferences) but will reappear when compared to a third one. Hence, the intrinsic qualities of t_i are related to those qualities that never appear at the same time and to some particular beliefs and ways of thinking[3].

II.3. The Walrasian involuntary unemployed worker's behaviour.

The Walrasian involontary unemployed worker is such as, in the equilibrium, his earnings are null (i.e. $< w^* \cdot t_i > = 0$). He is also *globally* indifferent between the null vector of R^l and a positive supply τ. We can sum up the Walrasian involuntary unemployed worker's behaviour as follows :

1- $\chi(c/0)_i = \chi(c/\tau)_i$

2- $< w^* \cdot 0 > = < w^* \cdot \tau > = 0.$

For a given consumption, c_i, defined from the budget constraint (saturated by GSP), the agent is indifferent between all profiles of tasks that correspond to a null wage. Between 0 and τ, the agent is coherent because his local indifference leads to a global indifference. Beyond τ, this local indifference is no more equivalent to a global indifference ; hence, the utility levels are not constant. Nevertheless, the agent remains rational since the first projection implies the satisfaction deriving from these profiles to be greater than the one corresponding to the other profiles.

Example : For a given consumption c, knowing that for 0, t' and t'', the earnings $< w \cdot t >$ are null in the equilibrium, the agent's preferences correspond to :

- $\mathcal{P}(0,t') = \mathcal{P}(t',0) = \mathcal{P}(t',t'') = \mathcal{P}(t'',t') = \mathcal{P}(0,t'') = \mathcal{P}(t'',0) = \xi.$

- $\forall t \in \{0,t',t''\}$: $\text{Max}_T[\mathcal{P}(t,.)] = \xi.$

This means : $\forall l \in T - \{0,t',t''\}$, $\mathcal{P}(l,.) < \xi.$

Indifference concerns the particular set $\{0,t',t''\}$ but as soon as we approach the other profiles, the level of relative qualities decreases.

The Walrasian involuntary unemployed worker's behaviour is : globally indifferent bet-

3 We can notice that the catholic tradition badly considers the unemployment (apart from all economic analysis). For a long time, unemployment was envisaged as one of the possible forms of idleness. In the Christian traditional economies, it is not absurd to suppose the intrinsic preference for employment to be often greater than the one for unemployment. (See Durkheim [1912], [1960] about the social perceptions of labour according to religious environments.)

ween 0 and τ, the agent *remembers* both degrees of reflexivity and chooses τ if its degree of reflexivity is greater than that of 0.

Generally (that is without FLD), a consumer-worker i is a Walrasian involuntary unemployed worker when he satisfies the three following characteristics : he supplies τ if and only if :

$$\text{(A) } Arg\{\text{Max } \mathcal{X}(c/t)_i \,/\, EC_i\} = [(c/0)_i],$$

$$\text{(B) } \text{Max}_{(C/T)_i}[\mathcal{P}_i((c/0)_i, .)] = \text{Max}_{(C/T)_i}[\mathcal{P}_i((c/\tau)_i, .)] \text{ and}$$

$$\text{(C) } \mathcal{P}_i((c/0)_i, (c/0)_i) < \mathcal{P}_i((c/\tau)_i, (c/\tau)_i).$$

(A) means the agent's optimal choice under his budget constraint to be the indifference class of $(c/0)_i$. (B) means $(c/\tau)_i$ to belong to the indifference class of $[(c/0)_i]$. (C) means that the agent i assigns a reflexivity degree to $(c/\tau)_i$ that is greater than $\mathcal{P}_i((c/0)_i, (c/0)_i)$. It means that his effective decision is the profile $(c/\tau)_i$.

Malinvaud [1986] wrote about discouraged unemployed workers : "*People who do not actively search for being employed, but who still want to work if they were offered to (...) can correspond to the notion of "discouraged unemployed worker"*". In our analysis, those agents are workers who satisfy (A) and (B) but not (C). They become voluntary unemployed workers by discouragement, which is revealed by the fact that the intrinsic qualities of τ become lower than the ones of a null supply : the intrinsic satisfaction for the announcement has disappeared.

II.4. Voluntary, involuntary and partial unemployed workers

We can give a precise characterization of both first types of workers by slightly shading the concept of voluntary unemployed workers according to the notion of discouraged ones.

II.4.1. The Walrasian voluntary unemployed worker

He can be defined as follows :

$$\boxed{Arg\{\text{Max } \mathcal{X}(c/t)_i \,/\, EC_i\} = (c/0)_i}$$

We can notice $(c/0)_i$ to be the very element not the indifference class : there is no global indifference between $(c/0)_i$ and another profile of $(C/T)_i$.

II.4.2. The discouraged voluntary unemployed worker

He can be defined as follows :

$$\begin{array}{|l|}\hline (A)\ Arg\{\mathrm{Max}\, \chi(c/t)_i \,/\, EC_i\} = [(c/0)_i], \\ (B)\ \mathrm{Max}_{(C/T)_i}[\mathcal{P}_i(c/0)_i, .)] = \mathrm{Max}_{(C/T)_i}[\mathcal{P}_i(c/\tau)_i, .)], \\ (C)\ \mathcal{P}_i(c/\tau)_i, (c/\tau)_i) < \mathcal{P}_i(c/0)_i, (c/0)_i). \\ \hline \end{array}$$

The indifference class of $[(c/0)_i]$ corresponds to the agent's optimal choice, since there is a global indifference between both profiles. In that sense, the agent *i* is an involuntary Walrasian unemployed worker according to definition 2. But, he has no intrinsic satisfaction for the announcement ; hence, his decision is $(c/0)_i$ which finally leads him to become a voluntary unemployed worker.

II.4.3. The Walrasian involuntary unemployed worker

He corresponds to the three following equations :

$$\begin{array}{|l|}\hline (A)\ Arg\{\mathrm{Max}\, \chi(c/t)_i \,/\, EC_i\} = [(c/0)_i], \\ (B)\ \mathrm{Max}_{(C/T)_i}[\mathcal{P}_i(c/0)_i, .)] = \mathrm{Max}_{(C/T)_i}[\mathcal{P}_i(c/\tau)_i, .)] \\ (C)\ \mathcal{P}_i(c/0)_i, (c/0)_i) < \mathcal{P}_i(c/\tau)_i, (c/\tau)_i). \\ \hline \end{array}$$

The only equation to differ from the definition of a discouraged voluntary unemployed worker is (C). It means that there is no satisfaction for the announcement.

Remark : The voluntary unemployed worker and the discouraged one supply the same profile $(c/t)_i$. It means that they take the same decisions even though their preferences are different. The one that we call *voluntary discouraged unemployed worker* corresponds to the "involuntary" unemployed worker consistent with a usual preorder, i.e. without a fuzzy preference system. He is therefore "voluntary" in his supply behaviour.

II.4.4. The partial Walrasian unemployed worker

He is the hardest to grasp : some of the tasks he decides to supply are free. Here, he can choose to supply them or not, depending on whether he assigns an important level of intrinsic qualities to a non-null tasks supply or not. Another analysis can be developed which is to consider (as it is logically the case in a Walrasian model), that consumers-workers are forced to exchange the tasks they supply in the equilibrium. Hence, we can envisage two symmetric notions : *voluntary* and *involuntary* partial unemployed workers.

According to this constraint of transactions, partial unemployed workers can be forced to freely supply some of the tasks whose marginal productivity is null. Then, we can consider that there is an implicit pressure of unemployment upon the wages. In that sense, the partial unemployed workers really "draw" a wage which is independent of the number of excess tasks, hence of balanced tasks.

Final remarks

We tried to introduce involuntary unemployment inside a Walrasian general equilibrium in order to analyze the relevance of some paradoxical equilibria.

Finally, we are going to define two possible limits of our approach.

1- Are all involuntary unemployments consistent with our model ?

No.

These involuntary unemployed workers are particular individuals whose *inward* structure lead them to persist in supplying free tasks. These tasks correspond to null marginal productivities ; it is therefore an involuntary unemployment whose nature is *technical.* In other words, a global demand increase, by forcing the commodities supply, would not reduce these labour excess. Apart from this remark, we know two agents having the same preferences to be always in the same situation. The involuntary aspect of these unemployed workers does not derive from their preferences : we do not recover the basic results of the standard analysis in terms of rationing. Nevertheless, in the *standard* Walrasian case, the only way to introduce involuntary unemployed workers is to demonstrate the theoretical relevance of a persistent supply of labour when the wage-rates are null.

2- Who are the employed workers in a *LCE* ?

Their first characteristic is to supply the only balanced tasks. Next, either their preferences satisfy both assumptions, GSP and FLD, therefore, they are just coherent even though "short -sighted", their relations of preference are fuzzy preorders, i.e. reflexive (F.s.) and f-transitive relations, any local indifference can evolve according to quantities, or they are *crisp*, their preferences are usual.

It suggests a relation between the usual coherence (preferences rationality) and the fact of not being a unemployed worker. On the contrary, an agent who is coherent in choice but who has a reflexive (F.s.) and *f*-transitive fuzzy relation of preference, when considered in a situation of unemployment, is not necessarily going to be a voluntary unemployed worker. In other words, there are some involuntary unemployed workers that are coherent but not *crisp*.

General Conclusion

Our purpose is to introduce fuzziness in microeconomics thanks to fuzzy preferences.

There is an important methodological point which deals with the limits of what we called *fuzzyfication*, i.e. the choice of concepts that one would expresses in fuzzy terms.

Ponsard's approach of fuzzy economics wants to attain two particular aims : first, ameliorating the description of choice behaviour by introducing fuzziness, then modelling the consumer's subjective imprecision or producer's one. Ponsard's will is based on an existence theorem for the equilibrium of an economy where goals and constraints are fuzzy. In Ponsard's models, there is a *fuzzyfication* of concepts according to a theoretical improvement that is economically awaited.

In Aubin's models, fuzziness is introduced thanks to coalitions. He assumes agents to belong more or less to coalitions. All the other assumptions remain quite traditional and therefore membership structures are modified in order to technically convexify the set of feasible coalitions. The introduction of fuzzy coalitions comes from a purely mathematical and not "*economic*" desire. Aubin wants to increase the possibilities of blocking to reduce the number of equilibria. The mathematical tool precedes the economic innovation.

The economic purpose is absent from Butnariu's works. He generalizes some Boolean results (fixed points theorems, correspondence, relation), and then uses generalizations in order to illustrate them. Here, the mathematical tool is the main target and not economics.

According to the three preceding approaches which form the main contribution of what is called fuzzy microeconomic theory (related to the theory of value), it seems quite illusory to talk about a single fuzzy economic theory. If we try to order those theoreticians in an increasing *scale of fuzzyfication*, Aubin would be behind Ponsard who himself would be behind Butnariu. Ponsard starts from an economic thought and leads to *fuzzyfication* of goals ; Aubin starts from a technical problem and solves it with fuzzy coalitions ; Butnariu generalizes without trying to solve a specific problem. To sum up, we could say that some authors have an economic intuition (Ponsard), others a technical intuition (Aubin), and finally, Butnariu no particular applied intuition, except the great flexibility of the mathematical tool.

If we try to place our own approach inside the existing theories, it seems that we could be placed between Aubin and Ponsard in the sense that our initial intuition is somewhat economic but that we have focused on behaviours. We share with Ponsard the conviction that the Boolean choice behaviour is a reducing of reality and we try, like Aubin, to change the concepts in order to obtain some paradoxical (new) results in regard to the usual theory.

The limits that we imposed ourselves when fuzzifying come from the delicate arbitrage between economic intuition and technical problems. We have the intuition that it is possible to describe an *incoherent* behaviour even though we try to obtain a Walrasian under-employment equilibrium. We have the intuition that dictatorship and majority rule are two *limits* of a single principle which is the planner's requirement while we look for the conditions under which a game with a usual empty core allows to balance an exchange economy. *Incoherence* of behaviours and step of choice involvement are economic intuitions. However, existence theorems that we propose for Walrasian under-employment equilibria and for nonemptiness of the peripheral core are somewhat technical.

We have reached our goals. Fuzziness can be introduced into the preference theory in order to define a new economic theory of equilibria. We hope the fuzzy behavioural standard that we considered inside the theory of value to be an important improvement. Hahn [1973] writes : "*The one who studies general equilibrium analysis thinks that he gets the starting point from which it is possible to progress towards a descriptive theory*". Blaug [1982] adds : "*Continuous refinements of general equilibrium analysis during the last thirty years, by weakening its axioms and generalizing the limit conditions, do not help us to get closer to such a descriptive theory*".

At the end of this book, we have the feeling that introducing fuzzy preference behaviours, far from just weakening the axioms and generalizing the limit conditions, allows the general equilibrium analysis to become more realistic without loosing closeness.

ANNEXES

ANNEX I

LEMMA 4 (Hammond) : $\forall(x,y) \in X^2, \forall u(.) \in \mathcal{U}(X)$, *if SWF W satisfies [P1], [P2] and [P4], then if :* $u_S(x) = u_S(y), \exists\sigma(.)$, *a permutation of* S, *such that :* $\forall i \in S, u_i(x) = u_{\sigma(i)}(y)$.

Proof : Let us consider the simple case where only two agents exchange their satisfaction levels. Let us suppose then, that for the two agents i and j, both belonging to society S, the following relation is satisfied :

$$u_i(x) = u_j(y) = \alpha \text{ and } u_j(x) = u_i(y) = \beta,$$

while, $\forall g \in S - \{i,j\} : u_g(x) = u_g(y) = \gamma$. Let us choose two other functions of fuzzy utility, $u^1(.)$ and $u^0(.)$, belonging to $\mathcal{U}(X)$, such that, $\forall g \in S - \{i,j\}$, the satisfaction level γ remained in any situation and let us write for the two agents $\{i,j\}$:

$$\forall z \in X - \{x,y\},\ u_i^0(z) = u_j^0(z) = u_i^1(z) = u_j^1(z).$$

The following table describes their complete preferences :

	$u(.)$		$u^0(.)$		$u^1(.)$	
	i	j	i	j	i	j
x	α	β	α	β	β	α
y	β	α	β	α	α	β

We are going to show that if x is preferred to y, then there is an inconsistency.

Let us suppose that $u_S(x) > u_S(y)$. [P1] implies $u_S^1(x) > u_S^1(y)$. Now, lemma 1 which proves that, if W satisfies [P1] and [P2], then W satisfies [P3], implies $u_S^0(y) > u_S^0(x)$, which is absurd. Hence, we have just to establish a sequence of n permutations on the agents in order to obtain the result.

□

This proof is adapted from d'Aspremont & Gevers [1977].

ANNEX II

LEMMA 5 (Strasnick): $\forall(x,y) \in X^2$, $\forall u(.) \in \mathcal{U}(X)$, $\forall C \subseteq S$, *a coalition such that:* $C = \{j \in S, u_j(x) < u_j(y)\}$. *If the SWF W verifies [P1], [P2] and [P5], if there exists an agent* $i, i \in S$, *such that :* α- $u_i(x) > u_i(y)$, β- $u_j(x) > u_j(y)$, *then :* $u_S(x) > u_S(y)$.

Proof: *First step* : The case $S = \varnothing$ is excluded since $| S | \geq 3$. Then, let us suppose the coalition C to be empty. It implies $\forall i \in S$, $u_i(y) < u_i(x)$; with [P2], $u_S(x) > u_S(y)$.

Second step : Let us suppose now C to be nonempty and :

(i) $C = \{j \in S \; ; \; u_j(x) < u_j(y)\}$, (definition of C).

(ii) $\exists i \in S \; ; \; u_i(x) > u_i(y)$.

(iii) $\forall j \in C \; ; \; u_j(x) > u_j(y)$.

Let any agent $k \in C$ and let us define $D = C - \{k\}$. Let us assume the lemma to be true for D. Moreover, for any fuzzy utility function, $u^0(.)$, $u^0(.) \in \mathcal{U}(X)$, if for $(x,y) \in X^2$, [$u_D^0(x) > u_D^0(y)$] , then [$u_S^0(x) < u_S^0(y)$]. In other words, we assume D to be *non p-decisive* on X. Let us take an object $z \in X - \{x,y\}$ and build up a fuzzy utility function $u^0(.)$ in the following way :

(iv) [P1] holds for X and for $X - \{x,y\}$.

(v) $\forall j \in C \; ; \; u_j^0(x) > u_i^0(z)$.

(vi) $u_i^0(x) > u_i^0(z) > u_i^0(y)$.

(vii) $u_k^0(x) = u_k^0(z)$.

(viii) $\forall j \in S - \{i,k\} \; ; \; u_j^0(y) = u_j^0(z)$.

It is obvious that such a fuzzy utility function $u^0(.)$ exists.

A- Let us show firstly : $u_S^0(x) > u_S^0(z)$, by proving :

(Ai) $\forall d \in D, u_d^0(x) < u_d^0(z)$.

(Aii) $\exists i \in S, u_i^0(x) > u_i^0(z)$.

(Aiii) $\forall j \in S - \{i,k\}, u_j^0(x) > u_i^0(z)$.

We can see that (Aii) is a part of (vi), that (Aiii) is derived from (v) since $D \subseteq C$. So, we have only to prove (Ai).

$u_j^0(z) > u_j^0(x)$ means, following (vi), (vii) and (viii) :

$$u_j^0(y) > u_j^0(x) \text{ where } j \in S - \{i,k\},$$

which means, with (iv) :

$$u_j(y) > u_j(x) \text{ where } j \in S - \{i,k\}.$$

This reveals, when we consider (i), that j belongs to C. But, this last equation is only defined upon $S - \{i,k\}$. Hence, it implies $j \in C - \{k\}$ ($i \notin C$ *trivially*, from (ii)), in other words :

$$j \in D.$$

We have shown (Ai), (Aii) and (Aiii) to be consistent. Therefore, we can conclude :

$$u_S^0(x) > u_S^0(z).$$

B- Let us prove $u_S^0(z) > u_S^0(y)$. We are going to use [P5]. As we assume the axiom of minimal equity, we have only to show :

(Bi) $u_i^0(z) > u_i^0(y)$

(Bii) $u_k^0(z) < u_k^0(y)$

(Biii) $\forall j \in S - \{i,k\}, u_j^0(y) = u_j^0(z)$

(Biv) $u_k^0(z) > u_i^0(z)$

(Bv) $u_k^0(y) > u_i^0(y)$

We can resolve these five propositions thanks to the last equations we have established. Thus, (Bi) is a part of (vi) and (Biii) corresponds to (viii). We know that k belongs to C, so (i) implies $u_k(y) > u_k(x)$ and then, including (iv) and [P1], $u_k^0(y) > u_k^0(x)$. We can also write, using (vii) : $u_k^0(y) > u_k^0(z)$, which confirms (Bii). From (i) and (iii), we know that $u_k(y) > u_k(x) > u_i(y)$. Hence, from (iv), it follows that $u_k^0(y) > u_i^0(y)$ which confirms (Bv). The five propositions are consistent : we can conclude from [P5] : $u_S^0(z) > u_S^0(y)$.

C- We have shown $u_S^0(x) > u_S^0(z)$ and $u_S^0(z) > u_S^0(y)$. By f-transitivity, obviously consistent for X connected and continuous fuzzy preferences :

$$u_S^0(x) > u_S^0(y).$$

We can conclude from (iv) and more specifically from [P1] that :

$u_S(x) > u_S(y)$.

□

This demonstration is adapted from Hammond [1976] and based on an argument of Strasnick [1976].

ANNEX III

Now, we have to verify the *SWF* W^L, which corresponds to the leximin principle, to satisfy the two following axioms : strong-Pareto [P2] and minimal equity [P5]. We must do it before proving that W^L axiomatically derives from [P1], [P2], [P4] and [P5]. Proving theorem 2 consists in generating W^L essentially from [P1] and [P4]. In order to show that W^L indeed satisfies [P2] and [P5], we need four preliminary propositions.

Proposition 1 : Let $\sigma(.)$ *be a permutation of* N*, where* N *is a set of ranks. If* $r > k \geq \sigma(r)$ *and* $r \in N$*, then there exists a rank* $s \leq k$ *such that* $\sigma(s) > k$.

Proof : Let us demonstrate this proposition, ad absurdum : we assume $r > k \geq \sigma(r)$ while $\sigma(s) \leq k$ (s goes from s to k), then :

$$\sigma(\{1,2,3,\ldots,k\} \cup \{r\}) \subseteq \{1,2,3,\ldots,k\}.$$

But, we know $|\{1,2,3,\ldots,k\} \cup \{r\}| = k+1$ while the same set, without r, has only a cardinal which is equal to k. This means $\sigma(.)$ not to be a permutation. Hence, it is a contradiction.

□

Proposition 2 : Let $\sigma(.)$ *be a permutation of* N*. If for* m *(* m *from* 1 *to* $|S|$ *),* $u_r(x) \geq u_{\sigma(r)}(y)$*,* $\forall u(.) \in \mathcal{U}(X)$*, then* $u_r(x) \geq u_{\sigma(r)}(y)$.

Proof : For each rank r, $(r{:}1,\ldots,m)$, there are two cases.

1- $\sigma(r) \geq r$; this would mean $u_r(x) \geq u_{\sigma(r)}(y) \geq u_r(y)$ which could lead us to conclude : $u_r(x) \geq u_r(y)$.

2- $\sigma(r) < r$; we decide k of the first proposition to correspond to $r-1$. Hence, it means that there exists an $s < r$ such that $\sigma(r) \geq r$, from which it follows that $u_r(x) \geq u_s(x) \geq u_{\sigma(s)}(y) \geq u_r(y)$ which allows us to conclude : $u_r(x) \geq u_r(y)$.

□

Proposition 3 : $\forall u(.) \in \mathcal{U}(X)$, $\forall r \in (1,...,m)$; *let* $\eta(.)$ *be a permutation of* N. *If* $u_r(x) = u_r(y) \geq u_{\eta(r)}(y)$, *then* $u_r(x) = u_{\eta(r)}(y)$.

Proof : We have only to demonstrate that : $u_{\eta(r)}(y) \geq u_r(y)$. Thus, let us suppose it is wrong ; this means : $u_r(y) > u_{\eta(r)}(y)$. So, we can write that there exists a rank k such that $r > k \geq \eta(r)$ and from the leximin principle, it follows that $u_{k+1}(y) > u_k(y)$. The first proposition teaches that there is a rank $s \leq k$ such that $\eta(s) > k$. Hence, $\eta(s) \geq k+1$ is possible. In that case, we deduce :

$$u_{k+1}(y) > u_k(y) \geq u_s(y) > u_{\eta(s)}(y) \geq u_{k+1}(y),$$

which generates a trivial contradiction : $u_{k+1}(y) > u_{k+1}(y)$.

□

Proposition 4 : $\forall u(.) \in \mathcal{U}(X)$, $\exists j \in S$; $u_j(x) > u_j(y)$, $\forall i \in S - \{j\}$, $u_i(y) > u_i(x)$, *where* $u_i(x) > u_j(x)$, *then for* W^L *the leximin principle*, $u_S(.) = W^L[u(.)]$, $u_S(x) > u_S(y)$.

Proof : Let us define $\eta(.)$ a permutation of N, the set of ranks : $\forall i \in S, r_i^y = r_{\eta(i)}^x$, where r_i^y corresponds to the rank of agent i in society, relative to the level of satisfaction issued from the object $y \in X$. Let $t = r_j^x$, such that $\eta(t) = r_j^y$. Since we have the proposition [$u_j(x) > u_j(y)$], we can deduce : $u_t(x) > u_{\eta(t)}(y)$. In the same way, taking $r = r_i^x$ and $\eta(r) = r_i^y$, the assumption of the proposition implies :

$$\forall r \in N, u_{\eta(r)}(y) > u_r(x) \Rightarrow u_r(x) > u_t(x).$$

Then :

$$\forall r \in N, u_{\eta(r)}(y) > u_r(x) \Rightarrow r > t.$$

Thus, we can write now : $u_r(x) \geq u_{\eta(r)}(y)$, $\forall r \in \{1,2,\ldots,t\}$. Applying the result of proposition 2, it follows that for $(r:1,\ldots,t)$, $u_r(x) \geq u_r(y)$.

Let us suppose now, that $u_r(x) = u_r(y)$ for $r \in \{1,2,\ldots,t\}$. Let us show how absurd this is : if it were true, since $u_r(x) \geq u_{\eta(r)}(y)$ ($r \in \{1,2,\ldots,t\}$), we could apply the result of proposition 3 which implies : $u_r(x) = u_{\eta(r)}(y)$. That is a contradiction of $u_t(x) > u_{\eta(t)}(y)$, which corresponds to one assumption of the proposition.

Thus, for $m \in \{1,2,\ldots,t\}$, $u_m(x) > u_m(y)$, while, for $m \in \{1,2,\ldots,m\}$, $u_r(x) \geq u_r(y)$, which implies : $u_S(x) > u_S(y)$.

□

THEOREM : *If W is the SWF-leximin ($W = W^L$), W satisfies axioms [P2] and [P5].*

Proof : *First step* : Let us suppose that :

$$\forall i \in S - \{j\}, u_i(x) \geq u_i(y),$$

$$\exists j \in S; u_j(x) > u_j(y).$$

We can see that the assumptions of proposition 4 are satisfied and thus $u_S(x) > u_S(y)$. It follows that, for $u_S(.) = W^L[u(.)]$, W^L satisfies [P2], the strong-Pareto principle.

Second step : Let us suppose that :

$$\exists (i,j) \in S^2,\ u_i(y) > u_i(x) \text{ and } u_j(x) > u_j(y),$$

$$u_i(y) > u_j(y) \text{ and } u_i(x) > u_j(x)$$

$$\forall k \in S - \{i,j\},\ u_k(x) = u_k(y).$$

This means the conditions of proposition 4 to be satisfied, then : $u_S(x) > u_S(y)$. It follows that W^L satisfies [P5], the minimal equity axiom.

□

Bibliography

Abdi H., Barthelemy J.P. & Luong X. [1980]. "Information Préordinale et Analyse des Préférences", in *Data Analysis and Informatics*, North-Holland, Amsterdam.

Arrow K.J. [1951], [1963]. *Choix collectif et Préférences Individuelles*, 2nde Edition, Calmann-Lévy, Paris.

Arrow K.J. [1979]. "The Division of Labour in the Economy, the Polity and the Society", in *A. Smith and Modern Political Economy*, G.P. O'Driscoll Ed, Ames, Iowa State University Press.

Arrow K.J. & Debreu G. [1954]. "Existence of an Equilibrium for a Competitive Economy", *Econometrica*, **22**, 265-290.

Arrow K.J. & Hahn F.H. [1971]. *General Competitive Analysis*, Mathematical Economics Texts, San Francisco Holden-Day, Edinburgh Oliver & Boyd.

d'Aspremont C. & Gevers L. [1977]. "Equity and the Informational Basis of Collective Choice", *Review of Economic Studies*, **44**, 199-209.

Aubin J.P. [1974]. "Coeur et Valeur des Jeux Flous", *Compte-rendus de l'Académie des Sciences de Paris*, **279**, 891-894.

Aubin J.P. [1976]. "Fuzzy Core and Equilibrium in Games Defined in Strategic Form", in *Directions in Large Scale Systems*, Y.C. Ho & S.K. Miller, Plenum Press.

Aubin J.P. [1979]. *Mathematical Methods in Economics and Game Theory*, North-Holland, Amsterdam.

Aubin J.P. [1981]. "Locally Lipschitz Cooperative Games", *Journal of Mathematical Economics*, **8**, 241-262.

Aubin J.P. [1986]. *L'analyse Non-Linéaire et ses Motivations Economiques*, Masson, Paris.

Aumann R.J. [1964]. "Values of Market with a Continuum of Traders", *Econometrica*, **43**, 611-646.

Azariadis C. [1985]. "Implicit Contracts and Under-Employment Equilibria", *Journal of Political Economy*, **83**,1183-1202.

Babbage C. [1832]. *On the Economy of Machinery and Manufactures*, Charles Knight, Londres.

Badard R. [1984]. "Fixed Point Theorems for Fuzzy Numbers", *Fuzzy Sets and Systems*, **13**, 291-302.

Baily M.N. [1977]. "Wages and Unemployment under Uncertain Demand", *Review of Economic Studies*, **41**, 37-50.

Balasko Y. [1976]. *L'Equilibre Economique du Point de Vue Différentiel*, Université Paris-IX, Dauphine.

Barret C.R., Pattanaik P.K. & Salles M. [1985]. "On the Structure of Fuzzy Social Welfare Functions", Séminaire de l'Institut de Mathématiques Economiques, Université de Dijon.

Barthelemy J.P. [1979]. *Propriétés Métriques des Ensembles Ordonnés, Comparaison et Agrégation des Relations Binaires*, Thèse de Doctorat d'Etat, Besançon.

Barthelemy J.P. & Montjardet B. [1979]. "Ajustement et Résumé de Données Relationnelles : les Relations Centrales", in *Data Analysis and Informatics*, North-Holland, Amsterdam, 645-653.

Barthelemy J.P. & Mullet E. [1986]. "Choice Basis : A model for Multi-Attribute Preference", *British Journal of Mathematical and Statistical Psychology*, **39**, 106-124.

Batteau P.,Blin J.M. & Monjardet B. [1981]. "Stability and Aggregation Procedures, Ultrafilters and Simple Games", *Econometrica*, **49**, 527-534.

Bazu K. [1984]. "Fuzzy Revealed Preference Theory", *Journal of Economic Theory*, **32**, 212-227.

Becker G.S. [1976]. *The Economic Approach to Human Behavior*, University of Chicago Press, Chicago.

Bellman R.E. & Zadeh L.A. [1970]. "Decision-making in a Fuzzy Environment", *Management Science*, **17**, 141-154.

Benassy J.P. [1984]. *Macroéconomie et Theorie du Déséquilibre*, Dunod, Paris.

Berge C. [1959]. *Espaces Topologiques*, Dunod, Paris.

Bernheim B.D., Peleg B. & Whinston M.D. [1987a;1987b]. "Coalition-Proof Nash Equilibria : Concepts and Applications", *Journal of Economic Theory*, **42**, 1-29.

Bezdek J.C. & Harris J.D. [1978]. "Fuzzy Partitions and Relations : An Axiomatic Basis for Clustering", *Fuzzy sets and Systems*, **1**, 117-118.

Billot A.B. [1986]. "A Contribution to a Mathematical Theory of Fuzzy Games" in *Fuzzy Economics and Spatial Analysis*, C. Ponsard & B. Fustier Eds, Dijon, Librairie de l'Université, 47-56.

Billot A.B. [1987a]. "Myopic Planner, Aggregation of Fuzzy Preorders and May's Theorem with Minimal Step of Implication", Working-paper n°96, Institut de Mathématiques Economiques, Dijon, published in 1991 under the new title "Aggregation of Preferences ; the Fuzzy Case", *Theory and Decision*, **30**, n°1, 51-93.

Billot A.B. [1987b]. *Préférences et Utilités Floues*, Travaux et Recherches de l'Université de Droit, d'Economie et de Sciences Sociales de Paris, Presses Universitaires de France, Paris.

Billot A.B. [1987c]. "Tâches, quasi-salaire et sous emploi", in *Flexibilité, Mobilité et Stimulants Economiques de l'Emploi, Actes du Colloque A.F.S.E. 1986*, Nathan, Paris.

Billot A.B. [1988]. "Peripheric Core and α-Nucleus of an Exchange Economy", 4th International Conference on the Foundations and Applications of Utility, Risk and Decision Theories, Budapest, June 6-10, published in 1990 in *Multiperson Decision Making Using Fuzzy Sets and Possibility Theory*, Kacprzyck J. & Fedrizzi M., Klüwer Academic Publishers, Boston, 331-335.

Black D. [1948]. "The Decision of a Committee Using a Simple Majority", *Econometrica*, **16**, 246-261.

Blair D.H., Bordes G., Kelly J.S. & Suzumura K. [1986]. "Impossibility Theorems without Collective Rationality", *Journal of Economic Theory*, **13**, 361-379.

Blaug M. [1982]. *La Méthodologie Economique*, Cambridge Surveys of Economic Literature, Economica, Paris.

Böhm V. [1974]. "The Core of an Economy with Production", *Review of Economic Studies*, **41**, 429-436.

Bondareva O.N. [1963]. "Some Applications of Linear Programming Methods to the Theory of Cooperative Games", *Problemy Kiberneteki*, **10**, 119-139.

Border K.C. [1982]. "The Core of a Coalitional Production Economy", Social Science Working Paper n°461, California Institute of Technology.

Border K.C. [1985]. *Fixed Point Theorems with Applications to Economics and Game Theory*, Cambridge University Press.

Bordes G. [1979]. "Some More Results on Consistency, Rationality and Collective Choice", in *Aggregation and Revelation of Preferences*, J.J. Laffont Ed, Amsterdam, North-Holland.

Bordes G. [1980]. "Procédures d'Agrégation et Fonctions de Choix", in *Analyse et Agrégation des Préférences (dans les Sciences Sociales, Economiques et de Gestion)*, Economica, Paris.

Bose R.K. & Sahani D. [1987]. "Fuzzy Mappings and Fixed Point Theorems", *Fuzzy Sets and Systems*, **21**, 53-58.

Bourbaki N. [1970]. *Eléments de Mathématiques : Topologie Générale*, Hermann, Paris.

Brouwer L.E.J. [1912]. "Uber Abbildung von Mannigfaltikeiten", *Mathematische Annalen*, **71**, 97-115.

Burdett K., Kieffern M., Mortensen D.T. & Neumann G.R. [1984]. "Earnings, Unemployment, and the Allocation of Time Over Time", *Review of Economic Studies*, **51**, 559-578.

Butnariu D. [1978]. "Fuzzy Games. A Description of the Concept", *Fuzzy Sets and Systems*, **1**, 181-192.

Butnariu D. [1979]. "Solution Concepts for *n*-Person Fuzzy Games" in *Advances in Fuzzy Set Theory and Applications*, M.M. Gupta, R.K. Ragade & R.R. Yager Eds, 339-359.

Butnariu D. [1980]. "Stability and Shapley Value for *n*-Persons Fuzzy Games", *Fuzzy Sets and Systems*, **7**, 63-72.

Butnariu D. [1982]. "Fixed Points for Fuzzy Mappings", *Fuzzy Sets and Systems*, **7**, 191-207.

Butnariu D. [1985]. "Non-Atomic Fuzzy Measures and Games", *Fuzzy Sets and Systems*, **17**, 39-52.

Butnariu D. [1986]. "Fuzzy Measurability and Integrability", *Journal of Mathematical Analysis and Applications*, **117**, 385-410.

Butnariu D. [1987]. "Values and Cores of Fuzzy Games with Infinitely Many Players" , *International Journal of Game Theory*, **16**, 43-68.

Calvo G. [1979]. "Quasi-Walrasian Theories of Unemployment", *American Economic Review*, **69**, 102-107.

Cassel G. [1932]. *Theory of the Social Economy*, Harcourt Brace, New-York.

Chakraboty M.K. & Das M. [1985]. "Reduction of Fuzzy Strict Order Relations", *Fuzzy Sets and Systems*, **15**, 33-44.

Chakraboty M.K. & Sarkar S. [1987]. "Fuzzy Antisymmetry and Order", *Fuzzy Sets and Systems*, **21**, 169-182.

Chang C.L. [1968]. "Fuzzy Topological Spaces", *Journal of Mathematical Analysis and Applications*, **24**, 182-190.

Chang S.S. [1985]. "Fixed Point Theorems for Fuzzy Mappings", *Fuzzy Sets and Systems*, **17**, 181-187.

Chichilinsky G. [1980]. "Continuous Representation of Preferences", *Review of Economic Studies*, **47**, 959-963.

Chichilinsky G. [1982]. "Social Aggregation and Continuity", *The Quarterly Journal of Economics*, **97**, 337-352.

Chitra A. & Subrahmanyam P.V. [1987]. "Fuzzy Sets and Fixed Points", *Journal of Mathematical Analysis and Applications*, **124**, 584-590.

Clause M. [1982]. *Choix Collectifs dans un Contexte Imprécis*, Thèse de 3ème Cycle en Economie Mathématique et Econométrie, Université de Dijon.

Cornwall R.R. [1984]. *Introduction to the Use of General Equilibrium Analysis*, Amsterdam, North-Holland.

Deb R. & Blau J.H. [1977]. "Social Decision Functions and Veto", *Econometrica*, **45**, 871-879.

Debreu G. [1956]. "Market Equilibrium", *Proceedings of the National Academy of Sciences*, **38**, 886-893, in Debreu [1983].

Debreu G. [1959], [1984]. *Théorie de la Valeur*, 2nde Edition, Dunod, Paris.

Debreu G. [1974]. "Excess Demand Functions", *Journal of Mathematical Economics*, **1**, 15-21.

Debreu G. [1975]. "The Rate of Convergence of the Core of an Economy", *Journal of Mathematical Economics*, **2**, 1-7.

Debreu G. [1983]. *Mathematical Economics : Twenty Papers of Gerard Debreu*, Cambridge University Press.

Debreu G. & Scarf H. [1963]. "A Limit Theorem on the Core of an Economy", *International Economic Review*, **4**, 235-246.

Debreu G. & Scarf H. [1972]. "The Limit of the Core of an Economy", in *Decision and Organization*, C.B. Mc Guire and R. Radner Eds, North Holland, Amsterdam.

Deschamps R. & Gevers L. [1978]. "Leximin and Utilitarian Rules : a Joint Characterization", *Journal of Economic Theory*, **17**, 143-163.

Dixmier J. [1981]. *Topologie Générale*, Mathématiques, Presses Universitaires de France, Paris.

Dreze J.H. & Gabszewicz J.J. [1971]. "Syndicates of Traders in an Exchange Economy", in *Differential Games and Related Topics*, North-Holland, Amsterdam.

Dreze J.H. & Gabszewicz J.J. & Postlawaite A. [1977]. "Disadvantageous Monopolies and Disadvantageous Endowments", *Journal of Economic Theory*, **16**, 116-121.

Dreze J.H. & Greenberg J. [1980]. "Hedonic Coalitions : Optimality and Stability", *Econometrica*, **48**, 987-1003.

Dubois D. [1980]. "Un Economiste Précurseur de la Théorie des Possibilités : G.L.S. Shackle", *Busefal*, **2**, 70-73.

Dubois D. [1983]. *Modèles Mathématiques de l'Imprécis et de l'Incertain en vue d'Applications aux Techniques d'Aide à la Décision*, Thèse de Doctorat d'Etat es Sciences, Mathématiques Appliquées, Grenoble.

Dubois D. [1985]. "Generalized Probabilistic Independence and Utility Functions", *Busefal*, **23**, 83-91.

Dubois D. & Prade H. [1979]. "Fuzzy Real Algebra : Some Results", *Fuzzy Sets and Systems*, **2**, 327-348.

Dubois D. & Prade H. [1980]. *Fuzzy Sets and Systems : Theory and Applications*, Academic Press, New York.

Durkeim E. [1897], [1960]. *De la Division du Travail Social*. 7ème Edition, Presses Universitaires de France, Paris.

Dutta B. [1977]. "Existence of Stable Situations, Restricted Preferences and Strategic Manipulations under Democratic Group Decision Rules", *Journal of Economic Theory*, **15**, 99-111.

Eaves B.C. [1971]. "Computing Kakutani Fixed Points", *Journal of Applied Mathematics*, **21**, 236-244.

Edgeworth F.Y. [1881], [1961]. *Mathematical Psychics*, 3ème Edition, A.M. Kelley.

Ekeland I. [1979]. *Eléments d'Economie Mathématique*, Hermann, Paris.

Farreny H. & Prade H. [1981]. "La Programmation Floue : Pourquoi et Comment ? Quelques Exemples et Suggestions", in *Actes Congrès AFCET Informatique*, 283-292.

Fenchel W. [1956]. "Convex Cones, Sets and Functions". Department of Mathematics, Princeton University.

Feron R. [1979]. "Ensembles Flous, Ensembles Aléatoires Flous, Economie Aléatoire Floue", *Publications Econométriques*, **9**, fasc 1.

Feyerabend P. [1979]. *Contre la Méthode*, Seuil, Paris.

Fishburn P.C. [1973]. *The Theory of Social Choice*, Princeton University Press.

Fung L.W. & Fu K.S. [1975]. "An Axiomatic Approach to Rational Decision-Making in a Fuzzy Environment", in *Fuzzy Sets and their Applications to Cognitive and Decision Processes*, L.A. Zadeh, K.S. Fu, K. Tanaka & M. Shimura Eds, Academic Press, New-York, 227-256.

Fustier B. [1982]. "Une Introduction à la Théorie de la Demande Floue", Working-paper, n°55, Institut de Mathématiques Economiques, Dijon.

Gale D. [1955]. "The Law of Supply and Demand", *Mathematica Scandinavica*, **37**, 155-169.

Gerard-Varet L.A., Prevôt M. & Thisse J.-F. [1976]. *Analyse Mathématique pour l'Economie : Topologie*, Dalloz Mathématiques, Paris.

Gioia M. [1815]. *Nuovo Prospetto Delle Scienze Economiche*, Presso Guis, Lugamo, Ruggia.

Goguen J.A. [1967]. *Axioms, Extensions and Applications for Fuzzy Sets*, University of California, 1-71.

Grandmont J.M. [1977]. "Temporary General Equilibrium Theory", *Econometrica*, **45**, 535-572.

Grandmont J.M. [1978]. "Intermediate Preferences and the Majority Rule", *Econometrica*, **46**, 317-330.

Grandmont J.M. & Laroque G. [1976]. "On Temporary Keynesian Equilibria", *Review of Economic Studies*, **43**, 53-57.

Granger G.G. [1955]. *Méthodologie Economique*, Presses Universitaires de France, Paris.

Grodal B. [1975]. "The Rate of Convergence of the Core of a Purely Competitive Sequence of Economies", *Journal of Mathematical Economics*, **2**, 171-186.

Grossman H.I. [1972]. "Was Keynes a Keynesian ? A Review Article", *Journal of Economic Literature*, **10**, 26-30.

Guilbaud G.T. [1952]. "Les Théories de L'intérêt Général et le Problème Logique de l'Agrégation", *Economie Appliquée*, **5**, 502-584.

Haak S. [1974]. *Deviant Logic*, Cambridge University Press.

Hahn F.H. [1973]. *On the Notion of Equilibrium in Economics : An Inaugural Lecture*, Cambridge University Press.

Hahn F.H. [1987]. On Involuntary Unemployment", *The Economic Journal (Conference)*, **97**, 1-16.

Halevy E. [1903]. *La Formation du Radicalisme Philosophique*, Thèse, Université de Paris.

Hammond P. [1976]. "Equity, Arrow's Conditions and Rawls Difference Principle", *Econometrica*, **44**, 793-804.

Harsanyi J.C. [1973]. "Can the Maximin Principle Serve as a Basis for Morality : A Critique of John Rawls's Theory", Document de Travail CP-351, Center for Research in Management Science, University of California in *American Political Science Review*, **69**.

Hashimoto H. [1983]. "Szpilrajn's Theorem on Fuzzy Ordering", *Fuzzy Sets and Systems*, **10**, 101-108.

Heilpern S. [1981]. "Fuzzy Mappings and Fixed Point Theorem", *Journal of Mathematical Analysis and Applications*, **83**, 566-569.

Heuchenne C. [1970]. "Un Algorithme Général pour Trouver un Sous-Ensemble d'un Certain Type à Distance Minimum d'une Partie Donnée", *Mathématiques et Sciences Humaines*, **30**, 23-33.

Hicks J. [1956]. *Revisions of Demand Theory*, Oxford Clarendon Press.

Hildenbrand W. [1971]. "Random Preferences and Equilibrium Analysis", *Journal of Economic Theory*, **3**, 414-429.

Hildenbrand W. [1974]. *Core and Equilibria of a Large Economy*, Princeton University Press.

Hildenbrand W. [1975]. "Distributions of Agents Characteristics", *Journal of Mathematical Economics*, **2**, 129-138.

Hildenbrand W. [1983]. "On the "Law of Demand"", *Econometrica*, **51**, 997-1019.

Hildenbrand W. & Kirman A. [1976]. *Introduction to Equilibrium Analysis*, North-Holland, Amsterdam.

Hosomatu Y. [1978]. "Zero-Sum Condition : A Necessary and Sufficient Condition for a Transitive Voting System", *Journal of Economic Theory*, **18**, 294-300.

Ichiishi T. [1981]. "A Social Coalitional Equilibrium Existence Theorem", *Econometrica*, **49**, 369-377.

Ichiishi T. [1982]. "Non-Cooperation and Cooperation", in *Games, Economic Dynamics and Time Series Analysis*, M. Diestler, E. Furst & G. Schwodiauer Eds, Vienne, Physica-Verlag.

Jevons W.S. [1871], [1909]. *The Theory of Political Economy*, French Translation, Giard, Paris.

Kakutani S. [1941]. "A Generalization of Brouwer's Fixed Point Theorem", *Duke Mathematical Journal*, **8**, 416-427.

Kalai E. & Ritz Z. [1980]. "Characterization of the Private Alternatives Domains Admitting Arrow Social Welfare Functions", *Journal of Economic Theory*, **22**, 12-22.

Kaleva O. [1985]. "A Note on Fixed Points for Fuzzy Mappings", *Fuzzy Sets and Systems*, **15**, 99-100.

Kannai Y. [1974]. "Approximation of Convex Preferences", *Journal of Mathematical Economics*, **1**, 101-106.

Kaplan M.A., Burns A. & Quandr R. [1960]. "Theorical Analysis of "Balance of Power"", *Behavioral Science*, **5**, 240-252.

Kaufmann A. [1973]-[1980]. *Introduction à la Théorie des Sous-Ensembles Flous*, Tomes I et IV, Masson, Paris.

Kendall M.G. [1962]. *Rank Correlation Methods*, Hafner, New-York.

Kim J.B. [1983]. "Fuzzy Rational Choice Functions", *Fuzzy Sets and Systems*, **10**, 37-43.

Kim K.H. & Roush F.W. [1981]. "Effective Nondictatorial Domains", *Journal of Economic Theory*, **24**, 40-47.

Kolm S.C. [1973]. *Justice et Equité*, Editions C.N.R.S., Paris.

Kolm S.C. [1980]. "Choix Social, Choix Collectif, Optimum Social", *Revue d'Economie Politique*, **3**, 246-254.

Lefaivre R. [1974]. "Fuzzy Problem Solving", Technical Report n°37, University of Wisconsin.

Lemaire J. [1981]. "Agrégation Topologique des Données de Préférences", in *Analyse et Agrégation des Préférences*, Economica, Paris.

Liebenstein H. [1957]. *Economics Backwardness and Economic Growth*, John Wiley, New-York.

Liu Y.M. [1977]. "A Note on Compactness in Fuzzy Unit Interval", *Kexue Tongbao*, **25**, 33-35.

Liu Y.M. [1985]. "Some Properties of Fuzzy Convex Sets", *Journal of Mathematical Analysis and Applications*, **111**, 119-129.

Lucas R.E.B. [1972]. "Hedonic Price Functions", *Economic Inquiry*, **13**, 157-178.

Luce R.D. [1956]. "Semi-Orders and Theory of Utility Discrimination", *Econometrica*, **24**, 178-191.

Luo C.Z. [1986]. "Fuzzy Relation Equation on Infinite Sets", *Busefal*, **26**, 57-66.

Lukasiewicz J. [1922]. "A Numerical Interpretation of the Theory of Propositions", *Ruch Filozoficzny*, **23**, 92-94.

Lydall H. [1968]. *The Structure of Earnings*, Oxford University Press.

Malinvaud E. [1975]. *Leçons de Théorie Micro-Economique*. 3ème Edition, Dunod, Paris.

Malinvaud E. [1977]. *The Theory of Unemployment Reconsidered*, Basil Blackwell, Oxford.

Malinvaud E. [1986]. *Sur les Statistiques de l'Emploi et du Chômage (rapport au Premier Ministre)*, La Documentation Française, Paris.

Mantel R. [1974]. "On the Characterization of Agregate Excess Demand", *Journal of Economic Theory*, **7**, 348-353.

Marchal J. [1952]. *Cours d'Economie Politique*, Tome I, Librairie de Medicis, Paris.

Mas-Colell A. [1974]. "An Equilibrium Existence Theorem without Complete or Transitive Preferences", *Journal of Mathematical Economics*, **1**, 237-246.

Mas-Colell A. & Sonnenschein H. [1972]. "General Possibility Theorems of Group Decisions", *Review of Economic Studies*, **1**, 237-246.

Mathieu-Nicot B. [1986]. *Espérance Mathématique de l'Utilité Floue*, Librairie de l'Université, Dijon.

May K.O. [1952]. "A Set of Independent, Necessary and Sufficient Conditions for Simple Majority Decision", *Econometrica*, **20**, 680-684.

Mc Kenzie L.W. [1959]. "On the Existence of General Equilibrium for a Competitive Market", *Econometrica*, **27**, 54-71.

Menger C. [1871], [1976]. *Grundsätze der Volkswirtschaftslehre*, Translation *Principes of Economics*, New-York University Press.

Mongin P. [1985]. "Simon, Stigler et les Théories de la Rationalité Limitée". Document de Travail n°106 de l'Ecole Normale Supérieure, Laboratoire d'Economie Politique.

Montero F.J. [1986]. "Measuring the Rationality of a Fuzzy Preference Relation", *Busefal*, **26**, 75-83.

Montero F.J. & Tejada J. [1986]. "Some Problems on the Definition of Fuzzy Preference Relations", *Fuzzy Sets and Systems*, **20**, 45-53.

Mookherjee D. [1986]. "Involuntary Unemployment and Worker Moral Hazard", *Review of Economic Studies*, **53**, 739-754.

Moon J.W. [1968]. *Topics on Tournaments*, Holt, New-York.

Mortensen D.T. [1970]. "A Theory of Wage and Unemployment Dynamics", in *Micro Economic Foundations of Unemployment and Inflation Theory*, E.S. Phelps Ed, New-York, 167-211.

Morviller M.S. & Lepage D. [1974]. "Applications des Concepts Flous : Description Dynamique d'un Ensemble de Données et son Utilisation en Langage Naturel", Mémoire Institut Informatique d'Entreprise. C.N.A.M.

Moscarola J. & Roy B. [1976]. "Procédure Automatique d'Examen des Dossiers Fondée sur un Classement Trichotomique en Présence de Critères Multiples", Document de Travail du LAMSADE, Université de Paris-IX, Dauphine.

Moulin H. [1977]. "How to Manipulate Two Persons Voting Schemes", Cahier de Mathématiques de la Décision n°7709, Université de Paris-IX, Dauphine.

Moulin H. [1979]. "Dominance-Solvable Voting Schemes", *Econometrica*, **47**, 249-269.

Moulin H. [1981]. *The Strategy of Social Choice*, Laboratoire d'Econométrie de l'Ecole Polytechnique, Paris.

Moulin H. [1982]. *Choix Social Cardinal*, Laboratoire d'Econométrie de l'Ecole Polytechnique, Paris.

Moulin H. [1983]. *Le Choix Social Utilitariste*, Laboratoire d'Econométrie de l'Ecole Polytechnique, Paris.

Moulin H. [1985]. "Egalitarianism and Utilitarianism in Quasi-Linear Bargaining", *Econometrica*, **53**, 49-67.

Moulin H. & Fogelman-Soulie F. [1979]. *La Convexité dans les Mathématiques de la Décision*, Hermann, Paris.

Mullet E. [1986]. "Choix dans l'Alternative et la Recherche de Covariation", *L'Année Psychologique*, 383-402.

Munier B. [1973]. *Jeux et Marchés*, Presses Universitaires de France, Paris.

Nahmias S. [1980]. "Fuzzy Variables", *Fuzzy Sets and Systems*, **1**, 97-110.

Nakamura K. [1975]. "The Core of a Simple Game with Ordinal Preferences", *International Journal of Game Theory*, **4**, 95-104.

Nash J. [1950]. "The Bargaining Problem", *Econometrica*, **18**, 155-162.

Negishi T. [1962]. "The Stability of a Competitive Economy : A Survey", *Econometrica*, **30**, 635-669.

Negoita C.V. & Ralescu D.A. [1978]. "Applications of Fuzzy Sets to System Analysis", *Fuzzy Sets and Systems*, **1**, 155-167.

von Neumann J. & Morgenstern O. [1944], [1970]. *Theory of Games and Economic Behaviour*, 4th Edition, Princeton University Press.

Orlovsky S.A. [1978]. "Decision Making with Fuzzy Preference Relation", *Fuzzy Sets and Systems*, **4**, 155-167.

Orlovsky S.A. [1980]. "On Formalization of a General Fuzzy Mathematical Problem", *Fuzzy Sets and Systems*, **3**, 311-321.

Ovchinnikov S.V. [1981]. "Structure of Fuzzy Binary Relations", *Fuzzy Sets and Systems*, **6**, 169-195.

Owen G. [1982]. *Game Theory*, 2nd Edition, Academic Press, London.

Pagano U. [1985]. *Work and Welfare in Economic Theory*, Basil Blackwell, Oxford, New-York.

Pattanaik P.K. & Salles M. Eds [1983]. *Social Choice and Welfare*, Contributions to Economic Analysis n°145, North-Holland, Amsterdam.

Peleg B. [1978]. "Representations of Simple Games by Social Choice Functions", *International Journal of Game Theory*, **7**, 81-94.

Phelps E.S. [1970]. "Money Wage Dynamics and Labor Market Equilibrium" in *Micro Economic Foundations of Employment and Inflation Theory*, E.S. Phelps Ed, New-York, 126-166.

Piatecki C. [1986]. "La Notion d'Effort et sa Place dans l'Histoire de la Pensée Economique", Journée d'Etude de l'Equipe de Recherche sur l'Emploi, les Marchés et la Simulation (ERMES), University of Paris 2.

Ponsard C. [1974], [1975]. "L'Imprécision et son Traitement en Analyse Economique", Working-paper n°4, Institut de Mathématiques Economiques, Dijon, in *Revue d'Economie Politique*, **1**, 17-37.

Ponsard C. [1980]. "Fuzzy Economic Spaces", First World Regional Science Congress, Harvard University, Cambridge, Massachusetts, June, 15-25.

Ponsard C. [1981]. "L'Equilibre Spatial du Consommateur dans un Contexte Imprécis", *Sistemi Urbani*, **3**, 107-133.

Ponsard C. [1982a]. "Producer's Spatial Equilibrium with Fuzzy Constraints", *European Journal of Operational Research*, **10**, n°3, 302-313.

Ponsard C. [1982b]. "Partial Spatial Equilibria with Fuzzy Constraints", *Journal of Regional Science*, **22**, 159-175.

Ponsard C. [1984], [1986]. "A Theory of Spatial General Equilibrium in a Fuzzy Economy", Second International Congress of Arts and Sciences, Regional Science Sessions, Erasmus University, Rotterdam, The Netherlands, Working-paper n° 65, Institut de Mathématiques Economiques, Dijon, in *Fuzzy Economics and Spatial Analysis*, C. Ponsard & B. Fustier Eds, Dijon, Librairie de l'Université, 1-28.

Ponsard C. [1986]. "Foundations of Soft Decision Theory", in *Management Decision Support Systems Using Fuzzy Sets and Possibility Theory*, J. Kacprzyk & R.R. Yager Eds, Verlag T.U.V., Rheinland, 27-37.

Ponsard C. [1987]. "Fuzzy Mathematical Models in Economics", *Fuzzy Sets and Systems*.

Ponsard C. & Fustier B. Eds [1986]. *Fuzzy Economics and Spatial Analysis*, Librairie de l'Université, Dijon.

Popper K. [1967]. "La Rationalité et le Statut du Principe de Rationalité", in *Les Fondements Philosophiques des Systèmes Economiques*, Payot, 142-152.

Prevôt M. [1977]. *Sous-Ensembles Flous : Une Approche Théorique*, Sirey, Collection de l'Institut de Mathématiques Economiques, Paris.

Quine W.V.O. [1972], [1984]. *Méthodes de Logique*. 3ème Edition, Armand Colin, Paris.

Rawls J. [1971], [1987]. *Théorie de la Justice*, Seuil, Paris.

Reza A.M. [1975]. "Geographic Differences in Earnings and Unemployment Rates", *Review of Economics and Statistics*, 201-208.

Robbins L. [1930]. "On the Elasticity of Demand for Income in Terms of Effort", *Economica*, **10**, 123-129.

Roberts K. [1980]. "Interpersonal Comparability and Social Choice Theory", *Review of Economic Studies*, **47**, 409-420.

Roberston D.H. [1926]. *Banking Policy and the Price Level*, P.J. King & Sons.

Rosen S. [1974]. "Hedonic Price and Implicit Markets", *Journal of Political Economy*, **82**, 34-55.

Rosen S. [1978]. "Substitution and Division of Labor", *Economica*, **45**, 113-128.

Rosen S. [1982]. "Authority, Control, and the Distribution of Earnings", *The Bail Journal of Economics*, **13**, 311-323.

Rosen S. [1983]. "Specialization and Human Capital", *Journal of Labor Economics*, **1**, 43-49.

Rosenmüller J.S. [1981]. *The Theory of Games and Markets*, North-Holland, Amsterdam.

Rosenthal R.W. [1971]. "External Economies and Cores", *Journal of Economic Theory*, **3**, 182-188.

Roubens M. & Vincke P. [1985]. "Fuzzy Preferences in an Optimisation Perspective", Colloque I.M.E. 1985, Dijon.

Roubens M. & Vincke P. [1986]. *Preferences Modelling*, Lecture Notes in Economics and Mathematical Systems n°250, Springer Verlag, Berlin, New-York.

Roy B. [1985]. *Méthodologie Multicitère d'Aide à la Décision*, Economica, Paris.

Rubinstein A. [1981]. "Perfect Equilibrium in a Bargaining Model", *Econometrica*, **50**, 97-110.

Saari D.G. [1986]. "Price Dynamics, Social Choice, Voting Methods, Probability and Chaos", FUR III Conference, Aix en provence.

Salles M. & Wendel R.E. [1977]. "A Further Result on the Core of Voting Games", *International Journal of Game Theory*, **6**, 35-40.

Salop S.C. [1979]. "A Model of the Natural Rate of Unemployment", *American Economic Review*, **69**, 117-144.

Samuelson P. [1947], [1948]. *Foundations of Economic Analysis*, Harvard University Press, Cambridge.

Satterhwaite M.A. [1975]. "Startegy-Proofness and Arrow's Conditions : Existence and Correspondence Theorems for Voting Procedures and Social Welfare Functions", *Journal of Economic Theory*, **10**, 187-217.

Scarf H. [1967]. "The Core of an *n*-Person Game", *Econometrica*, **35**, 50-69.

Scarf H. [1971]. "On the Existence of a Cooperative Solution for a General Class of *n*-Person Games", *Journal of Economic Theory*, **3**, 169-181.

Scarf H. [1973]. *The Computation of Economic Equilibria*, Yale University Press, New-Haven.

Schumpeter J.A. [1954]. *Capitalisme, Socialisme et Démocratie*, Payot, Paris.

Schleicher H. Ed [1979]. *Jeux, Information et Groupes*, Economica, Paris.

Schmidt C. [1985]. *La Sémantique Economique en Question*, Calmann-Levy, Paris.

Schofield N. [1977]. ""Transitivity of Preferences on a Smooth Manifold of Alternatives", *Journal of Economic Theory*, **14**, 149-171.

Schotter A. & Schwödiauer G. [1980]. "Economics and the Theory of Games : A Survey", *Journal of Economic Literature*, **18**, 479-527.

Schwartz T. [1972]. "Rationality and the Myth of the Maximum", *Theory and Decision*, **1**, 89-106.

Schwartz T. [1980]. *The Logic of Collective Choice*. University of Texas-St Austin.

Sen A.K. [1969]. "Quasi-Transitivity Rational Choice and Collective Decisions", *Review of Economic Studies*, **36**, 381-393.

Sen A.K. [1970]. *Collective Choice and Social Welfare*, Holden-Day, San Francisco.

Sen A.K. [1974]. "Information Basis of Alternative Welfare Approaches, Agregation and Income Distribution", *Journal of Public Economics*, **3**, 387-403.

Sen A.K. [1977]. "Social Choice Theory : A Re-Examination", *Econometrica*, **45**, 53-89.

Sen A.K. & Williams B. Eds [1982]. *Utilitarianism and Beyond*. Cambridge University Press.

Shackle G.L.S. [1961], [1971]. *Decision, Order and Time in Human Affairs*. Cambridge, 2nd Edition, Translation, Dunod, Paris.

Shaked A. & Sutton J. [1984]. "Involuntary Unemployment as a Perfect Equilibrium in a Bargaining model", *Econometrica*, **6**, 1351-1364.

Shapley L.S. [1973]. "On Balanced Games without Side Payments", in *Mathematical Programming*, T.C. Hu & S.M. Robinson Eds, Academic Press, New-York, 261-290.

Shapley L.S. & Shubik M. [1966]. "Quasi-Cores in a Monetary Economy with Nonconvex Preferences", *Econometrica*, **34**, 805-827.

Shapley L.S. & Shubik M. [1969]. "On Market Games", *Journal of Economic Theory*, **1**, 9-25.

Shapley L.S. & Shubik M. [1972]. "The Assignment Game I : The Core", *International Journal of Game Theory*, **1**, 111-130.

Shubik M. [1971]. "The Bridge Game Economy : An Example of Indivisibilities", *Journal of political*, **79**, 909-912.

Simon H. [1955]. "A Behavioural Model of Rational Choice", *Quarterly Journal of Economics*, **69**, 99-118.

Simon H. [1964]. "Rationality", in *A Dictionary of the Social Sciences*, J. Gould & W.L. Kolb Eds, Free Press, Glencoe, 573-574.

Shimura M. [1973]. "Fuzzy Sets Concepts in Rank-Ordering Objects", *Journal of Mathematical Analysis and Applications*, **43**, 717-733.

Slutsky S. [1979]. "Equilibrium Under α-Majority Voting", *Econometrica*, **47**, 1113-1127.

Sonnenschein H. [1973]. "Do Walras' Identity and Continuity Characterize the Class of Community Excess Demand Functions", *Journal of Economic Theory*, **6**, 345-354.

Stigum B.P. [1969]. "Competitive Equilibrium Under Uncertainty", *Quarterly Journal of Economics*, **11**, 224-245.

Strasnick S. [1976]. "The Problem of Social Choice : Arrow to Rawls", *Philosophy and Public Affairs*, **5**, 241-273.

Sugden R. [1986]. "Evolutionarily Stable Strategies in the Prisoner's Dilemma and Chicken Games", FUR III Conference, Aix en Provence in *The Economics of Rights, Cooperation and Welfare*, Basil Blackwell, Oxford, New-York.

Tamura S., Huguchi S. & Tanaka K. [1971]. "Pattern Classification Based on Fuzzy Relations", *IEEE Trans*, SMC-1, 61-66.

Tanaka K., Okuda S. & Asai A. [1974]. "On Fuzzy Mathematical Programming", *Journal of Cybernetics*, **3**, 37-46.

Thurstone L.L. [1927]. "A Law of Comparative Judgement", *Psychological Review*, **34**, 273-286.

Todd M.J. [1976]. *The Computation of Fixed Points and Applications*, Lectures Notes in Economics and Mathematical Systems, Springer-Verlag, New-York.

Topel R.H. [1984]. "Equilibirum Earnings, Turnover, and Unemployment : New Evidence", *Journal of Labor Economics*, **2**, 500-522.

Topel R.H. & Welch F. [1980]. "Unemployment Insurance : Survey and Extensions", *Economica*, **47**, 541-559.

Usawa H. [1960]. "Preference and Rational Choice in the Theory of Consumption", *Proceedings of a Symposium on Mathematical Methods in Social Sciences*, Stanford University Press.

Vuillemin J. [1984]. *Nécessité et Contingence : l'Aporie de Diodore*, Les Editions de Minuit, Paris.

Wald A. [1951]. "On Some Systems of Equations in Mathematical Economics", *Econometrica*, **19**, 368-403.

Walras [1874], [1904]. *Eléments d'Economie Politique Pure*, 4ème Edition. Librairie de Droit et de Jurisprudence, Paris.

Weber S. [1979]. "On ε-Cores of Balanced Games", *International Journal of Game Theory*, **8**, 241-250.

Weintraub E.R. [1980]. *Fondements Microéconomiques*, Cambridge Surveys of Economic Literature, Economica, Paris.

Weiss M.D. [1975]. "Fixed Points, Separation and Induced Topologies for Fuzzy Sets", *Journal of Mathematical Analysis and Applications*, **50**, 142-150.

Winch P. [1958]. *Idea of a Social Science*, Routlegde & Kegan Paul, Londres.

Wittgenstein L. [1921], [1961]. *Tractatus Logico-philosophicus*, Gallimard, Paris.

Wittgenstein L. [1983]. *Remarques sur les Fondements des Mathématiques*, Translation, Gallimard, Paris.

Wooders M.H. [1980]. "The Tiebout Hypothesis : Near Optimality in Local Public Good Economies", *Econometrica*, **48**, 1467-1485.

Wooders M.H. [1983]. "The Epsilon Core of a Large Replica Game", *Journal of Mathematical Economics*, **11**, 277-300.

Wooders M.H. & Zame W.R. [1984]. "Approximate Cores of Large Games", *Econometrica*, **52**, 1327-1350.

Zadeh L.A. [1965]. "Fuzzy Sets", *Information and Control*, **8**, 338-353.

Zadeh L.A. [1971a]. "Toward a Theory of Fuzzy Systems" in *Aspects of Network and System Theory*, R.E. Kalman & N. De Claris Eds, Holt, Rinehart and Winston, New-York, 469-490.

Zadeh L.A. [1971b]. "Similarity Relations and Fuzzy Orderings", *Information Sciences*, **3**, 177-200.

Zimmermann H.J. [1985]. *Fuzzy Set Theory - and its Applications*, Klüwer, Nijhoff Publishing, Boston.

Vol. 307: T.K. Dijkstra (Ed.), On Model Uncertainty and its Statistical Implications. VII, 138 pages. 1988.

Vol. 308: J.R. Daduna, A. Wren (Eds.), Computer-Aided Transit Scheduling. VIII, 339 pages. 1988.

Vol. 309: G. Ricci, K. Velupillai (Eds.), Growth Cycles and Multisectoral Economics: the Goodwin Tradition. III, 126 pages. 1988.

Vol. 310: J. Kacprzyk, M. Fedrizzi (Eds.), Combining Fuzzy Imprecision with Probabilistic Uncertainty in Decision Making. IX, 399 pages. 1988.

Vol. 311: R. Färe, Fundamentals of Production Theory. IX, 163 pages. 1988.

Vol. 312: J. Krishnakumar, Estimation of Simultaneous Equation Models with Error Components Structure. X, 357 pages. 1988.

Vol. 313: W. Jammernegg, Sequential Binary Investment Decisions. VI, 156 pages. 1988.

Vol. 314: R. Tietz, W. Albers, R. Selten (Eds.), Bounded Rational Behavior in Experimental Games and Markets. VI, 368 pages. 1988.

Vol. 315: I. Orishimo, G.J.D. Hewings, P. Nijkamp (Eds), Information Technology: Social and Spatial Perspectives. Proceedings 1986. VI, 268 pages. 1988.

Vol. 316: R.L. Basmann, D.J. Slottje, K. Hayes, J.D. Johnson, D.J. Molina, The Generalized Fechner-Thurstone Direct Utility Function and Some of its Uses. VIII, 159 pages. 1988.

Vol. 317: L. Bianco, A. La Bella (Eds.), Freight Transport Planning and Logistics. Proceedings, 1987. X, 568 pages. 1988.

Vol. 318: T. Doup, Simplicial Algorithms on the Simplotope. VIII, 262 pages. 1988.

Vol. 319: D.T. Luc, Theory of Vector Optimization. VIII, 173 pages. 1989.

Vol. 320: D. van der Wijst, Financial Structure in Small Business. VII, 181 pages. 1989.

Vol. 321: M. Di Matteo, R.M. Goodwin, A. Vercelli (Eds.), Technological and Social Factors in Long Term Fluctuations. Proceedings. IX, 442 pages. 1989.

Vol. 322: T. Kollintzas (Ed.), The Rational Expectations Equilibrium Inventory Model. XI, 269 pages. 1989.

Vol. 323: M.B.M. de Koster, Capacity Oriented Analysis and Design of Production Systems. XII, 245 pages. 1989.

Vol. 324: I.M. Bomze, B.M. Pötscher, Game Theoretical Foundations of Evolutionary Stability. VI, 145 pages. 1989.

Vol. 325: P. Ferri, E. Greenberg, The Labor Market and Business Cycle Theories. X, 183 pages. 1989.

Vol. 326: Ch. Sauer, Alternative Theories of Output, Unemployment, and lnflation in Germany: 1960–1985. XIII, 206 pages. 1989.

Vol. 327: M. Tawada, Production Structure and International Trade. V, 132 pages. 1989.

Vol. 328: W. Güth, B. Kalkofen, Unique Solutions for Strategic Games. VII, 200 pages. 1989.

Vol. 329: G. Tillmann, Equity, Incentives, and Taxation. VI, 132 pages. 1989.

Vol. 330: P.M. Kort, Optimal Dynamic Investment Policies of a Value Maximizing Firm. VII, 185 pages. 1989.

Vol. 331: A. Lewandowski, A.P. Wierzbicki (Eds.), Aspiration Based Decision Support Systems. X, 400 pages. 1989.

Vol. 332: T.R. Gulledge, Jr., L.A. Litteral (Eds.), Cost Analysis Applications of Economics and Operations Research. Proceedings. VII, 422 pages. 1989.

Vol. 333: N. Dellaert, Production to Order. VII, 158 pages. 1989.

Vol. 334: H.-W. Lorenz, Nonlinear Dynamical Economics and Chaotic Motion. XI, 248 pages. 1989.

Vol. 335: A.G. Lockett, G. Islei (Eds.), Improving Decision Making in Organisations. Proceedings. IX, 606 pages. 1989.

Vol. 336: T. Puu, Nonlinear Economic Dynamics. VII, 119 pages. 1989.

Vol. 337: A. Lewandowski, I. Stanchev (Eds.), Methodology and Software for Interactive Decision Support. VIII, 309 pages. 1989.

Vol. 338: J.K. Ho, R.P. Sundarraj, DECOMP: an Implementation of Dantzig-Wolfe Decomposition for Linear Programming. VI, 206 pages.

Vol. 339: J. Terceiro Lomba, Estimation of Dynamic Econometric Models with Errors in Variables. VIII, 116 pages. 1990.

Vol. 340: T. Vasko, R. Ayres, L. Fontvieille (Eds.), Life Cycles and Long Waves. XIV, 293 pages. 1990.

Vol. 341: G.R. Uhlich, Descriptive Theories of Bargaining. IX, 165 pages. 1990.

Vol. 342: K. Okuguchi, F. Szidarovszky, The Theory of Oligopoly with Multi-Product Firms. V, 167 pages. 1990.

Vol. 343: C. Chiarella, The Elements of a Nonlinear Theory of Economic Dynamics. IX, 149 pages. 1990.

Vol. 344: K. Neumann, Stochastic Project Networks. XI, 237 pages. 1990.

Vol. 345: A. Cambini, E. Castagnoli, L. Martein, P Mazzoleni, S. Schaible (Eds.), Generalized Convexity and Fractional Programming with Economic Applications. Proceedings, 1988. VII, 361 pages. 1990.

Vol. 346: R. von Randow (Ed.), Integer Programming and Related Areas. A Classified Bibliography 1984–1987. XIII, 514 pages. 1990.

Vol. 347: D. Ríos Insua, Sensitivity Analysis in Multi-objective Decision Making. XI, 193 pages. 1990.

Vol. 348: H. Störmer, Binary Functions and their Applications. VIII, 151 pages. 1990.

Vol. 349: G.A. Pfann, Dynamic Modelling of Stochastic Demand for Manufacturing Employment. VI, 158 pages. 1990.

Vol. 350: W.-B. Zhang, Economic Dynamics. X, 232 pages. 1990.

Vol. 351: A. Lewandowski, V. Volkovich (Eds.), Multiobjective Problems of Mathematical Programming. Proceedings, 1988. VII, 315 pages. 1991.

Vol. 352: O. van Hilten, Optimal Firm Behaviour in the Context of Technological Progress and a Business Cycle. XII, 229 pages. 1991.

Vol. 353: G. Riccil (Ed.), Declslon Processes In Economics. Proceedings, 1989. III, 209 pages 1991.

Vol. 354: M. Ivaldi, A Structural Analysis of Expectation Formation. XII, 230 pages. 1991.

Vol. 355: M. Salomon. Deterministic Lotsizlng Models for Production Planning. VII, 158 pages. 1991.

Vol. 356: P. Korhonen, A. Lewandowski, J . Wallenius (Eds.), Multlple Crltena Decision Supporl. Proceedings, 1989. XII, 393 pages. 1991.

Vol. 358: P. Knottnerus, Linear Models with Correlaled Disturbances. VIII, 196 pages. 1991.

Vol. 359: E. de Jong, Exchange Rate Determination and Optimal Economlc Policy Under Various Exchange Rate Regimes. VII, 270 pages. 1991.

Vol. 360: P. Stalder, Regime Translations, Spillovers and Buffer Stocks. VI, 193 pages . 1991.

Vol. 361: C. F. Daganzo, Logistics Systems Analysis. X, 321 pages. 1991.

Vol. 362: F. Gehreis, Essays In Macroeconomics of an Open Economy. VII, 183 pages. 1991.

Vol. 363: C. Puppe, Distorted Probabilities and Choice under Risk. VIII, 100 pages . 1991

Vol. 364: B. Horvath, Are Policy Variables Exogenous? XII, 162 pages. 1991.

Vol. 365: G. A Heuer, U. Leopold-Wildburger. Balanced Silverman Games on General Discrete Sets. V, 140 pages. 1991.

Vol. 366: J. Gruber (Ed.), Econometric Decision Models. Proceedings, 1989. VIII, 636 pages. 1991.

Vol. 367: M. Grauer, D. B. Pressmar (Eds.), Parallel Computing and Mathematical Optimization. Proceedings. V, 208 pages. 1991.

Vol. 368: M. Fedrizzi, J. Kacprzyk, M. Roubens (Eds.), Interactive Fuzzy Optimization. VII, 216 pages. 1991.

Vol. 369: R. Koblo, The Visible Hand. VIII, 131 pages.1991.

Vol. 370: M. J. Beckmann, M. N. Gopalan, R. Subramanian (Eds.), Stochastic Processes and their Applications. Proceedings, 1990. XLI, 292 pages. 1991.

Vol. 371: A. Schmutzler, Flexibility and Adjustment to Information in Sequential Decision Problems. VIII, 198 pages. 1991.

Vol. 372: J. Esteban, The Social Viability of Money. X, 202 pages. 1991.

Vol. 373: A. Billot, Economic Theory of Fuzzy Equilibria. XIII, 164 pages. 1992.